T0360935

Hornby's comprehensive guidebook will be of lasting value to experienced project managers and invaluable to those making the transition to commercial or business management positions. Drawing on extensive experience in software services, he critiques established tools and techniques, offering advice on when to follow and when to avoid or adapt. His professionalism, mastery of the subject, but above all his plain common sense, shine through. Hornby is sound on Risk, Estimating, and Quality. The book addresses the crucial question: how can services companies, especially software services companies, grow profitably and safely as the scale and number of the projects undertaken outstrips the ability of the founder business owners to take or even monitor every key decision? This reviewer exited profitably from two software start-ups. Hornby's insights on building a successful services firm might well have inspired and enabled us to grow rather than to sell.

Dr Alan Montgomery, founder and CEO of Integral
Solutions Ltd, ISL Decision Systems Inc.
and InferMed Ltd, UK

In *Commercial Project Management*, Robin Hornby, a project management authority and author, gives the reader a very complete view of the business management of projects from the professional service firm's perspective. His tips and templates on topics such as bidding, client engagement, and risk and quality management are practical and will help even the smallest vendor firm win more contracts and execute them successfully. His chapter on 'Building a successful services firm' is worth the price of the book alone. This is a must-have book for any small- to medium-sized services firm that wishes to improve their practices.

Dr Blaize Horner Reich, RBC Professor of Technology
and Innovation, Beedie School of Business,
Simon Fraser University, Canada

I don't know of a finer framework for delivering professional services-based projects, getting paid and making a profit, than Robin Hornby's. We implemented most of these processes and techniques presented in the book and reaped the benefits over the long run. Over time, we organized our entire operations around the main theme of *Commercial Project Management*, which is managing through all phases of the vendor lifecycle. This is a must-read for all who desire to implement superior commercial project management practices.

Jacques Tremblay, Vice President
of Hexagon, Canada

It is refreshing to find in this latest book, *Commercial Project Management* by Robin Hornby, a side of project management that is rarely tackled. In fact, it is not about project management per se, but rather about how to make money, or certainly not lose it, in the provision of real commercial project services in the course of 'Business as Usual'.

Robin's book is written in clear straightforward language and follows the natural work flow of this type of business. It includes an introduction to projects as a business and works its way through buyer/vendor relationships, the natural life span of managing a project contract in all its dimensions, to project-contract closure, including handling all of the financial side. Based as it is on his personal experiences, the book provides extensive practical and exhaustive advice to those working in the project management services industry with a view to making money, or contemplating doing so. Highly recommended.

R. Max Wideman, founder of the
(PMI) Project Management Body of Knowledge,
Past President of PMI (1987),
President AEW Services, Canada

Commercial Project Management

Selling and delivering a project to a satisfied client, and making a profit, is a complex task. Project manager and author Robin Hornby believes this has been neglected by current standards and is poorly understood by professionals in the field. *Commercial Project Management* aims to rectify this deficiency. As a unique 'how-to' guide for project and business managers, it offers practical guidance and a wealth of explanatory illustrations, useful techniques, proven checklists, real life examples, and case stories. It will give project managers a needed confidence boost and a head start in their demanding role as they go 'on contract'.

At the heart of Robin's approach is a vendor sales and delivery lifecycle that provides a framework for business control of projects. Unique elements include the integration of buyer and vendor project lifecycles, the recasting of project management as a cyclic set of functions to lead the work of the project, and the elevation of risk assessment from a project toolkit to a fundamental control process. Beyond project management, the book proposes a comprehensive template for the firm whose business is delivering projects.

This is a how-to book for project and business managers working in a commercial environment looking for practical guidance on conducting their projects and organizing their firm.

Robin Hornby worked in the information technology industry for over 35 years, migrating from systems engineering to project and then delivery management. He taught project management at Mount Royal University, Calgary, Canada, for 10 years and currently writes, consults, and conducts seminars. He pioneered many of the delivery practices described in this book.

Commercial Project Management

A Guide for Selling and Delivering
Professional Services

Robin Hornby PMP

Routledge
Taylor & Francis Group

LONDON AND NEW YORK

First published 2017
by Routledge
2 Park Square, Milton Park, Abingdon, Oxon OX14 4RN

and by Routledge
711 Third Avenue, New York, NY 10017

Routledge is an imprint of the Taylor & Francis Group, an informa business

© 2017 Robin Hornby

The right of Robin Hornby to be identified as author of this work
has been asserted by him in accordance with sections 77 and 78 of
the Copyright, Designs and Patents Act 1988.

British Library Cataloguing-in-Publication Data
A catalogue record for this book is available from the British Library

Library of Congress Cataloging-in-Publication Data
A catalog record for this book has been requested

ISBN: 978-1-138-23767-4 (hbk)
ISBN: 978-1-138-23768-1 (pbk)
ISBN: 978-1-315-29927-3 (ebk)

Typeset in Bembo
by codeMantra

Contents

Figures

Tables

Preface

Services projects, especially large software services projects, feature regularly in national and business news, and rarely for positive reasons. In no other industry has the cost of the raw material, computer hardware, or networked computing power shrunk so dramatically relative to the cost of the human services required to deliver the project. Fueled by this unprecedented increase in affordable capacity, exponential growth in the scope and complexity of the customer's ambition has inexorably driven up project costs. Simultaneously, a major shift to contracted services has occurred; projects that vendors typically bundled with hardware or software acquisitions are a thing of the past, and corporate projects previously managed internally, often ignoring internal labor costs, are now taking a commercial approach. These trends have done nothing to improve project success rates. What is it that makes these large projects fail so often? How can firms aiming to deliver these projects survive? In over 35 years of managing software services projects, I have observed impressive development and maturation of project management methods as they try to keep pace with ever more complex projects. At the same time, emerging professional services firms have struggled to evolve a business model to enable profitability in this challenging competitive environment. The model must leverage the firm's assets and senior resources, price with a margin, and then deliver to a satisfied customer at a profit. As a vendor and project manager, I have endeavored to understand and manage this target model for most of those 35 years and I write from that perspective.

Many firms fail at this target model, some spectacularly. Project managers are sometimes uneasy with business issues or unaware of their substance. Some think that the project is all about delivering what the client wants, not making a profit. On the business side, services firms are usually structured as sales organizations and their senior managers frequently come from a sales background. Their leadership may not be grounded in project management and may be unable or unwilling to balance sales entrepreneurship with the right degree of disciplined process.

I have seen the damage that these realities can inflict upon business success—a project manager and team unschooled in the importance of business principles and business people uncertain of the means whereby their promises can be delivered. That, in a nutshell, is the weakness I perceive in today's contracted projects, and why I believe it is necessary to match modern project management with the demands of commercial practice.

Standards

There are two preeminent standards for project management. The PMBOK®, or *Guide to the Project Management Body of Knowledge,* is published by the Project Management Institute. The Office of Government Commerce (UK) publishes PRINCE2® or *Managing Successful Projects with PRINCE2®.* In some regards, this guide may be interpreted as an extension to these methodologies. In general, when discussing project management, I strive to be consistent with PMBOK® terminology. I do not dwell on basics, as this would be repetitive with these works, and many other standard texts on the subject. The less experienced reader might appreciate keeping one of these texts available for reference and should also be aware of the extensive glossary at the end of the book.

Genesis

The material for this work has been slowly accumulated over the years, as it recycled from project to project and department to department. With each recycle, improvements got added, many designed to meet constructive criticism from colleagues and clients. Eventually, I was incented to self-publish a handbook titled *Projects for Profit.* This guide is refined and extracted from that original text and includes new material, greater clarity on the concept of a commercial project environment, and some restructuring.

Terminology

Inevitably, terminology is an issue, especially where there is no universal standard, or the context makes use of a standard sound awkward. These are the main conventions I have followed:

Vendor—is synonymous with seller, supplier, and firm. I use vendor most frequently, as that is the usual term in the market. If the discussion is within the PMBOK® context, I use seller. If the discussion is preoccupied with internal practices of the professional services firm or is outside of the market context, I use firm.

Client—is synonymous with customer and buyer. Professional services managers commonly use client. I might use buyer in a PMBOK® context.

Sponsor—has a very specific meaning in the standards and I adhere to that. Sometimes, it is also synonymous with client.

Pronouns—To avoid sexism, some writers use constructs such as 'he or she', or 's/he'. I have chosen to mix the pronouns randomly in the text, without significance, sometimes referring to 'he' and sometimes 'she'. If the sense allows, I use the plural 'their'.

Figures—Illustrations and tabular information are labeled with a figure or table number and title. The number is sequential within the chapter. Thus, the second figure or table in chapter 4 is labeled 4.2.

Acknowledgments

In my own career, during the lengthy process of evolving the practices of Commercial Project Management, there are three Calgary businessmen whose influence must be acknowledged. First is Russ Hall, who explained to me many years ago that a project was a slice of business and subject to the same rules of selling, delivery, and customer management as any other piece of business. The lesson finally sunk in. Then Doug Morrison, whom I have known almost as long and whose unflagging support, encouragement, and appreciation for what I was trying to achieve kept early implementation efforts going when the temptation was to take the easy way out. And Jim Wickson, who provided two critical years of sponsorship and so enabled a rare opportunity to take everything that had been formulated over the past two decades, refine it, and present it comprehensively from beginning to end. Finally, a tremendous debt of gratitude is owed to Tom Mitchell, who supplied his expertise to a painstaking technical review of my first draft. Tom is a friend and erstwhile colleague whose career and experience complement my own. He challenged many of my assertions and provided several corrections. But, at the end of a discussion round, Tom would always say, "well, it's your book, so make it as you want …" This means that I must be held fully accountable for any errors or misdirection that still remain in the text.

My sincere thanks to these gentlemen and to many others along the way who have challenged, critiqued, enhanced, and valued these ideas.

Robin Hornby
Calgary
2016

1 A summary of the guide

This is a 'how-to' book for project and business managers who work in a commercial or contracted project environment. Organized as a set of six core practices, this collection of practical advice, case histories, explanatory illustrations, useful techniques, and proven checklists will give vendor project managers the key information and the confidence to succeed in their demanding role. More than just project management, the book proposes a comprehensive template for the firm whose business is delivering projects.

Increasingly, projects are being delivered as part of a commercial arrangement between a buyer and a seller. The boom in outsourcing over the past 20 years is testimony to this fact. The trend is likely to continue. Despite this, project management standards fail to deal with the commercial context, although they do expand with every new edition in support of project management's attempt to take over the universe! Perhaps, my new guide is contributing to this impulse, though the modest intent is to simply avoid more black hole projects.

Intended audience

Any project manager (PM) of moderate experience who is transitioning to the world of commercial projects and seeking advice and guidance will find this book tailor made. It will also be useful to a manager or owner engaged in building a professional services firm, as the guide is a practical framework for such an endeavor. Managers in established firms can use the content to benchmark their internal policies, practices, and guidelines with a view to improvement. Those who supply corporate services internally can also find value here as they adopt more sophisticated commercial principles, possibly based on an internal economy where labor and other resource rates are priced on a cost-recovery basis and used for budgeting and internal charge-out.

Despite my background in information technology projects, the guide is not exclusively aimed at managers of software projects or IT firms. I believe the generalizations I have introduced make the text useful to all services firms, though some content will be discernable as originating from the software development discipline.

General scope

At the heart of my approach is a vendor sales and delivery lifecycle that subsumes the project lifecycle and provides a framework for business control of projects. Unique elements of this approach include the adoption of a unified project lifecycle, the recasting of project management as a cyclic set of functions, and the elevation of risk assessment from a project toolkit to a fundamental control process of the business. Also described are methods to promote client and vendor project integration, and essential, redeveloped practices for resource and quality management, scoping, estimating, and role definition.

I want to be clear that the book is about the business management of the project, not about managing customer business outcomes. Other writers have explored benefits management, which is a complementary but separate topic. An important early contribution to this field is Thorp's *The Information Paradox: Realizing the Business Benefits of Information Technology*.

Neither is this another treatise on conventional project management. For that, the interested reader may turn to the evolving international standards or one of many texts in the marketplace. The most comprehensive of these is probably Kerzner's *Project Management: A Systems Approach to Planning, Scheduling, and Controlling*. That does not mean important elements of project management are not discussed—far from it. As most artful project managers know, good project management mostly turns out to be good business.

Chapter synopsis

Following this summary, there are 11 chapters to cover the scope. Like project management books, the content is topic-driven so each can be read stand-alone, though Chapter 2 should probably be read first.

Chapter 2: Introduction to the business of projects

The professional services firm must take a disciplined business approach to the selling and delivery of commercial projects. PMs must understand that a project is also a profit center, and business managers must place more emphasis on the control of risk and commitment. This approach requires the firm to select core practices and a vendor lifecycle supported by core documents.

Available standards such as PRINCE2® and PMBOK® both avoid seller processes and do not fit well with commercial projects, requiring the adoption of a new architecture. The commercial project environment emphasizes the client's project lifecycle as the prime means of integrating the client and vendor. Project management is usefully viewed as four functions applied repetitively to the work of the project: plan, organize, control, and lead.

The deliverables and activities of both client and vendor PMs are mapped to the project lifecycle to achieve transparency and integration between project management and the work of the team. Core processes, deliverables, models, techniques, and checklists support the four project management functions.

Chapter 3: Buyer and vendor integration

There are many obstacles to building project unity after a contract is signed. The tendency is for client and vendor project silos to form. Project communications are complex, vendor and client are culturally distinct organizations, and the contract itself may be a source of discord between the parties. Contentious contract terms are explained and related risks are identified.

Perspectives on project management, such as the project scope, the role of the PMs and the sponsor, and the ownership of risk, will also differ in important ways. They must be resolved during project initiation. This clears the decks for the practice of lifecycle mapping, which is demonstrated using a sample project.

The parties are driven by success measures that may not be completely aligned. The client defines success as the achievement of project objectives documented in the charter. The vendor is obliged to deliver according to contract, make a profit, and leave the customer satisfied. An ideal, integrated model ensures that in the process of delivering to meet the client's objectives, the vendor automatically meets theirs.

Chapter 4: Evolution of a vendor lifecycle

The key activities of selling and delivering are straightforward and map logically into sequential phases to make an ideal waterfall lifecycle. The idea of treating the sales activities as a forward extension of delivery is critical, because it is during selling that commitments are made and risk factors often fail to be identified.

There are five phases in the vendor lifecycle. The first two are sales oriented: the opportunity and bid phases. The following three are delivery oriented: the initiation, execution, and completion phases. These phases may be repeated two or more times to deliver a complex project using multiple contracts.

The proposed lifecycle provides management control and shaping of the project by identifying phase exit criteria, approvers, and 15 core documents adapted from project management. By also deploying the six core practices in conjunction with the vendor lifecycle, the vendor introduces his business perspective into the project.

Chapter 5: Developing organizational responsibilities

The role of delivery manager is introduced to the vendor organization to counterbalance dominance by sales management. Delivery management brings sales and delivery concerns into balance and makes success more likely, more often. The firm's management responsibilities are aligned accordingly.

During project execution, ambiguous, ill-defined, incomplete, or ignored stakeholder responsibilities are the cause of a major share of failures. The vendor PM needs helpful models and techniques to rectify this failing.

The first model is responsibility, accountability, and authority (RAA). The firm must think about their key management positions from an RAA perspective. In the project context, examples show how vendor PMs can use the RAA model to ensure they only accept accountability commensurate with their delegated authority.

The second technique is the responsibility assignment matrix (RAM). Examples are used to document an unambiguous responsibility plan for the firm's management and a detail plan for a project's deliverables.

The third model is the organization structure chart. Structure charts illustrate the three basic project structures and their strengths and weaknesses. The chart is also used to show alternative vendor organizations and the link between growth and the evolution from decentralized to centralized organization.

Chapter 6: Risk as a guiding principle for management

Best practice for vendors is to design a risk *system* that takes a holistic view of the business, but with particular emphasis on the bid and execution phases. During the bid phase, there are two aspects to risk: the risk of not winning the bid and the risk of winning it but not adequately delivering and losing money. A systems approach to the firm's portfolio suggests a statistically optimum balance of risk and reward yields a 70% project success rate.

Risk models are especially useful for more advanced risk analysis. The 'known–unknown' model of risk has value when contemplating what risks can be identified and to what extent they impact the project. Other models include the familiar risk event model based on cause and effect analysis that is the source for the risk register and two innovative models designed to make the analysis process more accessible. The first is a risk factor model applied during the bid phase to determine a risk rank. The second is a risk indicator model used during the execution phase to assess the strength of performance chains and determine the risk alerts.

These models are valuable because they yield a set of metrics and can be embedded in the firm's operations. Risk rank conditions the firm's mitigation and bid review strategy. Risk alerts during execution trigger progressive levels of management support or, at the highest alert level, a red project review.

Chapter 7: Overcoming estimating anxieties

Development of a credible project estimate requires experience, knowledge, and discipline rarely found in one person; good estimators are valuable. Thus, methodology, feedback, and learning are needed to broaden the base of the firm's estimating expertise. Difficulties and anxieties faced by the estimator often arise from cultural behaviors within the firm, such as allowing sales pressure to influence estimates, ignoring risk factors, and making overly optimistic assumptions.

Improvement comes by implementing an estimating process and the cultural transition to support it. Planning elements, such as requirements and deliverables, must first be settled or assumed. At completion, project results must be recorded, compared to the estimates, and built into the knowledge base.

The estimating process embodies several techniques. Top-down, or expert, estimating uses comparisons with similar projects, or formulae (standard estimates) that the expert is confident can be applied. Bottom-up, or methodical, estimating uses either the activity list or the grid method for estimating deliverables. Rule of thumb (ROT) can be used as a quick method for elements such as project management and support, or for conditioning deliverable estimates based on productivity. Contingency is estimated based on the risk level, and an ROT based on probability theory is reviewed.

Chapter 8: Solving the quality conundrum

There are a variety of viewpoints on what quality represents, but they fall into two categories: the objective and subjective views. The vendor PM needs to be adept at translating the client's subjective view into an agreed set of measurable objectives. This dialogue also reveals the project's quality requirements. Some knowledge of the basic methodologies, such as Six Sigma, TQM, QFD, ISO9000, and requirements-centered techniques such as RTM, is helpful.

To deal with this quality smorgasbord, the firm must adopt three principles: the client pays for quality, a quality objective is only actionable if recognized by the client, and the firm must have a clear foundation for how they approach quality—a basic QMS.

A basic QMS positions the firm as a proponent of quality and enables a flexible, minimum-cost response in the absence of a specific client demand. Sets of checklists and models of quality can be referenced in dialogue with the client to help assemble a quality plan.

As the firm evolves, an expanded commitment to quality requires appointment of a quality manager. In this structure, the quality manager endorses each project's quality objectives and supports the vendor PMs by focusing on quality issues, which are consolidated and presented to the firm's management for action on continuous improvement.

In the final analysis, if management and the PMs have done their job, it comes down to the work of team members to deliver quality. Research shows that teams are motivated toward high-quality performance when the tasks are seen as significant, require a variety of skills performed autonomously, and are subject to constructive feedback.

Chapter 9: Managing the resource pool

The firm's resources are at the center of the business model, and at the same time, resource availability is a perennial risk factor found in project risk assessments. For this reason alone, concern for resource capability and active resource forecasting should be top priorities.

Managing the firm's resource assets starts with hiring practices, which in turn start with a carefully crafted statement of role for each position. Evaluation, selection, and interviewing methods should be consistently applied following proven guidelines.

Ongoing resource management and planning are an important aspect of the job of the Professional Services Manager (PSM), and a strong link must be established with their PMs' project resource plans. There are four metrics essential to this task: estimates, actuals, utilization, and availability. Effective resource management relies on systems that process these data and, with the sales forecast, feed into periodic management processes where allocation and planning decisions are made.

The PSM can rely on techniques and strategies to maximize morale, capability, and commitment of the resource pool. Some of these are unique to the services business; others are commonly known but carry a special emphasis. An important activity is resource contingency planning, which involves third-party relations, trap-line, and bench management. Performance management demands attention, as do a variety of techniques designed to ensure employee retention.

Chapter 10: Finance matters

The Finance Department of a large professional services firm carries significant project-related responsibilities. An awareness of financial matters by sales executives, vendor PMs, and senior practitioners is essential.

A model of the services business illustrates the relationships between the customer, the firm, their staff, and the firm's products and services. The model provides insights into how the business is driven and maintained, and hence the financial KPIs (key performance indicators) that Finance is responsible to track and report.

During the bid phase, sales executives and vendor PMs must understand the three most common types of contract: FP, T&M, and Cost Plus, plus common variations. The firm must have a logical framework for rate setting. Sales executives must be familiar with the cost S-curve and the cash flow chart for the proposed project. They must also be familiar with other financial concerns such as contractual penalties, performance bonds or holdbacks, and internal concerns like discounted bundled bids, or bids including a future product for which fair value cannot be demonstrated.

If the bid is won, the contract is negotiated, signed, and booked during the initiation phase. The vendor PM reviews project setup to ensure project accounting reports reflect the information to be tracked. The PM also takes an active role in initializing time reporting for the project and setting up the invoicing schedule.

During the execution phase, the vendor PM reports progress to Finance who recognize the revenue earned. The usual method is to estimate the project POC (percentage of completion) using accepted techniques. The PM must balance pressure to show an advancing POC that increases revenue against a realistic assessment of the work actually completed and still to be done. The PM enforces time reporting discipline, distinguishes billable and nonbillable time, and monitors utilization, expense claims, and invoice approvals.

Finally, during completion, the vendor PM conveys the project sign-off to Finance for final invoicing, completes remaining project administration, and packages the key contract files for archiving.

Chapter 11: Building a successful services firm

There is more to the firm's success than the practices and techniques described in this guide, which largely derive from the discipline of project management. For completeness, this chapter touches on additional internal management art that the firm must implement.

Core business concepts for professional services firms include understanding the supply versus demand management model; balancing the firm between seniors, intermediates, and juniors; implementing professional client management; setting billing multiples; and taking proper care of employees.

The firm must design and implement standard operating procedures, which also contribute to basic risk mitigation in line with a systems approach to risk. Important supporting components include training, authority tables for managers and senior staff, and document storage and retrieval.

Finally, an established firm that decides to augment their environment to match the principles and methods in this guide must pay attention to several important prerequisites. These include recognition of the probable need for culture change, proposition of alternatives for organizing delivery management, and demonstration of leadership and vision from the top.

Chapter 12: Toward collaborative procurement of services

This bonus chapter moves the discourse from vendor methods to a vision of a collaborative approach for the purchase and delivery of professional services. This is in response to the author's experience of avoidable loss, waste, and inefficiency associated with current methods, and a repeated emphasis in this guide on the importance of vendor and client integration practices.

Taking the commercial project environment from Chapter 2 as a base, a Total Collaborative Procurement (TCP) architecture is proposed that includes a description of five joint phases and six joint practices. These can eliminate the current inefficiencies but still permit a fair and competitive environment. They mirror the phases and practices already described, but with significant adaptations to support the collaborative approach.

This approach requires both client and vendor PMs to possess commercial skills and knowledge, and presumes trust as an essential ingredient for building productive commercial relationships. With these requirements established, a proposal for TCP implementation is outlined. Despite the righteous words on trust, a truly collaborative model can only be achieved by the sponsorship of a professional third party who assumes ownership of the TCP and maintains a registry of participants.

To bring this vision to reality will require considerable effort, partitioned into a series of six steps: feasibility assessment, constitution of the third party, pilot development and evaluation, version 1 development, implementation, and launch. The hope is that the productivity benefits, potentially of national significance, are recognized and the opportunity is seized.

Conclusion

I am confident that the growing services firm that can pause to implement the practices I have described will meet with success. Maybe not on every project, but on enough that the business will succeed. Contemplate the advice I received from a boss at my old consulting company who had a unique way of emphasizing the three priorities of the professional services firm: profit, customers, and employees.

"Success in this business is like juggling three balls: the profit, the customers, and the employees. If you drop one, I am not so interested in which one you dropped; just don't drop any!"

2 Introduction to the business of projects

Commercial project management involves a professional services firm (the firm) who supplies a vendor project manager (PM) and a team of practitioners to create a product for a sponsor, and at the same time makes a profit. It therefore follows that the vendor PM must operate within a business framework and follow business practices. He is in the front line in the effort to ensure the client is not merely pleased but will proudly reference the firm's services to others.

Overview of the situation

The introduction of a business relationship between a services firm, their project manager, and a sponsor who is now a customer has a salutary effect on the traditional project management role. Project managers with little experience in these situations manage less effectively, jeopardizing customer satisfaction and project profitability. At the same time, executives or owners of the firm are often unfamiliar with the disciplines of project management, especially at an early stage of their firm's evolution, and so their support for a struggling project manager is lacking and the firm may never gain the foundation for healthy growth or even survival. Managers and practitioners who work internally in a large corporation using project charge-out, often called an internal economy, have a similar dilemma, as they must deal with both business and project issues.

My generalized observations are:

- PMs lack experience and knowledge of business essentials, fail to run their projects as profit centers, and have difficulty understanding that their sponsor is also their customer; and
- Business owners are unaware of the potential for project management disciplines to enhance their business operations and are missing opportunities to gain much-needed business control.

Firms who have primed their PMs with business acumen and balanced an enthusiastic and skillful sales team with delivery management disciplines are rewarded with both successful projects and repeat business, which is the secret of a firm's profitability and longevity.

Project management vs. general management

It has always mystified me why there is such a divide between project and general management. A good project manager always has a grasp on general management (and leadership) principles. A good general manager also has a competence in things that are seen in the domain of project management, such as phasing of work, issue handling, decision analysis, risk and assumption assessments, and so forth. That isn't to say that there aren't PM specialties—Gantt charts, critical path analysis, and earned value are all important—but the PM spends less time on those tasks than you might imagine, especially in the commercial environment. A large part of the solution to bridge this divide is to promote some cross-fertilization, coaching PMs to think like profit center managers, and business managers to think of their firm's projects in terms of commitment phases and risk.

Resistance to process

Now the fun begins. In the minds of many managers, project management is synonymous with process, process, and more process. Regrettably, implementing process as a driver of business success has been out of fashion since the late 1990s and the bursting of the great quality bubble. The current trend seems to downplay or even marginalize process with the focus being on creativity and haste, freeing the talented employee from any form of discipline, and promoting results (what kind of results?) and a satisfied customer (for how long?) ahead of adherence to procedure. These are tempting options for the services firm that finds processes unappealing and relies instead on their above-average talent. They find reassurance in Tom Peters' infamous line in *The Pursuit of WOW!* where Peters quotes his colleague Richard Buetow who ironically suggested that a manufacturer of concrete lifejackets could be ISO certified so long as they were made following documented procedures and the next of kin were given instructions on how to complain about defects. I don't believe Peters was arguing against process but instead pleading for balance between freedom to innovate and business discipline.

Although talent in business is needed, there aren't enough talented people to go around, and even if there were, building a business totally dependent on superior people is at best a short-term strategy and at worst a recipe for disaster. The majority of long-term successful businesses are dependent on the application of intelligent process. This must also apply to the professional services business.

Now, a question that the project manager might ask: Why isn't classic project management enough? Why can't the firm's project managers be trained on a project management standard and turned loose? Well, naturally, they must have this knowledge. That is a 'given'. However, there is more to success than that. Success in this environment means winning the competitive bid for the project, accurately assessing the resources to do the work in the face of multiple uncertainties, consistently delivering what the customer wants within the cost budget, and making a profit for the firm. This requires skills and knowledge that go beyond the reach of traditional project management practice. The firm's management must also make their commitment to stand behind new organizational structures, authorities, and practices that determine how projects are bid and operated.

Having argued that more is needed, be cautioned that distributing a procedures manual to all and sundry is not going to work. Firms are essentially entrepreneurial, and sales people are instinctively hunters. A delicate touch must be applied, ensuring formalization is genuinely needed and can be appreciated by those who might resist. As the reader will discover, I generally avoid prescribing procedures and instead discuss practices (perhaps best practices), which leave more fluidity in the implementation than procedures and can be supported by a loosely coupled variety of techniques and checklists.

Project management standards have limits

In the foregoing, I affirmed the importance of formal training in project management. In today's world, it is a necessary, though insufficient, prerequisite for the job. So, without diminishing that declaration, I now must describe the difficulties encountered when attempting to apply these standards to a commercial situation.

There are two dominant standards in the world today: the PMBOK® and PRINCE2®. Both are now widely implemented, though PMBOK® had its origins in the United States and Canada, where it is prevalent, while PRINCE2® was developed in the United Kingdom and is stronger in Europe.

PMBOK®

This standard views project management as a collection of processes, with supporting techniques. There are two organizing principles for these 47 processes. They are allocated into each of 10 knowledge areas (such as scope, schedule, risk, and quality). They are also placed into five process groups: initiate, plan, execute, control, and close.

These process groups, illustrated in Section 3 of the PMBOK®, show a sequential flow from initiation through a cyclic process of planning and executing, ending with closing. Monitoring and controlling is represented as an overarching process group. Procurement is described as a knowledge area, though as purely a buyer process executed as part of the client's existing project.

An unfortunate side effect of the process group representation is that the groups are widely misinterpreted as part of a project lifecycle, even though the PMBOK® states that process groups are not project phases. It appears to be a hybrid, caught between sequential phases such as initiation and closing, and repetitive functions such as planning, executing, and controlling.

Both parties flounder with PMBOK® when the concept of a contract is introduced. It appears as though a new project is beginning and should go through initiation, but this cannot be true, as the project must already exist or there would be no procurement. Important preliminary deliverables such as the charter become ambiguous with no clear ownership.

Adherence to the PMBOK® process group cycle almost encourages the emergence of a new project every time a procurement is launched. Essential unity is lost, and the silo effect between the vendor team and the client team can become dominant.

PRINCE2®

The framework offered by PRINCE2® is based on eight interacting high-level processes: directing, start-up, initiating, planning, controlling a stage, managing delivery, managing stage boundaries, and closing. There are also eight components—organization, plans, controls, risk, quality, configuration management, change control, and business case—that can interact with all of the project management processes.

The major difficulty is that procurement is omitted from the scheme. This is explicitly acknowledged in the standard with the assumption that the PM and, presumably, the team already exist on contract, or alternately exist in-house. The buyer and seller processes to get to this point are absent.

These processes modeled in Section 2 of the PRINCE2® manual provide a comprehensive and unmistakable picture of management processes. The price of this is complexity. It is not improbable to imagine an extension to these processes and components that might accommodate buyer and seller activities to bid and execute a scope of work (or 'work package'), but at present they are not there.

The way forward

I have come to several conclusions when wrestling with these existing standards and how they might assist the goal of achieving wholesome integration between client and vendor project teams, and the need to bring structure to the fluid world of professional services.

The first conclusion is that imposing an operational standard on project management is counterproductive. Although standards have many benefits and over the past 20 years have resulted in appreciation and respect for the PM role, they have unfortunately contributed to the perception that project management exists in its own universe and is disconnected from the work of the project. The work of the project is expressed in a technique called the project lifecycle (aka the application lifecycle or the development lifecycle), and it is time to put project management back where it belongs—integrated with the actual work.

Another conclusion is that implementing the minutiae of process in a mixed team and between managers from different organizations is next to impossible. Things need to be defined and agreed to, but at a different level. Thus, specifying project management in terms of process, other than for those fundamentals called the core processes, is an uphill struggle. A much more productive view of the PM job, especially in the commercial world, is to see it as a set of functions. There are four functions: plan, organize, control, and lead, sometimes abbreviated as POCL. These functions interact with the people and their organizations to get the work done.

A final conclusion is that really nothing in the standards addresses the reality of the vendor's role in the bidding and delivery of projects to the client's order. A framework is needed. Project management's favorite technique comes to the rescue again and offers us the vendor lifecycle—opportunity, bid, initiate, execute, and complete. Just as with the project lifecycle, practices borrowed from project management can be applied to this lifecycle as well, to get the job done.

Solutions based on these conclusions are expanded in the chapters that follow, but the simple architecture diagram in Figure 2.1 introduces the concepts upon which this guide is based.

The architecture is founded upon the two lifecycles: one that describes the project work and the other, the vendor's sales and delivery cycle. The project lifecycle is managed by applying the four functions of project management and a small set of core processes. The vendor's lifecycle is supported by a set of core documents and practices. In the ecology are an array of techniques, deliverables, and so forth, to be employed as needed.

I hope the reader is persuaded by my conclusion, and perhaps their own experience, that working with the standard frameworks in a contracted project

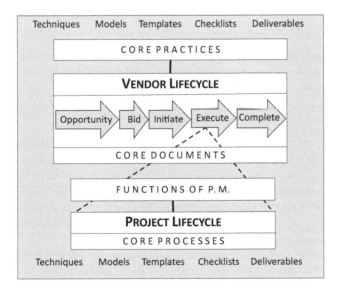

Figure 2.1 Architecture of the commercial project environment

is an exercise in frustration, and there is little to support the vendor. A custom architecture, as presented, is the most productive solution. But, the baby is not going out with the bathwater. Under the covers, most elements of sound project management are the same. Practices, techniques, checklists, and deliverables are shamelessly taken from the standards and adapted to meet our needs. They are just packaged into a more useful framework.

The commercial project environment

The CPE framework provides context for the methods deemed to contribute to commercial projects. The following descriptions illustrate how the model helps secure the aims of the project team and the success of the vendor.

The project lifecycle

The lifecycle most of us think of when considering this important but underappreciated technique is the project lifecycle, meaning a lifecycle appropriate for work in a specific industry or area of application. This might be construction, electronics, pharmaceuticals, software, aviation, and others. The client often hands the project lifecycle to the contractor as a detailed blueprint on how the specialized work of building the product is to be accomplished. Alternatively, the technical practitioners of the commercial firm provide their own. Regardless of the sourcing of the project lifecycle, it must become central to project management and must be used as a focus for meaningful integration between the client and vendor teams, and their PMs. It creates a communications bridge and a platform for management of the project.

> The project lifecycle is the most effective basis for integrating project management into commercial projects and promoting the concept of project unity.

During joint client/firm project planning sessions, the firm naturally presents their own lifecycle and preferred solutions to approaching the project, but remains open to accepting the client's proposals—as they should. The firm can do this without jeopardizing their own control, because, as we shall see later, the firm extracts key business-oriented project management deliverables that are universal to all their projects and links them to their own vendor lifecycle controlled by the firm.

Recognizing, communicating, and agreeing to the project lifecycle are so important, I want to give some examples. First, a definition: the lifecycle is simply a sequence of defined phases. The work of each phase of the project lifecycle is organized to meet the objectives of the phase and to develop the phase deliverables. The phase generally employs resources of the same type.

Clear phase completion criteria are usually established and data provided for project cost/benefit re-evaluation so that the project can receive progressive commitment through the lifecycle.

Project lifecycles are undergoing a transformation at present with the advent of Agile, which originated in the software development milieu where changes in requirements are a fact of life. These trends have influenced projects in other areas, but the sequential, step-by-step project lifecycle is still common and is chosen here as the base for discussion.

Such lifecycles are colloquially referred to as *waterfall* lifecycles, meaning one phase must be completed before the next is started. This emphasizes thoroughness and quality during each phase. In a waterfall, a return to a previous phase would suggest that a mistake had been made and should be rectified. An example of a waterfall lifecycle is shown in Figure 2.2.

Sometimes, to reduce the project lifecycle schedule, waterfall phases may be overlapped, though this naturally increases risk. That is, the phase completion criteria are consciously relaxed and the next phase started early. This version of the waterfall is called *fast tracking*, illustrated in Figure 2.3.

Another type of project lifecycle encountered in certain application areas is the *iterative* lifecycle. The iterative lifecycle acknowledges that some of the risk of phase overlap is removed by partitioning the product into components so the design phase is kept open as successive components are worked on. When a component is designed, it moves right away into the build phase. For example, Figure 2.4 shows a simple iterative lifecycle based on the six-phase lifecycle already discussed, but with three iterations planned during design/build, each building a different component of the product.

Project lifecycle designers have taken the concepts of the iterative lifecycle and further refined it into a spiral lifecycle and more recently into the agile

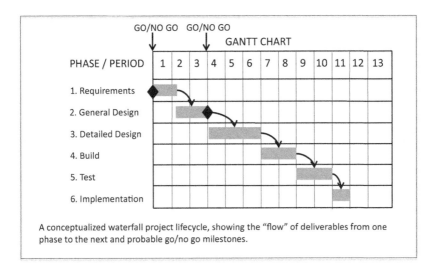

A conceptualized waterfall project lifecycle, showing the "flow" of deliverables from one phase to the next and probable go/no go milestones.

Figure 2.2 A classic waterfall lifecycle for a generic application

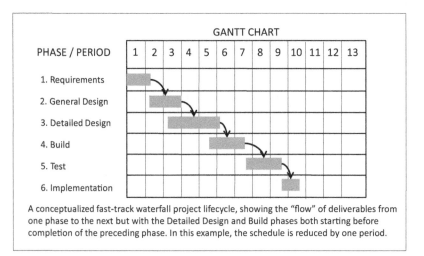

Figure 2.3 A waterfall lifecycle with fast-track

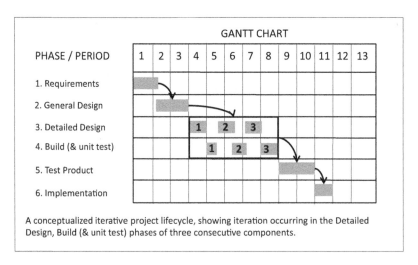

Figure 2.4 An iterative lifecycle

lifecycle. Consultants, product developers, and others with expertise in the application area have taken the concept of the project lifecycle, be it waterfall, iterative, spiral, or agile, and generated full-blown methodologies offered for sale in the marketplace. A contemporary example would be Fujitsu Consulting's *Macroscope* for software development.

With a project lifecycle base defined and agreed to by the client and vendor, the other key benefits of the CPE can come into play:

Mapping–The line linking the Project Lifecycle and the Functions of PM in Figure 2.1 represents the practice of mapping and allows the project managers to understand their exact responsibilities through each phase and clarify their accountabilities.

Common View of the Lifecycle–Aligns the vendor and client views of the project and promotes communication and joint processes where necessary.

Vendor's Business Lifecycle–The vendor is now free to institute an independent business lifecycle to subsume any type of project and retain necessary control of the business management.

The functions of project management

My preference for representing project management as a set of functions, not a set of processes, and certainly not a lifecycle, has been influenced by a definition of project management that impressed me many years ago. It is not in any standard literature that I can recall, but here it is and I commend it.

Project management is a structured approach to plan, organize, control, and lead the work of the project to meet project objectives.

Using this definition, the work of the project is organized (structured) into a lifecycle and the work of the project manager is characterized as four functions. The definition does not mention deliverables, though the project manager accomplishes many of her functions through the production of deliverables. To firmly bring project management into reality, these deliverables should also be considered as 'work of the project' and integrated with the project lifecycle rather than hived off into some theoretical project management structure.

A lifecycle aggregates project activities into sequential phases where each phase is distinctive in terms of the work being done by the team and the deliverables being produced. The work of the PM, on the other hand, is embodied in the functions of planning, organizing, controlling, and leading (POCL). These are repetitive and never-ending, as shown in Figure 2.5, and must not be confused with the sequential, phased work defined by the project lifecycle and set in place by the project manager to guide the team.

Another way of thinking about the concept of project management functions during the project lifecycle is to envision the project manager as continuously juggling her daily duties between POCL functions. Obviously, the emphasis placed on a specific function depends on the deliverables being worked and the current phase situation. For example, if the project is wrapping up a requirements phase and a project plan is being prepared, then the bulk of the day goes to planning, with the occasional hour or two on organizing. The next day, however, may bring a working session with the sponsor where it is discovered that expectations

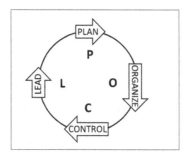

Figure 2.5 The four functions of project management

are misaligned and departments have conflicting objectives. Now is the time for the project manager to show leadership. In due course, plans are baselined and the emphasis moves to controlling, but details must still be worked and variances resolved, and so a day or two each week still goes to planning.

Deliverables of project managers

Deliverables is a rather odd word coined by project management and means result or product. It also has a useful shade of meaning, as deliverables may be intermediate, i.e., a stepping-stone to the end result. For example, a design report is an intermediate deliverable that is required before the product can be built. Despite the odd name, deliverables are a powerful technique of project management because they have tangibility and can be inspected, approved, and measured. These attributes make them dissimilar to activities. Deliverables are therefore an essential element in project planning and control and are produced during a specific phase of a lifecycle.

Some deliverables are defined in standards as the responsibility of the project manager, though, on larger projects, qualified team members may be assigned to work on them. PM deliverables include items such as the project charter, the scope of work, the status report, change requests, sign-off reports, and so on. These are comprehensively dealt with in the PMBOK® as a checklist under 'project documents'. Conversely, the majority of project deliverables reflect the output of the team, and they are allocated based on the practitioner's role and specialization. These deliverables are usually defined in the methodology for the project lifecycle being followed. Thus, an unnatural partition can be erected between the project management and the team deliverables, especially if two different reference books are being consulted, even though the project manager is ultimately accountable for *all* deliverables on the project, not just PM deliverables.

This partition is demolished during the planning at the beginning of the project using lifecycle mapping. The vendor and client PMs jointly map the required project management deliverables into the agreed project lifecycle phases, just like the team deliverables, and manage them accordingly.

PMBOK® does not tell exactly where these deliverables belong because, in the cause of universality, PMBOK® is neutral on the project lifecycle. The project manager's job is to use judgment to map the deliverables into the right phase.

> Both project management and team deliverables must be mapped to the project lifecycle.

Core processes

There are, from experience, an essential core group of processes that must be implemented on a commercial project independently from the methodology deployed, the practices described in this guide, or the corporate culture. There are project eventualities with business repercussions that can only be handled accurately by following a specified process, in the best interests of the client and the vendor. Vendor PMs might have slightly different ideas on the top eight; the list is my selection in order of criticality.

List of eight core processes

The statement of work (SOW) may include the following, and, ideally, they are agreed upon in the contract. For communication purposes, it is a good idea to assemble all customized processes into a *Project Procedures Manual*. The worst time to figure out a procedure is when you need it!

1 Change management
2 Issue management
3 Deliverable acceptance
4 Status and progress reporting to client
5 Discrepancy reporting
6 Project sign-off
7 Decision requests
8 Transition to operations/maintenance.

The vendor lifecycle

The vendor lifecycle is central to the commercial project environment (CPE). This is a higher-level lifecycle focused on the management of business risk and commitment. It is operated by the firm's delivery manager and is independent of the project lifecycle. Logical analysis of the professional services business, fully explained in Chapter 4, results in a straightforward five-phase waterfall lifecycle summarized in Figure 2.6.

The vendor lifecycle acts as a wrapper for the project lifecycle (where the work occurs) and provides the firm with a consistent approach to bidding, winning, and successfully executing their projects. This 'wrapper' concept explains

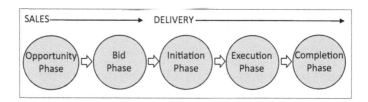

Figure 2.6 The phases of the vendor lifecycle

the dashed lines in the CPE (Figure 2.1) from the project lifecycle to the execute phase of the vendor lifecycle. This means that all contracted phases of work (e.g., design, develop, install) occur as part of the execution phase.

Equipped with its own business-friendly phases, key management deliverables or core documents, and built-in practices to match the interests of the vendor firm, the vendor lifecycle may be regarded as a rudimentary methodology. The core documents, being vendor confidential, are not normally visible to the customer, though I must reinforce that the vast majority of the vendor PM's deliverables are explicitly agreed to with the customer, mapped into the project lifecycle, and are very visible.

Practices

A practice is general-purpose guidance for the accomplishment of a task and will call upon the use of techniques, templates, checklists, and the like. In business, best practices are continually being identified in order to achieve best results. This is an area of specialization for consultancies.

At first sight, the practices might be confused with conventional project management, but that is not the case. The practices are the prime means of introducing business and vendor perspectives into the contracted project and are aimed at generating either a more effective bid or, when deployed during execution, a more effective project.

List of six core practices

A practice is open in its implementation and unlike a procedure does not funnel all projects into 'one-size-fits-all'. If formalization is required, the firm must write the procedure tailored to the firm. These are the six core practices in the sequence in which they are covered in the book:

1   Lifecycle Mapping–The practice of mapping all deliverables and the activities of POCL has been mentioned already—it is fully explained in Chapter 3.
2   Accountabilities Definition–Mixed teams operating under joint management need roles and responsibilities specified using the models and techniques in Chapter 5.
3   Risk Management–The concept of risk is expanded in the CPE to become a system applied to both project and business and is described in Chapter 6.

4   Estimating–The firm that fails to build its estimating expertise goes out of business fairly quickly. Chapter 7 covers the ground.
5   Quality Management–Quality often causes difficulties for the firm, and Chapter 8 presents a solution based on establishing a set of principles, a basic and inexpensive QMS, and a set of models to guide project quality decisions.
6   Resource Management–The most common complaint from PMs is not enough people with the right skills. The firm must be especially adept at managing this aspect, and Chapter 9 shows how.

The line linking core practices and vendor lifecycle shown in the CPE diagram (Figure 2.1) represents the requirement for each of these practices to support the work of each phase. The CPE also names common categories of problem-solving methods that support the core practices.

Models, techniques, templates, and checklists

The reader will find many of these problem-solving methods in the guide. Some are specialized in support of a practice, and others are helpful in many phases of both the vendor and project lifecycles. They are woven throughout the CPE and can be drawn on as required to support a core practice or a specific activity of the POCL functions. The following are categories that are most useful:

Models–I have always enjoyed the aphorism "a picture is worth a thousand words," and as most models are pictures, I use lots of them. In the CPE, they have a role in simplifying complexity, promoting decision making, and triggering the use of a technique. The model used in risk analysis to explain risk factors (Figure 6.5) is a good example.

Techniques–A commonly used term often confused with process or procedure. A technique is aimed at a solution and calls for a level of expertise, or tool use. These techniques are found in the expert's 'tool bag' or in the body of knowledge for the relevant profession or trade. For example, one technique to determine priorities is to draw up a list of needed, wanted, and desirable items. Another technique used often in estimating is a rule of thumb (ROT).

Templates–A template is a good example of reuse, an important quality technique. Templates are always a good idea for any repetitive document and are effective in enforcing standards. If regularly updated, the template keeps all users current with business improvements. Templates may be regarded as a form of stored knowledge that leverages the firm's experts.

Checklists–Another great example of reuse and stored knowledge. There are several to be found in this guide. In Gawande's excellent *The Checklist Manifesto* two types are described: the READ/DO and the DO/CONFIRM. Although right for surgical procedures and flight emergencies, they are too prescriptive for the flexible world of commercial projects. I prefer READ/SELECT.

3 Buyer and vendor integration

Project complexity has two dimensions: the complexity of the product being built and the complexity of the project itself. Technical experts have their own techniques for determining product complexity using assessments of the technical environment, degree of innovation, number of interfaces, performance demands, stability of specifications, etc. But what about the project itself? It doesn't seem to take very much product complexity for the project to get much more complicated than anticipated.

The impact of product or technical complexity is only the beginning. The commercial project is subject to other unique pressures. These promote the negative tendency for project silos to form. A divide forms between the vendor project and the 'other' client project. Every now and again they have to pay attention, but they would rather ignore each other. It's a joke, I know, but the after-work pub comment "this would be a really good project if it wasn't for the customer" carries an edge. In this chapter, I look at the factors behind this and some of the actions the leaders can take to bring these two entities together under a common goal to form an integrated project.

The vendor's challenges start in the bid phase and only increase into execution. Examples include estimating under conditions of marketplace free-for-all, regulatory and procurement policy constraints, zero sum contracting terms, arm's length stakeholders, hidden communication channels, and project delivery under commercial pressures, as well as the usual quota of technical and project management issues. These all serve to create a complex environment. If failure is not the occasional result here, then I have certainly witnessed unnecessary aggravation, expense, and inefficiency that seem endemic to many professional services contracts.

Most PMs are conversant with the common causes of project failure in their industry, and these form useful inputs into risk mitigation analysis. The nature of commercial projects not only adds a whole new list of causes but also exacerbates those already present. Table 3.1 includes failure causes from both categories. I have not yet seen a standard definition of advanced project management, but my guess is that any PM who can navigate his way through this list must be practicing it.

Table 3.1 Causes of failure

Failure causes	
Unrealistic expectations	Commercial pressure
Different perspectives	Inadequate resources
Hidden agenda	Miscommunication
Vendor arrogance	Ignored risks
Marketplace free-for-all	Political over-rides
Over-optimism	Bad experiences
Over-selling	Unexplored assumptions
Lack of priorities	Over-controlling
Lack of specificity, ambiguity	Inattention to responsibilities
Playing the vendor field	Surprise requirements
Inadequate client funding	Unsupportive policies
Lack of client consensus	Sponsor inaccessibility
Missing commitments	Immaturity
Inappropriate contracts	

Impediments to unified project management

The practice of lifecycle mapping, described later, gets to the root cause of many of the problems of joint management, but some common impediments can also be addressed by point solutions.

Uncontrolled communications

Things that are important to manage in a traditional project are doubly so in the commercial project, and if things go wrong, then the impact is similarly magnified. Obvious examples might be variances in delivery compared to plan, or scope escalation and a poorly implemented change control process. However, recalling the old adage that three things are critical in a project—communication, communication, and communication—I think the most underrated threat to the smooth running of the commercial project is uncontrolled communications. This is illustrated in Figure 3.1.

This appears as an extreme case with the number of central stakeholders at the higher end of the spectrum, but is actually quite representative in a large project scenario. The solid lines show formal communications that should be described in a communications plan. The dashed lines are informal, difficult to control, and a source of much of the difficulty.

Here are a few examples where miscommunication is easily amplified. The client PM inevitably talks with the vendor sales manager (or sales executive) though her formal line is with the vendor PM. Or, taking the reciprocal case, the client liaison person talks to the vendor PM though his formal line is to the client PM. A final example, which once caused me very serious grief, is a third party team member talking to the client team, who relayed to the client PM, bypassing the formal link.

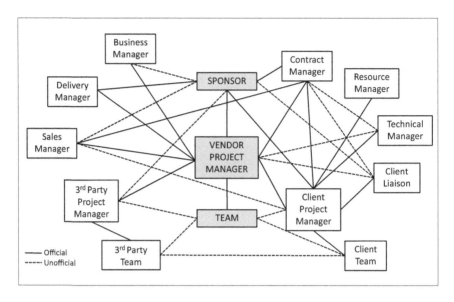

Figure 3.1 Communications nightmare

As implied earlier, this complex scenario absolutely begs for the discipline of a formal communications plan. This is preferably developed jointly by the client and vendor PMs (and third parties) as representing their organizations and should be agreed to and signed off. A useful template is shown in Table 3.2.

There is no harm and something to be gained, by jointly drafting a protocol to govern the informal communications links; to ban them is authoritarian and impractical. But, no matter what is agreed to in the plan, communications management remains a high priority for the vendor PM.

Cultural incompatibilities

Bringing together people who have never worked with each other before is an inherent characteristic of project work. A contracted project may now introduce the factor of organizations that have never worked together before.

Personal style

There is a fairly mature body of knowledge on methods of accommodating personality differences in teams. In the final chapter of *Ten Commandments of Project Management*, which also discusses conflict management, I give a summary of these analytical methods as they affect project management. As a manager and leader, it is very valuable to understand one's personality and how one 'comes over' to others. Likewise, there are quick methods of summing up

Table 3.2 Communications plan template

Communications plan					
Recipient of information	*What information?*	*Why is it needed?*	*When is it needed?*	*How is it delivered?*	*Who is responsible?*
Project team					
Name of stakeholder					
Name of stakeholder					
Etc.					
Client stakeholders					
Name of stakeholder					
Etc.					
External stakeholders					
Name of stakeholder					
Etc.					

a new person in your sphere of business. Almost all of these analytical methods are rooted in Myers–Briggs Type Indicator (MBTI), a model of personality typing, but for PMs, it is more useful to translate this detailed model into something immediately applicable to business interactions, such as that described in Merrill and Reid's *Personal Styles & Effective Performance.*

Social style determines how others perceive you. It is an individual's natural way of reacting to social situations. According to this theory, there are four basic styles evenly distributed throughout the population, though certain professions seem to attract more of one specific style than another:

1   Analytic–Tends to live life according to facts, principles, logic, and consistency; viewed as lacking enthusiasm, as cold and detached.
2   Driver–Gives the impression they know want they want, where they are going, and how to get there quickly.
3   Expressive–Appears communicative, warm, approachable, and competitive; involves others in their feelings, thoughts, and dreams.
4   Amiable–Places a high priority on friendships, close relationships, and cooperative behavior.

People are not necessarily trapped by the style dealt them by fate; they can choose to react to social situations in many different ways. However, the versatility to deviate from one's natural response requires a real effort of will and considerable practice. Such 'unnatural' behavior creates an internal stress that most prefer to avoid.

Versatility is obviously a desirable attribute—for a sales executive, a manager, and a PM. Versatility, in the context of social style, is primarily a tool to improve communications. All PMs can benefit from that.

Organizational style

Organizational differences are a different matter. Do organizations have a personality? Maybe not, but they do have a culture, which is how the organization 'comes over' to others. In fact, cultivating a culture seems a critical issue for start-up companies founded by millennials, which makes it a bit uncomfortable for a 50-year-old seeking a job there!

I have too many cases of the impact of not appreciating cultural differences. The one that hurt most concerned an attempt to establish a PMO directly reporting to a deputy minister (most senior bureaucrat) who knew little about projects. A parliamentary committee who doubted the ability of the ministry to manage a new multi-million program of recently funded projects decreed this position. This was done over the head of the department who would normally have that responsibility. My failure to appreciate the government culture I found myself in, and my inability to adapt my own behavior, led me to seeking a new contract 12 months later. The hurt came when I read a published interview with the department head who, without naming me, quite openly criticized the cost of spending public funds on expensive consultants who knew no more about program management than they did, and probably less.

A second case, which hurt almost as much, comes from the private sector. I was leading a senior group from our team in a joint meeting with the client to get a final decision that was costing time and money and long overdue. Regrettably, in frustration, I started to lose my control and asked the group to make up their minds, as we could not afford further delay, whereupon a member of the client team looked at me and said abruptly that I was trying to force the decision so I could "make my bonus"! Our culture was pay for performance, theirs was not. My firm fixed that issue, but the hurt remained.

Most situations are not as dramatic as that; it is the minor difficulties that arise during the prosaic day-to-day tasks of assigning activities with completion criteria and end-dates, determining priorities, requesting overtime work or extra resources, or getting deliverable sign-off. Significant insights to these situations can be gained from Taggart's *Project Management for Supplier Organizations*, wherein he draws many useful distinctions between supplier and owner organizations. These differences seem to be rooted in the finding that suppliers, or contracting organizations, are essentially task driven, attracting people with those characteristics and generally behaving accordingly. On the other hand, owner/operator organizations are likely to be functionally oriented and place a high priority on the attention paid to their own functional responsibilities. This would put high stress on the proper working of a matrixed project team, and provides an explanation for other common mixed team frustrations that Taggart goes on to diagnose.

Contractual hindrances

One of my wise bosses once told me that the only time you have to worry about the contract is when you get into trouble! Well, I know exactly what he meant. It's also worth recalling that if both parties agree to change a contract, then there is absolutely no reason why it cannot be changed.

Yet, instinct and experience drive me to conclude that if contracts can be designed to help a project, it's worth expending the effort to get it right. Just hoping for the best may be a cause for regrets when the client PM is forced into fighting for 'rights' under the contract and the vendor is likewise. This does not exactly promote the unified project concept.

Common terms and conditions arise in clients' standard contracts that are often 'one-size-fits-all' templates and can be tedious to negotiate as they deal with procurements different from the professional services world. Obviously, it behooves the firm to have their own template to put forward, and that's my recommendation. In the event that client terms must be dealt with, here are the ones that can cause most difficulty.

Business impact

Intellectual Property (IP). This is usually of crucial importance to the services firm. Interestingly, under Canadian law, unless agreed to otherwise, IP for work done under contract resides with the firm, even though it seems counterintuitive. Terms are frequently inserted to reverse this and assign IP to the client. The firm, with reference to their business model, must carefully scrutinize this. For example, the firm should protect custom software constructed with re-used common components for probable future use. The client's view is usually a simplistic "I've paid for it, it's mine." Indeed, the product is his, but not to use in violation of the vendor's rights. This is an example where interest-based negotiating can work well. If owning the IP is in the real interest of both parties, usually a compromise can be crafted that works for both. A common solution is to agree to some form of joint ownership with conditions of use spelt out.

Insurance. Most clients require their contractors to carry forms of insurance. These requirements must be looked at carefully and, if reasonable, any additional premium costs included in the bid financials. A common requirement is for professional liability insurance that the firm should be carrying in any case. The amount required should be checked; coverage can range from $1M to $5M and up.

Liability and Indemnity. These highly technical terms cover both the extent of the damages for which the firm can be held liable in the event of product malfunction or inadequate services, and the nature of any indemnities granted to the client. The firm should strive to limit any liability to the value of the contract; the client often proposes a term that suggests unlimited liability, including a term for consequential damages. Depending on the nature of the project and application area, these are very hard for the firm to agree to and can be deal breakers. Typical indemnities that can be negotiated include indemnifying the client against third party claims for copyright (or IP) infringements or other suspected illegalities that might arise from product use.

Non-Solicitation. Both parties may find it advantageous to include a term prohibiting active recruitment of each other's staff, though the firm may have a more direct interest, as its staff is its business. These terms are written to extend for a period of 6–12 months beyond contract completion. In practice, legal action is rarely contemplated in such cases, unless it is a blatant violation.

Escrow. Occasionally a client requires escrow and includes such a term in the contract. Escrow is a form of security in which a third party holds something of value provided by the first party (documents, money) that can only be released to the second party when certain conditions are met. A common example is the software COTS business when the client may require the source code to be placed in escrow and kept up-to-date, with a release condition being bankruptcy of the vendor. For business-critical applications, this assures the client that the product will be maintainable by his own staff in such an extreme eventuality.

Project impact

Performance Requirements. Occasionally a client places this contentious item into the contract. Technical opinions from the firm's expert must be sought and risk of penalties estimated. If obliged to agree to this clause, make sure it is only the firm's product to be tested (no inclusion of other products or services in the test) and that the test environment is specified and controlled.

Penalties. Faced with a large project and a critical completion date, the client may demand a penalty or other damages if the vendor fails to deliver on-time. This is a more common requirement in certain application areas (e.g., construction) and less so in others. The firm will accept this term reluctantly, and only when balanced by incentives for early delivery, but, when present, some form of delay management is required. In many application areas (e.g., software development), the achievement of deadlines requires *both* parties to meet their responsibilities on schedule. The purpose of delay management is to fairly assess the accountability for project delays incurred during execution and to have an agreed mechanism to adjust the penalty date accordingly. Financial mechanisms for dealing with penalties and holdbacks are discussed in Chapter 10.

Fit for Purpose. I have seen client contracts that close a long list of requirements with this catchall, discussed in Chapter 8. Remove it, or insist on detailed specifics. A related concern is the vendor responsibility to exercise professional care and avoid negligence. This does not have to be spelt out, it is implied. A judge will find against you if you did not meet the generally accepted standards for your profession.

Reporting Requirements. Most reporting requirements are reasonable, sometimes minimal. However, a highly detail-oriented client occasionally insists on something unreasonable that can put a measurable cost against the contract with no significant benefit to the project. I can recall a case when I spent a day a month updating an incredibly detailed and progressively incorrect project schedule that went two years into the future, because the Gantt chart (24 pages) was required for the contract, and it was to be appended to the periodic status report. Eventually, after six months, the futility was recognized and the requirement quietly lapsed. In general, though, status reporting to the client must follow their demands and formats. Internal reporting to vendor management is always a separate report as it contains financial and other privileged information.

Contract Termination. There are three basic ways in which a contract can terminate: the completion criteria are met and the contract ends normally, the contract is in breach and the injured party chooses to terminate 'with cause', and the client chooses to terminate 'without cause'. It is presumed that the vendor would never choose to terminate without cause and that a customer would probably not agree to such a term in any case. There are some things to look for in these terms—make sure that the client is obliged to advise in writing, referencing the paragraph in breach and detailing the reason. The term must also include a procedure for a 'cure period', whereby the vendor is allowed, say, 30 days to rectify the issue. Termination without cause, although seemingly a harsh term to inflict on a vendor, is not unusual, and the client generally expects the firm's agreement. It might be possible to negotiate some compensation for loss of project revenue, though, more likely, the best that can be agreed on is payment up to the stop work order on a T&M basis.

Force Majeure. Although not classified as a termination clause, *force majeure* (sometimes also called an 'Act of God') does provide a mechanism for defined shutdown of the contract if the vendor meets with insuperable difficulties totally outside of his control.

Dispute Resolution. More and more contracts are specifying ADR (alternative dispute resolution) as an alternative to immediately seeking legal recourse. These methods, such as mediation and binding arbitration, are generally much less expensive and less confrontational. Try to ensure such a clause is included.

These are the more legalistic terms the vendor PM must understand. The normal project matters of pricing, payment, scope, acceptance, and so forth are dealt with in Chapter 10.

Negotiation

Terms and conditions and other matters usually require negotiation meetings, and so give some thought to strategy. Strategy can cover such seemingly simple matters as where the meetings are to be held and whether they should conclude with a social component. My conviction is that lawyers do *not* attend these meetings—they can dance in the wings or be formally consulted, but the meetings are first and foremost business meetings and attended by business people. Other matters that the firm should think about include how many people attend and who. I have found that two well-briefed representatives from each side can be most efficient. The firm should think out the role each person plays and who can make the call on which issues. As a general rule, I would not include the senior decision-maker in these meetings; this can actually increase pressure on the firm and may raise expectations for immediate agreement. Best to keep your senior player in reserve at head office. Use of timeouts for private discussion and consultation should also be part of the process.

Divergent perspectives

Inevitably, the client and the vendor have different views on project work, on the best way to approach the project in hand, and on theory of management. Although the discussion on the contract was framed to sound like the contract was a problem, it is also a solution when both parties negotiate and document a compromise on their opposing views. However, there are frequent differences encountered in perception that create conditions for miscommunication and misunderstanding. Finding common ground is helpful before launching into the lifecycle mapping practice.

Role of the PM

This starts with establishing whether the client has a project management practice and has assigned a PM to the project. Sometimes, the vendor reports to a procurement manager, or a functional manager in the application area of the project whose job is to oversee the contract. Unless the contract is simple, the vendor would prefer to see a client PM assigned.

A client PM, if assigned, may have responsibilities ranging from project coordinator to fully empowered PM. It helps to understand the level to which the PM reports. Naturally, the vendor PM reports to the client PM, but this reporting may be exclusive or may be shared with dotted lines to one or more senior client staff.

Regardless, although the vendor PM possesses less organizational authority than the in-house PM, his authority on the project is usually strong. After all, the vendor PM is likely the firm's most senior representative consistently on the client-site.

These facts, though useful to understand, do not yield a clear definition of management responsibilities for a project with two project managers. The solution is to use the techniques in Chapter 5, such as RAM and RAA, in order to jointly develop an unambiguous set of responsibilities and authorities for both PMs.

Role of the sponsor

It is hard to admit, but I have managed many a vendor project where I never set eyes on the sponsor, never met her, and may even have doubted her existence. The question is, despite the valid conventional wisdom, must the PM really have a project relationship with the sponsor in a commercial setting? There is an instinctive need to be connected with the person paying the bills, but in the typical corporate jungle that person is tough to identify and organizational charts hard to come by. Even if an identifiable sponsor can be isolated within the client organization, access by the vendor PM is restricted and closely managed by the client PM.

On top of this reality, the vendor must follow the authorities defined in the contract. These inevitably specify the client PM as the delegated client contact for all project matters. Senior managers named in the contract frequently include the procurement manager and the director of the application area of the project. For example, an IT project references the director of IT. A construction project references the director of construction. This position is unlikely to represent the sponsor, but does carry an executive responsibility. The contract may also identify a delegate of the sponsor who has been nominated to play a role in the management of project and contract; this may be the closest the vendor can get to meaningful sponsor engagement.

Is this dilemma worth getting fussed about? I don't think so. Remember, the client may see this as just a contract to be managed, not a project. They may think, with some justification, that the role of the sponsor has served its purpose in getting to this stage, and that reaching into the depths of the contracted project is inappropriate and not required. That is why they have the client PM and the procurement manager. Delegation of issues such as budget authority is a matter between the sponsor and client PM.

The vendor PM should focus on building formal and informal client relationships primarily with the client PM, implementing effective issue and change management processes, and operating them jointly with the client.

The existence of a contract with a scope and a price really removes the vendor from many of the issues that involve the sponsor. Maybe, then, it is a non-issue, and if the sponsor actually sends out a message that she wants to meet you when you arrive on-site, accept that as a bonus.

Project charter

A common question that arises in commercial projects is the need for a project charter. Many vendor PMs, usually those with a fresh certification, are rightly concerned with getting the project off to a good start and seem convinced that their first task is to develop their own project charter. The existence of a contract changes that requirement.

The purpose of the charter is to authorize the project and mandate the role of the PM. It was actually written when the project started, before the procurement. The charter must include within its boundary the entire project from the client's perspective. It is not meaningful to exclude a component from the described project just because it may be subcontracted.

The project charter is therefore signed, sealed, and settled before the vendor even shows up on the scene. Now, it is also probable that the references to the vendor in the charter are vague or cast in very general terms. This is because the client expects, as part of the procurement process, that the mandate of the vendor and their entire scope and responsibility will be laid out in the future contract and its schedules. The vendor contract thus acts as a charter, though only from the vendor's perspective.

The best solution from the client's perspective is to update the original charter with the essentials of the new vendor contract and submit for re-approval.

There can only be one charter for a project.

Risk ownership

By means of the contract (presumably FP), the client intended and to a degree succeeded in passing risk to the firm. The temptation is for the client to think of project risk as 'your problem'.

Having essentially moved the financial risk, perceptions of risk are profoundly altered and influence risk conversations between the parties. Discussing the details of the firm's risk management process may be of little interest to the client. Faced with this, two parallel processes are often established. The firm takes care of their risks internally, and the client takes care of theirs. The ideal, which can make a real improvement to project operations, is a joint risk management process between the firm and the client.

Chapter 6 is devoted to risk management from the vendor's viewpoint. If the client is open to joint risk management, the vendor's techniques and templates can be modified for project use. This can facilitate the collaborative approach to risk management and promote unified project management.

The statement of work

The statement of work (SOW) is the most important document involved in the contract. It is usually appended as a 'schedule'—Chapter 10 provides an account of contract structure and document precedence. Incidentally, the SOW abbreviation can also mean scope of work and is sometimes thought of as synonymous, though scope description is much narrower than the

Table 3.3 Universal statement of work (SOW) checklist

Vendor statement of work	
1 Executive summary	10 Roles and responsibilities (RAM charts)
2 Background to project	11 Resource usage plan
3 Vendor's understanding of the project—project objectives, requirements, success factors, constraints	12 Communications plan
4 General approach	13 Quality plan
5 Scope description	14 Risk plan
6 Work breakdown structure (WBS)	15 Project procedures
7 Deliverables	16 Customer provided facilities
8 Schedule and milestones	17 Standard business terms, pricing, payment schedule, other T&C
9 Estimates and assumptions	

intention of the SOW. To ensure readers have a common view, Table 3.3 offers an outline of a SOW checklist for commercial practice.

There can be further terminology and perception issues over the positioning and authorship of the SOW. Some standards use the term to describe the plan for the project issued shortly after initiation. Some use the term to mean the sponsor's early description of her requirement and its feasibility. Clearly the usage in the commercial context, however, refers to the subcontracted work of the vendor.

Authorship of the SOW is also open to interpretation. The PMBOK® suggests it is a buyer's document. Conversely, the usual commercial meaning of SOW is a *response* to specifications received from the buyer as part of an RFP.

The SOW is best defined as a major component of the vendor's proposal, submitted to the buyer to confirm the vendor's understanding of what is required and how it is delivered; it is a comprehensive, budgeted, scheduled, and scoped plan for the subcontracted work for evaluation and approval by the client.

The client's project management standard

Larger and more sophisticated clients could be operating PRINCE2®, PMBOK®, a proprietary system, or their own in-house project management methodology. Many clients have spent thousands of dollars investing in it. Is this a material issue for the services firm?

Presuming reasonableness, the vendor must follow the client's process. It's probably in the contract. There are no perceptual issues here. The issue is how does the firm prepare and train for this.

When working under the hood, the moving parts of project management are pretty much all the same. So, for this reason, the POCL functional model of project management should be the foundation for vendor PM training. This is the base level of abstraction of project management and is truly universal. It equips the vendor PM to quickly adapt to any client project methodology, and to communicate fluently without getting confused between conflicting frameworks.

Nonetheless, frameworks are important and are hard to shake off when one has been trained to see things a certain way. It's difficult to believe one is driving a Porsche if it looks like a VW Beetle. The firm would be wise to ensure their staff are familiar with the structure of extant standards, and encourage individuals to certify in the prevalent standard. The firm should not invest in building their own project management methodology unless they are in the methodology business. That just adds to the conflict when another standard is encountered.

Finally, with POCL knowledge and experience, the vendor PM will be confident she can put together the deliverables, use the techniques, and follow any procedures as the situation demands. In any event, it is the client PM who is responsible for navigating through the labyrinth of project management process the client might have established.

The practice of lifecycle mapping

The purpose of lifecycle mapping is to achieve a joint understanding of the management and operations of the project. The specific objectives are to integrate the POCL activities plus *all* deliverables with the phases of the project lifecycle. This practice helps both parties understand exactly what the planned project looks like and how they will work together. It is effective with any project lifecycle. The resultant map can also serve as a foundation for other integrative initiatives.

Starting the map

As an example, I use the simple project lifecycle in Figure 2.2 with six formal phases from requirements to implementation and two checkpoints. These go/no go decision points align with the need for progressive commitment—at the beginning of the project, when the preliminary cost/benefit is being assessed, and after general design, when scope and costs are better known. For simplicity, I assume the project is starting from scratch and the client and vendor PMs are working on this jointly. The mind-set of the PM is to focus on the work to be done using the project lifecycle that has already been discussed and agreed on, and to think of the POCL functions being applied repetitively during each phase of the lifecycle. It helps to have some training and access to project management checklists that can be used as memory joggers. As many project lifecycles are similar, previous maps can also be reused as templates.

The map template up to the first checkpoint looks like Table 3.4.

Four columns are drawn to record the primary activities necessary to accomplish the function during each of the phases. In a fifth column are shown the PM's deliverables produced during that phase, and in an adjacent column, not shown, would be the team deliverables specified by the project methodology. Treating the PM's deliverables as subject to a planning process, just like any other deliverable, is a major contribution to integration.

Table 3.4 Project lifecycle mapped to checkpoint 1

	Project lifecycle mapping				
Phase of lifecycle	*Functions of project management*				*Sample PM deliverables mapped to phase*
	Plan	*Organize*	*Control*	*Lead*	
Feasibility study	It is unlikely that a project management role is established during feasibility study.				None
Go/no-go checkpoint					

The first map is delightfully simple. A feasibility study is used by most organizations to provide an initial estimate of costs and benefits as a basis for the first go/no go decision, though there is no general rule for this. In some cases, the framework for the cost/benefit is defined ad hoc by the sponsor or may follow a standard prescribed by the accountants; it may also be codified and built into the first phase of the project lifecycle.

Mapping requirements and general design phases

The requirements phase marks the start of the project and this is a busy and critical phase for project management. The PM is focused on ensuring solid requirements documentation, and a grasp of priorities and other management information. The PM defines the roles and responsibilities of stakeholders, and the scope and focus of the small team currently on-hand. The project charter, the first and most significant PM deliverable, is likely issued during this phase and provides the PM with a mandate and preliminary scope definitions. For commercial projects, this is updated with agreements in the contract. A draft project procedures manual should also be tabled during this phase. Working with the sponsor, a good PM shows leadership as needed by validating and promoting awareness of the customer's cost/benefit case and the project objectives.

The general design translates the needs of the user into a solution. This is a creative phase requiring contribution from subject matter experts (SMEs) and cross-functional teams. Communication, always an issue, is critical as design revisions and possible new approaches are tried and maybe adopted. The PM, in the role of prime guardian of the project objectives, must be positioned to knowledgably oversee approvals of the evolving design as being the best way of meeting the sponsor's prioritized needs within the triple constraint (cost, schedule, and scope) and quality. Leadership skills are needed to build the emerging teams, reconcile inevitable stakeholder conflicts, and keep the results aligned with the business. The goal of the

Table 3.5 Project lifecycle mapped to checkpoint 2

	Project lifecycle mapping				
Phase of lifecycle	*Functions of project management*				*Sample PM deliverables mapped to phase*
	Plan	*Organize*	*Control*	*Lead*	
1 Requirements	Develop mandate. Plan the activities. Establish priorities.	Define responsibilities and procedures.	Evaluate activity completion. Provide feedback.	Verify CBA. Set objectives. Align stakeholders.	Project charter. Project procedures manual. Responsibility assignment matrix. Requirements sign-off.
2 General design	Plan the activities. Set design direction.	Induct team members. Establish communication.	Approve designs. Trace to requirements.	Build team. Fit to business.	Project plan. Communications plan. Design sign-off. Project status report.
Go/no-go checkpoint					

PM is to publish the full project plan for official approval as part of the go/no go documentation.

The map template to Checkpoint 2 is shown in Table 3.5.

Mapping detailed design, build, test, and implementation phases

Team issues and peak project burn rate typify the detailed design and build phases. This dictates an increased attention to project progress/status reports centered on control of milestones and deliverable effort, and on control of scope using change control protocols. A requisite for success includes maximum clarity on how the work is to be performed, and practical implementation of efficient work methods. The preoccupation of the PM is the leadership to build and maintain team efficiency. Visible support of the team also sustains morale. This means proactive removal of obstacles and a maximum level of team empowerment. The stance of the effective PM during these phases must be that success is being achieved and that achievement is highly valued. The PM continually seeks full team commitment and recognizes every accomplishment. This is not meant to imply that he buries his head in the sand. If off-plan situations arise, then the PM must show determination and strength of character to face down the obstacles or make the necessary tough decisions, but the secret is—good leaders accentuate the positive and always show confidence.

The test phase introduces the challenge of maintaining effectiveness during a phase that has a life of its own and often is deep into technicalities. Good documentation must be maintained and a perspective on defects retained by allocating priorities. *Ad hoc* planning and contingency management help maintain control and clarify the choices when problems are encountered. Ensuring good metrics and measurement processes are in operation, and using them to provide progress visibility and decision support is very helpful. In this challenging phase, the PM leads by expressing the determination of the whole team, balanced with a show of flexibility if it is obvious that trade-offs need to be made.

The implementation phase brings the project into production. The PM, in conjunction with the sponsor, must confirm the criteria and associated activities needed for sign-off. This is no time for surprises; all players must understand their responsibilities. The PM must create an atmosphere of inevitability—the belief that the jointly agreed plan leads to success.

The map template to the end of the project is shown in Table 3.6.

This brief example touches on only a few features of project methodology. The point being made is that project management must *integrate* with the nature of the work phase being managed—acknowledging the demands of the phase, and the best practices of the methodologies being used. The functional PM model is a generic and comprehensive way of thinking about project management and sparks the right conversations between vendor and client. Note that what is right for one project may not be for others.

Table 3.6 Project lifecycle mapped to end of project

| Phase of lifecycle | Functions of project management | | | | Sample PM deliverables mapped to phase |
	Plan	Organize	Control	Lead	
3 Detailed design	Plan the activities. Focus on quality.	Invoke methodology.	Deliverables effort. Milestones. Scope.	Ensure delegations. Clear obstacles.	Project status report. Change request. Issue log. Continuous improvement report.
4 Build	Plan the activities. Manage standards. Focus on dependencies.	Optimize work flow.	Deliverables effort. Milestones. Scope.	Demonstrate successes. Promote achievements. Show determination. Meet adversity with confidence.	Project status report. Change request. Issue log. Continuous improvement report.
5 Test	Plan the activities. Focus on contingencies.	Documentation. Alternatives. Backups.	Trend charts. Metrics.	Flexibility. Determination.	Test progress chart. Test scenario sign-off. Defect reports. Project status report.
6 Implementation	Plan the activities. Focus on criteria.	Define responsibilities and procedures.	Joint with sponsor.	Inevitability.	Completion report. Project sign-off.

Project lifecycle mapping

Realities that impact lifecycle mapping

The preceding account was rendered as a tutorial and ignored some of the realities that intrude in the real world of project procurement.

Project managers not assigned

The composition of a feasibility phase is highly dependent upon customer practice. As the project has no existence at this stage, assignment of a client PM is unlikely and a vendor PM is improbable. The sponsor should be encouraged to engage vendor expertise to provide planning-level estimates and development templates.

The requirements phase is the beginning of the project, and is a critical time for the client PM, who should now be appointed. However, the vendor PM may not be engaged at this point. In fact, it is common for requirements specifications developed by the client to be used as the basis for procurement documents such as an RFP. These are issued to competing services firms who assign the vendor PM. The vendor PM faces a major challenge when the contract is awarded, namely, taking the contracted project through planning and organizing activities associated with initiation despite the sponsor having already approved initiation documents generated at the beginning of the requirements phase.

This issue arises from the parties having different views of the lifecycle and entering the lifecycle at different phases. Like most problems, recognition is half the solution, and using the lifecycle mapping practice, both parties can arrive at a common understanding.

Commercial conflict

The completion of the general design phase is another crucial moment for the vendor, as the upcoming go/no go decision will be highly dependent upon the cost estimates generated for the balance of the project. Unlike her client counterpart, the vendor PM is constrained by contractual budgets, most likely the demand for fixed price commitment that impacts the dynamics, teamwork, and politics of the project. Obviously, the pressure from the client is to reduce costs to keep the cost/benefit viable, whereas the pressure from the firm is to ensure the rest of the work is bid profitably.

This scenario is, in essence, the same as the initial pressure during the RFP response, and the solution lies in the disciplines of a vendor lifecycle and assigning delivery management accountabilities, which are the topics of Chapters 4 and 5.

Divergent views on scope

The final challenge for the vendor PM is successful navigation of the test and implementation phases. On any sizable project, the client is looking at a much broader scale of activity during these phases than the vendor PM. The client is training end-users and operational staff, conducting tests with other interfaces, involving third party products not previously identified, preparing for commissioning, and often dealing with a community of stakeholders who have suddenly awoken to the fact of imminent implementation. This immediately creates a conflict of priorities and potential for scope arguments. Issues associated with the contracted deliverables that could be glossed over during the design phases (such as integration with client or third party products, and design of the user acceptance test process) now have to be confronted. A project methodology that is insufficiently granular would not have identified and dealt with these issues in previous phases. Costly overruns are likely.

An agreed lifecycle with joint deliverables and mapped POCL activities is an excellent start to management of a contracted project. Communication, clarity of plan, and coordination benefits are evident. The map can also act as a high-quality prerequisite to developing the RAM part of the accountabilities definition practice described in Chapter 5.

Other integrative initiatives

The discussion on project integration has overviewed the common impediments with suggestions on how they can be handled, leading up to the centerpiece practice of lifecycle mapping. Branching from that topic, further important initiatives can be considered. These are recommendations that address the vendor/client working relationship, the issue of business delegation, and finally, an important survey on the meaning of success.

Recommendations on the working relationship

Mutual Communication. There should be absolutely no reluctance to share every available piece of information that describes how each party works their projects, and the specifics of the PM's role. Any concerns over confidentiality can be resolved by executing non-disclosure agreements independently of any main contract.

Flexibility with the Details. In the usual case, where the vendor project is a subset of the client project, there has to be some flexibility from both parties for the whole enterprise to work properly. The devil, truly, is in the details, and there must be a willingness to adapt methods so that the project integrates efficiently. A good example of this is the RAM. The client's matrix inevitably looks different from the vendor's version unless they are integrated and reconciled. This is an obvious example where attention to detail and flexibility in approach pays dividends. Others include procedures, approvals, phase-end determination, baseline definition, and test case definition.

Sort It Out Up-Front. The best time to communicate the parties' methodologies, project management roles, and all the expectations arising is at the beginning of the contracted project, preferably before the contract is signed. This can take the form of a one-day planning session during which various perspectives are explained; gaps, overlaps, and disconnects identified; and solutions (or at least action plans) created to resolve them.

Business delegation

A difference in all organizations is the level of delegation given to project managers. If the delegation authority is unmatched to the size and value of the contract, and presumably the experience or seniority of the PM, delays and frustrations will occur. It certainly does not contribute to the sense of one project marching toward a common goal.

Delegation covers matters like hiring, compensation, promotion, bonuses, assignments, time-off approval, vacation, overtime, and special awards and events, but the issue of most concern is financial approval. If two project managers can't wrap up a long and intense discussion because the outcome requires approval by one or both of a $5000 expenditure they are not delegated to approve, the project is not working efficiently.

The best context for a joint assessment of delegation is during review of the change control process at the beginning of the project. What changes do both organizations agree can be approved by the project managers, and which must be submitted to a change control board? The vendor probably defines their PMs' limits of authority as a part of their standard operating procedures discussed more fully in Chapter 11.

The meaning of success

There is a question embedded in my psyche because it was asked repeatedly by one of my more diligent bosses over and over during proposal preparation and during rough times on the project. That question was "how will we know when we are successful?"

That question should be asked by all PMs, especially on commercial projects when the answers inevitably given by the vendor PM and the client PM are somewhat different.

Success for the firm

Success is defined with three core objectives:

1   Delivering within the cost budget allocated to the vendor PM and used in calculating the project financials;
2   Performing the work in-line with the firm's expectations and standards;
3   Creating, or retaining, a satisfied customer who will reference the firm and use their services again.

> Project success for the firm means on time, on budget, and to customer satisfaction.

As firms get larger and management hierarchies are formed, the focus moves to the outcome of these success factors, namely revenue and margin. There are a large number of projects to keep track of, and although summary reporting and dashboard displays have a role to play, the reality is that the dominant metric for services performance is project margin. The firm must know how to estimate project costs and revenue, how to deliver to meet these targets, and how to aggregate into an annual plan. Prediction of project wins, and the outcome of won projects, is a problem for risk analysis in Chapter 6.

Success for the customer

The customer is, as a rule, not very concerned about the firm's financial success. The customer is driven by a broader view of the meaning of success, and one that doesn't always consider the vendor as a stakeholder. If the customer is following good project management practice, then success must be defined as the attainment of project objectives. Those objectives must be supportive of the overall business goal of the client and must be defined and approved in the project charter or scope statement. A checklist of typical objectives is shown in Table 3.7.

There should be clarity between the client and the vendor PM on the degree to which the attainment of the project objectives has been delegated to the firm. This delegation by the client is, of course, a risk transference technique, and if not properly understood during the bid phase becomes a source of unestimated risk and unanticipated responsibility that could jeopardize success.

The cleanest approach to complex, multi-objective projects is for the vendor PM to work outwards from the deliverables that he is clearly responsible for preparing. The deliverable is then tagged with a sub-objective that the vendor must meet, but which is only a part of the objective to be met by the project as a whole. For example, the vendor PM is building a data server that must meet an average response time of 200 ms. This is a component of a total communication and display system that is designed for an average response of 500 ms. These statements make the accountabilities of the vendor PM and the client PM crystal clear.

In practice, the clean dissection of objectives and deliverables between client and vendor is not always so easy, and this risks an imperfect contract. To the degree they have been specified, the vendor PM must ensure he has been granted authority and budget to match these assigned responsibilities. In this case, as in so many others, a teamwork approach works much better than one driven by strict contractual interpretation. It is often said that a successful project is one in which the contract is signed and then never referred to

Table 3.7 Project objectives checklist

Objective	Description
1 Business specific	The project may have some very precise business objectives that derive from the overall goal. For example, to reduce departmental costs by 10%.
2 Functionality	A high-level statement of the functional requirements for the project, as this is closely linked to project scope.
3 Cost	The customer's cost will include their own variable costs and fixed costs such as the contracted fixed price project.
4 Schedule	There will be end-date objectives and probably interim dates to be attained in order to match cyclic business events, optimize benefits, comply with regulations, link with external events, or meet internal political requirements.
5 Technical	Projects may be required to implement specific technologies within the developed product.
6 Performance	The product must operate within a specified performance envelope in a specified environment (speed, endurance, capacity, economy, responsiveness, and so forth).
7 Quality	Explicit quality targets may have to be met such as residual defects, MTBF, or related requirements such as ease of use, maintainability, and durability.
8 Process	There may be a need to follow a specific process, for example, to ensure auditability, or to meet ISO certification.
9 Standards	The project or product must be in compliance with specified standards, for example, using templates or meeting building codes.
10 Environmental	There may be an objective related to environmental issues (footprint and disturbance, resource usage, sustainability, etc.).
11 HR/safety	Certain projects may have mandatory training requirements, safety targets, or other HR objectives.

again. This sentiment might be unrealistic, but there is little doubt that most successful projects occur when the parties have a clear sense of their mutual responsibilities and also make every effort to collaborate and support each other to attain objectives, with the business impacts being dealt with fairly and in the background.

> The ideal model for the success of a commercial project is that when driven to meet agreed client objectives, the firm automatically meets theirs.

I think King Ferdinand II of Spain was on the right track, if a little crass, when he reputedly said, "He serves his king the best, who also serves himself."

4 Evolution of a vendor lifecycle

Project managers are problem solvers who use models and frameworks derived from their own and others' experience to solve the big problem of how to deliver the project. Vendor PMs have that problem, but with the added demand to work within two organizations—the client and the firm—and to make a profit.

The lifecycle is a very good model for examining how to get from the beginning to the end of a project, the two most significant events for the vendor PM. The lifecycle, that most ubiquitous of all project management techniques, is so closely associated with the idea of project management in the minds of onlookers that many believe the lifecycle *is* project management. I hope by now, however, that any notion of project management as a lifecycle has been banished. The idea of centering attention on the buyer's project through the project lifecycle and applying project management represented by POCL functions has already been discussed. In this chapter, I am going to develop another lifecycle, one that does not concern the client but that forms the basis for management of the vendor's business.

> The vendor lifecycle is focused on business issues and gives control of risk and commitment.

The vendor lifecycle encloses the project lifecycle within an overarching framework regardless of the industry, the client view of project management, the type of project lifecycle, or the number of project phases to be bid. It appropriates deliverables and uses phase controls implied by the PMBOK® process groups without excuses. These core documents are a fundamental subset of project management deliverables plus innovations applicable to bidding and managing commercial projects. This creates a positive framework for vendor management—repeatable, essential, and consistent. The reader may wish to refer back to Figure 2.1 to review the overall CPE architecture of which the vendor lifecycle is a major part.

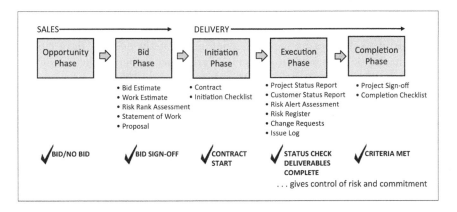

Figure 4.1 A vendor lifecycle and core documents

Phases of the vendor lifecycle

Back to the beginning for a moment. A professional services firm sets up in business with two priorities—sell the service and deliver the service—in that order. The business logic needed to break that down into component phases is straightforward:

Selling–Identify and hunt down an opportunity, then develop and present a proposal or bid. Win the bid!

Delivering–Negotiate and sign the contract, assemble the PM and team, execute the work, place the deliverables into the client's hands, and complete all the stipulations of the contract. Get paid!

These are grouped logically into the five phases of the lifecycle shown in Figure 4.1 and elaborated with the core documents and other important phase attributes. This diagram provides a reference base for the phase descriptions that follow.

Phase 1: Opportunity

The purpose of the opportunity phase is to qualify the project opportunity and to make the bid decision. This phase is the responsibility of the sales executive in whose territory the opportunity lies.

Systemization of the sales process is a tricky issue. Understandably, sales people regard it as a constraint on their responsiveness to the customer or on their flexibility in a competitive environment. The excuse heard when attempting to implement such procedures is that they "don't have time." There has to be clear benefit in terms of sales success before the sales force actively support these attempts. Otherwise, the best that can be achieved from sales executives is lip service or reluctant compliance. Even customer relationship management systems that on the surface offer sales benefit fall into disuse unless continually promoted and even demanded by senior management.

In the face of this experience, requirements for deliverables, written call reports, or formal status assessments are minimized. They are left to the discretion of sales management. The optimum amount of documentation during the sales process is less rather than more, and so judgment rather than prescription is the rule.

The exit criterion from this phase is simple—the decision to bid or no bid. This requires an audit trail because the bid decision authorizes the expenditure of resources to prepare the proposal and arrange demonstrations and other actions to secure the win. Principles of accountability require management approval for this estimated cost, set against the uncertainties of actually winning the business.

Phase 2: Bid

This phase marks the real entrance into the specifics of the vendor lifecycle. There are two sides to the phase purpose: to prepare and submit a winning proposal and to ensure that the proposed project can be delivered. Thus, although this is a sales process and the sales executive remains accountable for the success of this phase, the responsibility is shared with the professional services team often represented by a delivery manager.

Recognizing the split of these responsibilities—a winnable and deliverable project—is a critical success factor for the typical services firm, and getting it wrong is a root cause of many subsequent project challenges. The solution, supported by the firm's senior management, lies in a clear delineation of roles and responsibilities and an open, analytic approach to the identification and management of risk.

Five bid steps

Following the decision to bid, a generic bid phase may be separated into five basic steps, some of which may be executed in parallel:

1　Plan the response to the customer's RFP.
2　Do a risk assessment.
3　Build the proposal response.
4　Prepare the bid estimate.
5　Gain approvals.

These steps may be iterated and/or elaborated as the bid phase progresses. Much of the early work in Step 1 is focused on establishing a clear understanding of the scope of work, the environment in which the work is performed, and the nature of the competition. This is crucial to the three related elements that underpin the bid: the risk, the estimate (including contingency), and the assumptions.

There are five core documents expected from the bid phase. Four are interim documents: the statement of work (SOW), the risk assessment, the work estimate, and the bid estimate. These documents, with additional information, are edited and consolidated into the proposal. Supporting documents are always subject to the principle of progressive response to avoid unnecessary work. This means, for example, that high-risk projects must include a preliminary risk register, though it is discretionary for projects of moderate or low risk.

The exit criterion for this phase is the submission of the bid to the customer. Both the sales executive and delivery manager should approve the submission, though the business unit manager has final say. Good practice in making these approvals meaningful is to build proper review processes into the phase. For large bids, this would include review of SOW/estimate, review of risk, and review of the final bid.

Phase 3: Initiation

If the proposal is accepted, the lifecycle enters the initiation phase and responsibility moves from the sales executive to the vendor PM, who by now must certainly be appointed. Management of this transfer of responsibility is a subtext for the initiation phase, though the specific purpose is to agree on the contract and set up the project for success. There may, in this phase, be a chance to negotiate around errors made in the bid phase, though this emphatically should not be relied on.

Table 4.1 A project initiation checklist

	Vendor project initiation	
1	Bid/work estimate	10	Change requests
2	Contingency	11	Issues
3	Contracts	12	Deliverable approval
4	Booking	13	Project acceptance criteria
5	Time reporting	14	Key client
6	Status reporting (PSR, CSR)	15	Resources
7	Milestones	16	Metrics
8	Deliverables	17	Team briefing
9	Risk	18	Kickoff

Although responsibility shifts to the vendor PM, best practice is to retain accountability for sealing of the contract with the sales executive after resolving issues arising from legal and delivery reviews. Binding the firm to a contract is a question for the firm's policy, usually the business manager or board appointees. Whatever level of signature is required, the duality of responsibility between sales and delivery should continue to be respected.

The initiation phase is thus the first of the three delivery phases—initiation, execution, and completion. As might be expected, these phases draw proportionately more from the world of project management, to provide business control of the firm's commitment to deliver project services. The vendor lifecycle requires two core documents from initiation—primarily the contract or equivalent document committing the parties to the project, and the completed checklist that verifies all necessary setup actions have been performed. An example of an initiation checklist is shown in Table 4.1. Initiation is typically a brief phase, though on occasion, contract negotiations can be protracted, particularly on complex projects contracted with large bureaucracies.

The exit criterion from initiation is very concrete: formal execution of the contract or authorization to begin the project. This signals the unambiguous assumption of full project authority by the vendor PM, though some project-related responsibilities remain with the sales executive. The focus of the vendor PM during initiation is understanding and committing to the contract and relevant schedules (such as the SOW), clarifying the details prior to contract signing, and planning the agenda of the all-important joint kickoff meeting that signals to all stakeholders the official commencement of the contracted component of the project.

Phase 4: Execution

The project begins in earnest. The execution phase encapsulates the phases of the project lifecycle within the scope of the contracted project. The use of the vendor lifecycle handles the rolling wave very logically. As the project moves through the various waves, multiple contracts are enacted but the project remains one project. This is exactly how the client and vendor should regard it, to stay in synchrony.

Here is an example of a large client project tackled in two waves compliant with the rolling wave principle. Figure 4.2 shows the requirement for two contracts and two iterations of the vendor lifecycle.

The first wave, Requirements and General Design, would be contracted as Contract #1, enclosed within the first vendor lifecycle. Detailed Design, Build, Test, and Implementation would be contracted as Contract #2, enclosed within a second vendor lifecycle, though the opportunity phase may be diminished or non-existent on the second iteration as the project is obviously already identified.

Although the rolling wave is a logical and lower-risk approach, clients are not always persuaded of its merits and insist on issuing RFPs based on one contract from beginning to end. This 'big bang' approach increases the execution risk for the firm quite significantly, who would be wise to take additional mitigating action such as investing extra effort in requirements and design for inclusion in the response.

In any case, execution is where the real work of the project is performed and the vendor lifecycle may seem secondary to the disciplines required by the project lifecycle and project management. The interests of the firm are now centered on ensuring that the project unfolds as planned, specifically in regards to the triple constraint, much the same as any other stakeholder. Perhaps most significant is the firm's interest in revenue and margin. The firm's accounting staff consolidates project financials for monthly and quarterly

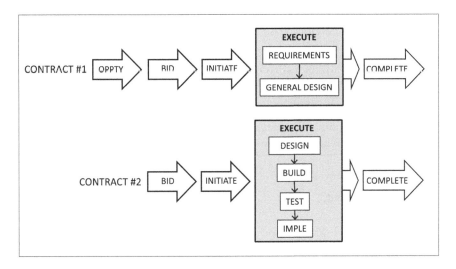

Figure 4.2 Two iterations of the vendor lifecycle for one project

Table 4.2 An internal vendor status report checklist

Vendor project status report	
1 Project description	7 Plans for next period
2 Risk rank	8 Milestone tracking
3 Alert indicators	9 Red flag issues
4 Accomplishments this period	10 Deliverable effort tracking
5 Activities not performed	11 Financial tracking
6 Out of scope	12 Invoice tracking

review, and the PM submits status reports with metrics that are consolidated into executive dashboard reports for monthly review.

The core documents required by this phase are, unsurprisingly, overlapped with the requirements of competent project management. These are a project status report (PSR), a client status report (CSR), change request reports, a risk register, and a risk indicator checklist. The PSR is a business-focused report intended for the firm's management; thus, it is inappropriate for distribution to the client. There is some work duplication, as the vendor PM must also prepare a CSR tailored for the client. Ideally, it is prepared as a joint project report with the client PM, but that is not always agreed on during lifecycle mapping. The change request process and requisite templates are usually found in the contract; otherwise, these too must be developed prior to kickoff. The risk register is central to risk analysis and was initiated during the bid phase. These and other documents form part of the vendor's practice for the containment of business risk.

Table 4.2 shows the content of a comprehensive PSR. The CSR is related, but for fixed price contracts the interest in cost is diminished as the client is virtually guaranteed a maximum cost for a given scope of work, no matter how much work is actually required. This might not be the case for other contract types.

Exit from the execution phase is least amenable to concrete criteria and decided primarily by the judgment of the vendor PM who must assess whether all activities to meet contract commitments have been finished, or are in the final stages of completion. I can perhaps paraphrase the criterion as "the end is in sight." This means all deliverables are believed to be complete or any variances that exist are definable and rectifiable. The best marker for transition from execution to completion is an agreement between the vendor PM and the client identifying the activities that move the project from its current status to full completion.

Phase 5: Completion

There is little doubt that moving a larger, more complex project through the completion phase to a successful conclusion is a major challenge for most vendor PMs. This is the phase that differentiates a skilled and experienced vendor PM from an inexperienced colleague. The reasons for this are not hard to imagine. Completion requires the customer to declare satisfaction with the results and to put this sentiment in writing. It's a rare project that executes every term of the contract precisely and unambiguously, and clearly demonstrates that to the buyer. Even when that goal is achieved, it is quite usual to discover small shifts in requirements leading to last minute change requests and other unplanned activities that need to be worked. Reporting and documentation discipline is essential to determine whether these items are defects that must be repaired at the vendor's cost or otherwise at the client's.

When these last-minute activities are added to the natural inclination of the project team to defer difficult issues to the last minute, and the concerns of the customer who wants to keep the team of experts around as long as possible to work on every potential issue, you can see why the completion phase can be a drawn-out misery. The '99% complete' syndrome is the most common project disease, known as the 'the tail of the dragon' in rather descriptive jargon (Figure 4.3).

The solution to this dilemma, as experienced vendor PMs have discovered, is to treat the completion phase as a mini-project in its own right. It is also reasonable to incent a reluctant customer by ensuring the contract stipulates that no production use of the product is allowable until sign-off. The contract should also make clear the obligation of the customer to sign off, unless her review and testing reveals a material defect that is identified in writing within an acceptable time period.

As the execution phase draws to an end, the vendor works with the customer to scrutinize contract requirements and acceptance criteria versus actual accomplishments, and to effectively negotiate the path to successful completion and sign-off. With this approach mutually agreed on, the vendor PM can move confidently toward end-of-job. Such an approach can be

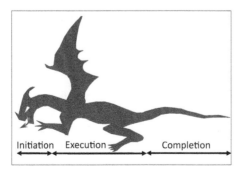

Figure 4.3 The tail of the dragon

Table 4.3 A project completion checklist

Vendor project completion			
1	Cost budget	10	Satisfaction
2	Revenue	11	Lessons
3	Margin	12	Team performance
4	Estimate	13	Transition
5	Schedule	14	Archive
6	Risk	15	Sign-offs
7	Quality	16	Subcontract
8	Scope	17	Invoices
9	Resources	18	Reference

dovetailed quite nicely with the commissioning and production planning that should be occurring during this stage, according to the project lifecycle.

The core documents of this phase focus on the project sign-off report and the plan needed to achieve it. These are central to the joint goal of both contractor and customer and are highly visible. Internally within the firm, a completion checklist shown in Table 4.3 should also be used to ensure that the numerous items surrounding business closure, such as outstanding invoices, are adequately addressed.

The exit criteria for closure are clear-cut, but occur in two stages. The first stage of completion is the signing and filing of the project sign-off and completion report. Both the vendor PM and an authorized representative of the customer sign this. This represents a release of the vendor's obligation (warranty issues excepted) and can trigger a number of events within the firm. The most significant are the final release of staff, sub-contractors, and final invoicing. The second stage of completion is internal to the firm and is represented by the finalization of all project financials, closure of the project accounts, team evaluations, and a review of lessons learned. This can occur some time after Stage 1, and is likely monitored by vendor operations management rather than the PM who has by this time been released from the project.

The responsibility for operating the vendor lifecycle and ensuring its efficiency belongs to a role that is properly introduced in the next chapter. This individual is the delivery manager.

Outline of a vendor methodology

The natural consequence of a sound vendor lifecycle is formalization and development of a comprehensive methodology. Based on experience and common sense, and the key activities and deliverables already identified from each phase, the summary of components in Table 4.4 provides a reasonable starting point.

Table 4.4 Vendor methodology components

Phase		1 Opportunity	2 Bid	3 Initiate	4 Execute	5 Complete
			Methodology based on vendor lifecycle			
Purpose		Bid justification	Winning bid submission	Getting started	Staying on plan	Delivering project and profit
Objectives		Risk screening Bid resources commitment	Responsive proposal Financially sound Risk managed Management approval	Fair contract terms Balanced risk Management approval Prompt booking Transition to PM Set-up for success	Team performance Risk managed Satisfied client Client approvals Utilization Budget Schedule Revenue	Agreed process Meet criteria Sponsor acceptance Settlements Production
Exit criteria		Bid/no bid: sales manager	Bid sign-off: business manager	Contract sign-off: business manager	Deliverables complete: PM	Project sign-off: PM Financial close: finance
Core documents (subset of deliverables)		None	Bid estimate Work estimate Risk rank assessment Statement of work Proposal	Contract Initiation checklist	Project status report Customer status report Risk alert assessment Risk register Change requests Issue log	Project sign-off Completion checklist
Processes (decompose to procedures)		Opportunity evaluation Bid decision	Bid planning Bid preparation Risk assessment Risk mitigation Bid review	Contract negotiation Order entry Project initiation Issue management Change management	Project work Business management Income generation Risk management Issue management Change management	Project acceptance Transition Financial management Administration Issue management Change management

Such a methodology could also include other useful tools. Process hierarchy charts guide the decomposition of process into sub-process and procedures, supported by techniques and checklists. Analysis using input–process–output charts contributes to the development of a full set of deliverables, supported by templates. Deployment flowcharts supported by a detailed RAM illustrate the responsibilities of the main actors in the firm.

Methodologies are always controversial. Complaints are heard about stifling creativity, or pandering to the less experienced, or defining 'make-work' and so forth. It is possible to design methodology that can handle these concerns and improve organizational productivity, but that is not the present intention.

The top-down approach implied by Table 4.4 would doubtless lead to a very complete model, but at a cost. The 80/20 rule suggests a shortcut almost as valuable; less complete but very flexible. This could be described as an *elementary* vendor methodology and is a practical subset based primarily on the deployment of best practices linked to the lifecycle phases and is proposed in the following chapters.

Finally, the reader interested in top-down analysis and methodology development may turn to Chapter 12. Collaborative procurement is an experimental methodology that explores the unification of the vendor and client lifecycles into methodology applicable to the complete procurement process.

5 Developing organizational responsibilities

Roles and responsibilities are a starting point for any newly born firm or project. People need to know who's in charge and who's counting the cash. Regarding projects, a sloppy lifecycle creates inefficiency, inadequately defined scope leads to un-estimated work, and lip service to risk reduces the odds of on-time, on-budget completion, but incomplete, poorly communicated, erroneous, or unaccepted responsibilities will stop a project in its tracks. In project recovery reviews, time after time I have found that inadequate definition of responsibilities is a consistent cause of failure. The purpose of this chapter is to describe basic organizational design tools and their usage, specifically within the services firm, so this can be avoided.

A reminder that the ultimate purpose of the commercial firm is to make a profit gives us a grand starting point for any business discussion on responsibilities. With sales generally focused on revenue, and the vendor PM on delivery, there are many opportunities for this fundamental to be overlooked. During the bid phase, the need to define a solution with acceptable risk, to price the bid to beat competition, to account for some contingency, and to produce a profit creates contradictory pressures. The firm's business management must keep engaged during this phase to ensure the profit requirement stays front-and-center. Another common scenario during the execution phase is when the perceived need for a technically perfect solution eats into profit margins in an alarming way. Everyone in the firm needs to be reminded that they share responsibility to generate profit; it is not a dirty word.

Organizational balance

When a services firm is founded, especially if its roots are in consulting or small-scale construction, the sales/delivery dichotomy does not exist. Why? Because the organization is naturally self-balancing when it is small. The partner proposing the work to the client is the same person as the senior consultant or craftsman performing the work. The project will evidently be bid to satisfy the objectives of the young business and to provide adequate resources for satisfactory delivery. If not, learning soon occurs, as the negative feedback will be felt personally and have the salutary effect. The trouble comes with growth and the evolution of the firm's business model to include specialized sales staff, whom we call sales executives. These new professionals have to be paid, requiring adjustments to the firm's fee, revenue, and margin structure. Their sales of services must be both profitable and capable of delivery (within the competence of the firm). Sometimes, this last requirement is referred to as services 'deliverability'.

Causes of sales dominance

The risk is that the imperative to 'make the sale' over-rides the need for services deliverability. This can have a number of causes:

- The probability that the sales executive has only limited experience in project estimation and scope definition. Naturally, her skills will be in selling, as that is her role.
- Financial incentives mean that the sales executive gets a fatter paycheck when a bid is submitted and won than when a no-bid is called or the bid is lost.
- The environment can be extremely competitive, sometimes leading to false optimism (for example, in assessment of risk) in order to reduce costs.
- Similarly, a competitive environment can lead to discounting pressures. In an effort to maintain a profitable rate structure, this can sometimes be diverted into pressure to reduce the effort estimate.
- Sometimes, the bid opportunity is so compelling that the sales priorities overwhelm all others, leading the sales executive to turn a blind eye to deficiencies in the proposal that will cost the firm heavily during execution. This is not just false optimism but more often a case of deliberately ignoring the firm's weaknesses in order to bid what are often termed 'strategic' opportunities.

I suppose the list could be made longer, but it's depressing enough already. The bottom line is that conflict between sales and delivery is a factor to be addressed. What is required is a senior advocate for the vendor PM, specifically in larger firms who employ specialized sales people. This function is commonly referred to as *delivery management.*

Delivery management

Delivery management is a function whose fundamental purpose is to validate services deliverability and then to ensure delivery. It sounds a lot like project management and certainly requires considerable project management experience, but the function is distinguished by being represented at the senior levels of the firm and carrying a global responsibility.

Differentiating services and delivery

A basic question must be addressed before going further. Isn't this role the same as the professional services manager—the person to whom practitioners and perhaps the vendor PM report? Often it is, but combining a delivery role with services management is a poor choice. There are several reasons:

- Adding overall delivery accountability to a job already busy with resource management, performance management, career management, sales interfacing, and technical currency creates an overload.
- Combining these roles can create, if not a conflict of interest, perhaps a dilution of interest.
- In all likelihood, a services manager's skills (primarily managerial and people skills) will not include the depth of project skills the delivery role demands. The vendor PMs may feel increasingly unsupported and detached from the firm's management process.
- These days, project teams are drawn from many different service units, meaning many services managers are involved. On what basis can one be selected for the delivery management role, and expect it to work?

Removing the delivery role from the Professional Services Manager (PSM) and assigning a focused Delivery Manager (DM) is not a brand-new idea and has been adopted by many of the established professional services firms. It may be implemented as a highly active role, where the PMs and perhaps a small Project Management Office (PMO) report directly to the DM. Or it may be a less active or matrixed role in which the vendor PMs participate in a dotted line relationship with the DM for reviews, project assessments, and risk assessments. In either case, for the concept to work, the DM must have a seat at the senior management table and must be empowered to approve bids. This resolves the sales bias.

Although the delivery role is best split from the professional services role, particularly as the firm gets larger, it is not always an intuitive move and difficulties of role definition can arise. These roles are delineated in Table 5.1. The table shows the role of the DM and PSM in a large, centralized firm. The danger in creating management focus is that silos are inadvertently formed. The answer is to encourage a teamwork approach, and not to rely exclusively on procedures and black and white role definitions. Be careful not to take Table 5.1 as a cookie cutter role template for all firms—the best solution is always tailored to the unique characteristics of a specific firm.

General description of the DM role

The DM role also resolves the continuity problem when the executing vendor PM is not available or simply not identified during the bid phase. To support his bid signoff responsibility, the DM validates the work on the details of the bid such as estimates. Through reviews and assessments, the DM retains

Table 5.1 Roles of the delivery manager and professional services manager

	Typical DM/PSM roles	
Role	Delivery manager	Professional services manager
Staff management	PMs in all the firm's offices report to DM.	Practitioners within an office or technical specialization report to the PSM.
Project management	Corporate expert, setting and maintaining standards, manager, reviewer, and coach to PMs.	Understands and represents PM requirements to staff, acts as PM on smaller projects if PM not assigned.
Customer attention	Maintains customer awareness and a point of escalation for project delivery issues.	Strong customer knowledge and responsiveness, point of escalation for general service issues.
Policy and procedure	Project delivery.	Performance, utilization, bench management, training, local sales support, career management.
Technical focus	General.	Manages practitioners within a specialization, maintains currency in that specialization.
Geography	Global (across the firm).	Local (location focus).

a level of accountability, allowing project responsibility to be passed to the executing PM when ultimately assigned. Clearly, the DM retains some 'skin in the deal' through this process. Although the best solution is to have the executing PM engaged during the bid phase, reality says this is not always possible. The concept of delivery management accountability is better than simply dumping the project in the lap of the executing PM who will have little commitment to the analysis and estimates that were done during the bid.

Once a project is awarded, the DM becomes the focal point of both regular and exception-driven reviews with the PM, engaging the sales executive and the PSM when customer and resourcing issues arise.

There are other important things a delivery manager can do that might be more difficult for the PSM:

• Hold the PM to account.
• Provide support for the PM and a link to senior management.
• Provide business and project management coaching.

These are important responsibilities, and when they are weak, the firm's projects eventually start to perform below par even with seemingly experienced vendor PMs. (On the flip side, strong delivery management can reinforce less experienced vendor PMs.) PMs must feel part of the business and believe that the upper levels of the firm appreciate the issues of project management. Someone who understands project management can interpret project status and project metrics. Someone who is aware of the disciplines and priorities can meaningfully reinforce the PM's accountabilities. Someone who is not, cannot.

The DM has a key role in ensuring that all involved in the project understand the commitments and the business priorities, and deliver them. For example, it is the role of sales to make the sale at a planned gross margin and the role of delivery management and the PM to deliver the project at that margin. It is not logical to sell a project at 10% margin and expect it to be delivered at 40% (but believe it or not, this expectation exists). Delivery at 10% should be seen as (and is) a complete success, as it meets the plan, regardless of the firm's expectation for considerably higher margins. Likewise, a project signed-off at 40% margin but delivered at 10% cannot, all other things being equal, be classed as a success.

As the project proceeds, the DM can often provide strategic and tactical advice to the vendor PM and act as a conduit from the practical rough-and-tumble of the project to central corporate functions such as Finance and Project Accounting. When the project goes through the completion phase, the DM is the natural function to ensure that lessons learned from the project (and there will be some) are assimilated as appropriate by fellow managers and sales executives and codified in procedures, checklists, or templates for future use.

Incentive plans

The introduction of delivery management as an antidote to excessive sales bias is not a panacea. Compensation plans and incentives also have a strong influence on sales, PM behavior and the achievement of a business balance. The point of most compensation plans is to incent behaviors that companies believe will align the individual's and the organization's success. Unfortunately, that ideal is often hard to achieve because unintended behaviors may not help the organization and can even be a detriment. For example, sales targets based on booked value alone are good for building a backlog, but not so good for ensuring revenue and profit. In the contractual context, incentives to the vendor PM for timely or ahead-of-schedule completion seem like a good idea (though they are usually balanced with penalties for delay!) but simply don't work on many types of projects, especially those where the vendor and client tasks are intermingled. It's also a drag on team building unless the same incentives are available to everyone. Design incentive programs with great care.

Responsibility, accountability, and authority

During project execution, ambiguous, ill-defined, incomplete, or ignored stakeholder responsibilities are the cause of a major share of failures. The

Figure 5.1 The three-legged stool for the RAA model

vendor PM needs helpful models and techniques to rectify this failing. One of the most useful models is the triplet of responsibility, accountability, and authority (RAA). This is often drawn as a three-legged stool as shown in Figure 5.1, suggesting that if one leg is removed the stool falls over.

To ensure these important terms are properly understood, following are some definitions and examples of use.

Responsibility

This one is easy. Responsibility is what you have agreed to do or are professionally expected to do as a duty. If you are responsible, then you must execute some task over which you have control, based on the level and nature of the responsibility. Assuming a simple project, which is to bury electric cable between two points and provide suitable terminations, this case explores the RAA for three types of resource: laborer, electrician, and perhaps a surveyor. The laborer needs to know the parameters of the trench, the deadline, and the costs he is allowed. His responsibility is to dig the trench within those parameters. It could also be his responsibility to advise the PM if his knowledge tells him that the task might be unsafe, or incorrectly specified. For example, the instructions are to dig three feet deep, but the laborer knows local code requires a depth of four feet. Now this last point is a bit gray, as it is unlikely to be shown on his activity list, but it is possible that the laborer would agree it's something he should report. Similarly, the other resources have their responsibilities defined, coordinated by the PM. The work of all three workers must be carried out correctly for the project to succeed, and as the PM manages this, she therefore has *overall* responsibility. Now, it is not particularly informative to see an activity called 'make sure the plan is executed correctly', but I would expect to see this responsibility made specific, for example, 'review and approve specifications', 'collect time and expense costs', 'review activity progress', and so on.

Accountability

Accountability is the other side of responsibility. If an assigned or implied responsibility is accepted, then you are accountable for the proper discharge of the responsibility and can be held accountable for the associated success measure. This is a fundamental and sometimes neglected principle of management. Holding people accountable requires that all parameters of the responsibility must be spelled out or professionally implied and that there are consequences if they are not met. Dealing with these situations is hard work, and skill is needed to do it fairly and productively. It would be unfair and unproductive to fire the trench digger for a late finish if the cause was unexpected obstacles. The laborer should be trained to bring these situations to the notice of the PM immediately and not wait for periodic review. The person holding you accountable receives your reports.

Now consider the ill-defined responsibility regarding local codes. Can the laborer be held accountable if the specifications for depth are wrong, but that's the way it's dug? In this case, I don't think so. It may be an expectation, but it is not an accountability that the PM could reasonably delegate. Accountability implies a consequence resulting from success or failure, and can never be totally delegated. Responsibility, however, can be segmented and delegated quite precisely and relates more to task performance than to overall success or failure.

Accountability flows down the chain of command, and success measures become narrower in focus because accountabilities can never be 100% delegated. The PM has partitioned the work and is holding the workers accountable; the sponsor is holding her accountable for the success of the project. What about the sponsor's accountability? Well, a company director should hold him accountable for achieving the benefits of this project.

Although the responsibility may lie with a member of the group, group accountability suggests all members can be held accountable. There are business examples, but the best-known example is from British government practice and is referred to as cabinet accountability. This practice holds that if an action or policy voted for in cabinet turns out badly for the nation, no matter how an individual voted, they are all held accountable. So turf the rascals out at the next election! There is always a consequence from failing to meet accountability.

Authority

Like accountability, authority flows down in an organization—sometimes, very silently! Authority is your mandate, your freedom of action. The greater your authority, the more freedom you enjoy. Freedom means the license to incur costs, to issue commands, to hire and fire, to present issues and solutions, and to make decisions, all on one's own account. This is the most difficult of our triplet to deal with because project management principles require authority to be clear and explicit, whereas general management can be uncomfortable with this. There is a common attitude among general management that authority should be earned. That is, when the employee has demonstrated they can handle additional delegation, *then* the authority necessary to be consistently successful will be granted. This makes sense to management, but is not logical.

A simple case from digging trenches explains this. If the PM had worked with the laborer before, and knew his capabilities went beyond wielding a shovel or operating a backhoe, then she might confidently delegate additional authority within limits of budget and schedule. She might tell the laborer he could hire an assistant, or rent additional equipment, or meet with the surveyor to propose improvement to the specifications. The laborer now has overall responsibility for trench digging, as he now has subordinates, and with additional authority comes added accountability. The PM must now hold him accountable for the decisions he makes under the umbrella of his broadened authority.

> Responsibility and the authority granted to achieve it represent boundaries on accountability, and define the success measures used to hold an individual accountable.

Practical examples of RAA

RAA is much more than interesting management theory. It provides the vendor PM and team members with a versatile framework that can be used to think about project roles in a practical way and identify and fix any deficiencies.

Case 1: Providing a large bid estimate

During the bid phase of a large and complex project, which will require the firm to propose technology where they lack familiarity, the responsibility for estimating the work is handed to a PM who has 50% of her time available. This is how the RAA model can be used to help her succeed in this assignment.

Responsibility–What exactly is she expected to provide? The estimating work to be done might include: raw work hours effort, type of resources, list of assumptions, expected duration, customer effort to be contributed, resource costs, expenses, fees and price to client, included contingency—and maybe more.

Accountability–To whom is she accountable for this work—to the sales executive, her services manager, a bid manager, or someone else? What will be considered the measure of success and how should it be reported? What about her existing accountability on her current work—can it be sustained, and if it cannot, what are the consequences and the back-up plan?

Authority–Is it clear from her level in the firm what her authority is, and is it sufficient, or should special authority be requested? For example, can she task others with specialized pieces of work? Can she engage technology expertise from outside the firm? Can she authorize a proof of concept exercise if it is needed to determine the feasibility of estimates?

Case 2: Managing a project

During the execution phase of a project, the PM needs confidence that his RAA assignments are in balance and provide the freedom of action to deal with situations expeditiously. (As an aside, I have seen considerably more PMs get into trouble because they have underestimated their authority than overstepped it.) Not just the PM but also his team members will have exactly the same concerns, albeit at a different level. It is the PM's job to address that, too.

Responsibility–The checklist in Table 5.2 might represent a full set of project management responsibilities within the mandate to deliver the project on schedule, on budget, meeting agreed objectives. Best practice is to check these responsibilities at the start of the project and confirm those that reside with the vendor PM and those that don't.

Accountability–Who is holding the vendor PM accountable and through what means? This is where complexity inevitably arises, because there are multiple interests in the outcome of the project, and many views on what success means. The sponsor, within the client organization, is paying the bill for services rendered, and expects the vendor PM to render them. The firm's business manager has authorized certain costs in the expectation of a margin, and the PM must deliver that. The sales executive wants a happy client and believes the PM is accountable for that. It's usual to find many stakeholders within the client, within the firm, and even third parties who believe the vendor PM is accountable to them for specific aspects of the project.

Authority–The authority of the vendor PM is not always clear-cut, and sometimes judgment has to be applied. Table 5.3 provides a generic list

Table 5.2 Checklist of project management responsibilities

Project manager responsibilities checklist	
1 Plan the project, establish and maintain project scope, objectives	9 Monitor progress and report status (schedule, budget, scope)
2 Manage the expectations of sponsor and steering committee	10 Detect variances (schedule, budget, scope) and take action
3 Design the project approach	11 Assess risk and take mitigating action
4 Prepare plans and budgets	12 Manage changes
5 Acquire resources, ensure staff orientation	13 Resolve issues, escalating as necessary
6 Organize teams, resources, procedures, etc.	14 Monitor and coach team performance
7 Obtain commitments	15 Enforce standards
8 Assign and supervise tasks	16 Feedback on team performance

Table 5.3 Checklist of project management authorities

Project manager authorities checklist	
1 Limit of authority for project expenses and costs	8 Task assignment
2 Limit of authority for project change requests	9 Implementation of risk mitigation
3 Hiring of staff or contractors	10 Scope of decision making and issue resolution
4 Staff re-assignment	11 Access to information
5 Staff development	12 Access to senior staff
6 Staff recognition	13 Modification of standards or operating procedures
7 Use of contingency or reserves	14 Management of performance

for reference. Inevitably, the PM must take the initiative and create his own authority framework deemed to balance the allocated responsibilities and accountabilities. This is then discussed and confirmed with the DM and the sponsor during initiation. Not all of this is feasible to document, but the essentials must end up in the project charter, contract, initiation checklist, or equivalent document.

Superiors are not always forthcoming on these matters, uncertain of the implications of explicitly delegating certain authorities. Nonetheless the vendor PM can only strengthen his position by using the RAA model in discussions. It is essential to avoid accepting responsibility and accountability for which adequate authority has not been given.

Case 3: Project coordinator

A common situation is being asked to perform as a PM but given a project coordinator role. Although the term 'project manager' is defined more or less consistently in the literature, the term 'project coordinator' is not. What I mean by it is a project management assignment with so little authority that the PM title is misleading. Few of the authorities listed in Table 5.3 might be granted, leaving the project coordinator in the position of continually finding out what is going on, translating it all into progress and issues, and then reporting it to the boss who will then either commandeer the matter, or grant authority piecemeal only for temporary use! Now, this is a perfectly legitimate (maybe inefficient) method of operating; it only becomes dysfunctional when there is mutual misunderstanding about the role. Having been there, I can say there are few frustrations worse than thinking you are PM when you are a project coordinator (except perhaps thinking you are project coordinator when you are PM).

Flexibility

The problem with describing responsibilities concisely is that it can create the misleading impression that every responsibility can be neatly assigned to a waiting, fully skilled individual. Alas, this is not always the case, and in project scenarios everyone, especially the PM, must be prepared to be flexible.

An example is the best way to explain. In IT projects, there seems to be a history of contention between the PM and the business analyst. In the perfect world, there is no doubt that gathering requirements is the job of the analyst, but on smaller projects, there are usually no analysts assigned to do the work. Thus, requirements analysis is an extremely valuable skill for a PM to possess, though it is perhaps not spelled out in her job description. The PM now doing a portion of business analysis does not mean this is defined as part of project management. The PM is demonstrating flexibility, perhaps out of necessity, by removing her PM hat and putting on her analyst hat—to get the job done.

The RAA model is a useful framework for identifying and analyzing the issues of a specific role, but it is not really a tool for actually designing project-specific responsibilities. To help with that task, we need to employ the RAM and the structure chart.

The responsibility assignment matrix

Project managers should crave clarity on important responsibilities, for themselves, their team, and project stakeholders, and that is exactly the job of the Responsibility Assignment Matrix (RAM). The purpose of the RAM is to document an agreed responsibility plan for the project (or firm) and, using a pre-defined coding structure, ensure adequate analysis. This excellent tool furnishes an uncomplicated analytic solution that can be succinctly documented.

> Every stakeholder should appear in at least one RAM chart as evidence of stakeholder analysis and for completeness of the responsibility plan.

The structure is a simple matrix, with the horizontal axis assigned to stakeholders and the vertical axis assigned to listing the deliverables, or business results to be created by the project. This arrangement is quite versatile; instead of deliverables, a more detailed matrix could list activities. A matrix can be created for each phase instead of the entire project. The matrix cells are then populated with a coding scheme showing the responsibility assignments. The vendor PM cannot prepare and publish this in isolation, but must consult with stakeholders and gain consensus.

There are two common coding schemes for RAM in general use. The first is referred to as RACI—responsible, accountable, consulted, and informed. The second is PARIS—participate, accountable, review, input, and sign-off. Although both can be successful, the PARIS scheme often gives best results for development projects, whereas RACI is more useful for consulting engagements. The examples explore the PARIS scheme in more detail, as it is more comprehensive and powerful.

Meaning of the PARIS coding

Participate–A Participant is a team member, responsible for activities to accomplish the result, who will look to the Accountable person for direction. To Participate means to 'do' and is similar to being responsible in the RAA model.

Accountable–The Accountable person assigned overall responsibility for the result (or activity or deliverable), has the necessary authority, and will be judged on the success of the endeavor. Organization theory suggests there only be one Accountable person per line item, but in rare situations this is not possible. Shared accountability is always a special case, and care and attention is required. An escalation procedure should be designed to resolve disagreements or conflict.

Review–A Review person has a strong role, with high expectations for its performance. This is not a quick, off-the-cuff opinion. Usually a Reviewer will have specialist knowledge, responsibilities or experience. Often, the Sign-off person will look to Reviewers for validation of approval.

Input–Input people provide data, information, techniques, and opinion, usually on request. An example would be a user who is asked to input their requirements. Not as strong a role as Participate or Review, and very specific or narrow in scope, meaning that Input people may not be considered core team members (Participants).

Sign-off–The Sign-off person ends the phase of work designed to get the result. It is a formal granting of approval or acknowledgment of completion, usually from the owner of the business result. There may, quite reasonably, be more than one Sign-off individual. For example, a system is completed and the invoice submitted. Engineering sign off to say it meets their needs, IT sign off to say their standards were complied with, and Finance sign off so the bill can be paid.

Practical examples of RAM

Examples of the technique are chosen from the opportunity and execution phases of the vendor lifecycle. An additional detailed example shows how RAM is applied to managing the project team's deliverables. The intent is to demonstrate the utility of the technique, and not to provide a definitive responsibility plan—that will depend upon the specifics of the firm, or the project.

Example 1: Bid/no bid

The high-level RAM in Table 5.4 serves to document the firm's policy based on bids estimated at different values, and makes the responsibility plan clear without the need for a detailed procedure manual.

Table 5.4 Responsibility plan for the bid/no bid decision

Business result	Stakeholder RAM for bid/no bid						
	Stakeholders						
	Sales executive	Vendor PM	Professional services manager	Sales manager	Delivery manager	Legal	Finance
Decide to bid >$500K	A,P	I	P	I,S	R	I	
Decide to bid <$500K	A,P,S	I	P	R	I		

This RAM may or may not be agreeable to you, or any other firm, but it is policy for this firm, and the RAM makes it clear:

• First, note that DM does not sign off on the decision, but they are given a review role for larger bids. The rationale may be that there is no delivery risk in deciding to bid.
• The sales executive retains accountability, always. That really means he's the person pushing for the decision, calling the meetings, allocating any specific responsibilities to dig out information etc. The vendor PM is expected to provide input, though the PSM is the participant.
• For smaller bids, matters are delegated to the sales executive and PSM, with the sales executive having sign-off (confirms/makes the decision). The sales manager reviews all such situations at the monthly sales meeting.
• Legal and Finance have no role for smaller bids, but on large bids that respond to RFP, Legal are asked for an opinion on terms and conditions.

Example 2: Project success through teamwork

What does successful execution mean to the services firm? And how does management work together as a team to create success? The wrong answer is to dump everything in the lap of the PM. The firm must create roles and responsibilities that support the vendor PM.

The RAM in Table 5.5 makes it real, dealing with the firm's three key success results described in Chapter 3:

1   Delivering within budget is clear enough. The vendor PM is the main player and accountable. The PSM participates, mainly in the resourcing process, and probably engages in periodic reviews in conjunction with the DM, who approves all relevant reports submitted.

Table 5.5 Responsibility plan for project success

	Stakeholder RAM for project success						
Business result	*Stakeholders*						
	Sales executive	*Vendor PM*	*Professional services manager*	*Sales manager*	*Delivery manager*	*Legal*	*Finance*
Deliverables within budget		A,P	P,R		R,S		I
Performance to standard	I	A,P	P,R	I	R,S		
Customer satisfaction	A,R,P	P	P,R	P,S	I		

2   Ensuring performance meets standards carries a similar responsibility plan but is broader and takes input from the sales executive and sales manager.

3   For customer satisfaction, some might be surprised to see accountability taken by the sales executive, but such clarity is the advantage of the RAM! The sales executive cannot sell services and abandon the customer, unless the firm employs a different sales model. In essence, the sales executive and vendor PM are teamed together—devising detailed responsibility plans on how difficult issues are handled (such as resources not being supplied by client, controversial change requests, maybe project performance issues). Perhaps the roles 'good cop, bad cop' overdramatize the case, but if the vendor PM remains focused on delivery, and the sales executive on customer satisfaction, then the dynamics of the situation result in the best solution. Having said this, in other firms with less focus on client management, the 'A' would indeed be with the PM.

Example 3: Completing a project deliverable

To conclude the RAM discussion, look at the responsibility plan in Table 5.6 showing how a rather detailed activity list might be allocated in order to produce a deliverable—for example, the specifications report. For simplicity, I have lumped all the team roles (chief designer, analyst, technician, etc.) into one column called 'Team'. In actuality, it would be split out into individuals and detailed PARIS codes assigned.

The vendor PM, team leader, and team are the firm's personnel, the rest are with the client. The operations manager (usually, but not always, a subordinate of the sponsor) accepts and operates the system. The vendor PM and sponsor carry a dual sign-off role. The sponsor doubtless relies on subordinates' reviews in order to grant his approval. Tasks that result in a conclusive physical deliverable (such as the specifications report itself) will carry a physical signature. In other cases, the approval may be less formal, such as an exchange of email.

Table 5.6 Responsibility plan for a specifications report

Specifications report activities	Stakeholders						
	Vendor PM	*Team leader*	*Team*	*Client technology rep*	*Operations manager*	*System users*	*Sponsor*
Prepare plan	A,P	P,R	P	I	I	I	S
Gather requirements	S	A,P	P	I	I	I	I
Validate requirements with contract	S,A,P	P			R		S
Ensure requirements are technically feasible	S,A,P	P		R			S
Prepare conceptual designs	S	A,P	P	I,R	I,R		S
Prepare specifications report	S	A,P	P	R	R	R	S

Stakeholder RAM for a project deliverable

Project team structure

An organization structure chart is a useful tool to clear away tangles when there are many client departments, contracted organizations, and managers with various spans of control. Effort should be made to agree a project structure during the bid phase, as it provides a framework for the detailing of responsibilities using descriptions and/or the RAM charts.

The services firm cannot determine the project structure unilaterally, as both the client and the firm must interface smoothly, and the management hierarchies must find a match. Both parties should understand the choice to be made between three management options, each of which can lead to a very different project. Often, the client will have made this decision already. The firm must ensure that the project can be successful with the chosen team structure, otherwise contractual conditions must be drafted that balance the vendor PM's RAA and allow for success.

The three options to be looked at are:

1 Parallel management teams
2 Technically led teams
3 Business led teams.

Each of these has strengths and weaknesses, and naturally there are also hybrid solutions that can be designed for specific circumstances.

Parallel management teams

This structure is not particularly integrated, but it is the most popular and the easiest to implement. There is lots of freedom on both sides to design the reporting details to suit their own needs, so long as effort is put into the communication and interface point(s) with the other team. Figure 5.2 shows a generic example of this structure and the typical management roles. The vendor PM and client PM form a joint management team, perhaps also including client business/user managers, each with their own deliverables and responsibilities.

Parallel management structures are common for fixed price contracts when the firm fully understands what they're building and do not need strong team integration, but seek independence and a high degree of control for the vendor PM.

The structure shows communication and hierarchical equivalence between the sponsor, DM, and sales executive. This is an idealized example, and the reality is highly situational. Either the delivery or services manager could sit on the steering committee. The dashed line to the sponsor indicates a point of equivalence for escalations. The existence of the steering committee is conjectured and is only usual on large and critical projects spanning several departments. The client PM makes reports to the steering committee, but may not be regarded as a voting member. The vendor PM plays a back-up role.

The drawback to this arrangement is the lack of integration. Joint team operations are made more complex by the separate reporting. Although not shown in the idealized chart, there is often a multiplicity of client PMs of indeterminate rank, representing the client's technical builders of the product, the eventual owner or operating manager, and the various departmental user teams. Although the firm should insist on identifying exactly whom they get their orders from, this is a possible weakness. The vendor PM rarely has direct links with the sponsor under this arrangement. Such communication is perceived as undermining to the client PM.

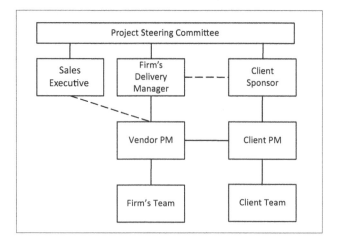

Figure 5.2 Parallel management team structure

> Parallel management teams are easy to assemble and the best option
> when team integration is less essential.

Technically led teams

Giving the lead to the technical PM is almost always the 'get it done' option. This is the way to go if time is of the essence. A technical PM is one who understands the nature and complexity of what is being built, and the methods, tools, techniques to build it. In other words, this is the vendor PM role, as shown in Figure 5.3. If a client PM is given this job, then the firm must look carefully at contractual commitments and ensure they have adequate authority to deliver.

This structure has some considerable strength. The vendor PM manages a joint technical team, which can be integrated where it counts and efficiencies improved. She also reports to the sponsor, giving the opportunity to build an effective relationship with the key decision maker. Perhaps most important is the relationship with the business manager who is likely an operations manager and the eventual owner of the project's product.

The diagram shows both roles at the same level, reporting to the sponsor, and with a communication link between them. This is a good model of a balanced supplier/acceptor structure and, with intelligent management, can give excellent results. The vendor PM's influence with the sponsor has to be earned, but usually the vendor PM will enjoy considerable authority to keep things moving. In the event of conflicting objectives that can't be easily resolved between the vendor PM and the business manager, access to the sponsor allows both to make their case and the decision made.

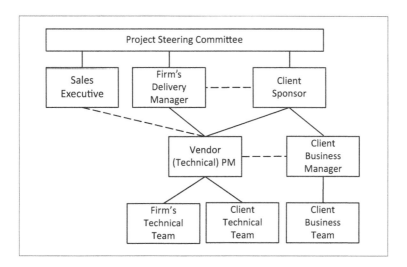

Figure 5.3 Technically led team structure

The major drawback is that clients are often unwilling to hand this degree of authority to a commercial firm. For example, the diagram shows a reporting of client project technical staff to the vendor PM. This allows for excellent coordination and response to priorities, but admittedly meets with client reluctance. Trust and openness are essential. Depending on the degree of team integration, and the predictability of workload in this environment, it may also be challenging to design a workable fixed price contract. Usually time and material (T&M) might be preferred. Alternatively, a hybrid approach with some management staff on T&M and selected deliverables committed on an FP basis can be agreed on.

> When results are needed quickly use a technically led team.

Business led teams

This solution, illustrated in Figure 5.4, is chosen when the client wants maximum assurance that the best possible product will be delivered, in terms of meeting the needs of the business. Paradoxically, this arrangement usually distances the sponsor from the project and may necessitate the DM to align with the business manager who is now acting as overall PM. Connections with the sponsor will tend to be picked up by sales management.

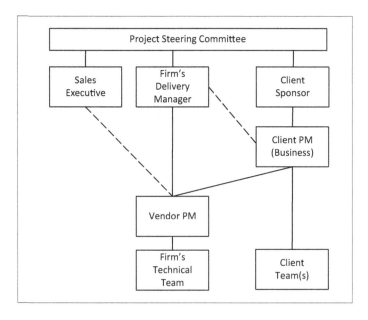

Figure 5.4 Business led team structure

Critical to operation of this structure is the business manager's feel for the technology issues, and a workable technical team relationship. In addition to co-ordinating the business teams contributing to the project, he must also be active in dealing with technical management to ensure their resources are properly deployed. The vendor PM always reports directly to the business manager in this structure, and the technical savvy of the business manager will be a success factor in that relationship. Unified management control, with the business in command, can make it difficult to find the right technical/business balance.

The main long-term drawbacks of this structure are loading the business manager with the extra technical responsibilities, and the evident redundancy between sponsor and business manager, causing the sponsor to reduce his involvement. Depending upon the situation, this can evolve into the business manager taking the role of PM plus de facto sponsor. There is no immediate counterbalance to force necessary trade-offs between business requirements and other priorities.

> When business needs and wants are paramount use a business led team.

Vendor organizational alternatives

Structure charts can also be used to illustrate and analyze organizational alternatives within the vendor firm. Such charts show all of the sales, services, and operational support groups, and the basis for their structural strengths and weaknesses.

The two structures are the decentralized model, and the centralized model. The decentralized model is described first, as that is the beginning point for the majority of firms. There are always overlaps and exceptions in implementation to accommodate special requirements but, nonetheless, there are two distinct organizing principles at work.

Decentralized model

Figure 5.5 shows a conceptualization of the decentralized model. This model is simple and easy to understand. Each operating unit, or office, has a manager in charge, and all staff in that office report to her. This is the natural starting point for any firm and is initially based on geographic location. As growth occurs, and work is being done further and further from base, a new manager is appointed at a second location who sets about building his own organization, perhaps modeled on office one, perhaps not. The decentralized model is easy to grow, and the character of the office manager sets the 'style' of each office. Accountability of each manager to the managing director is focused on financial results—revenue, costs, and margin. Planning is at the local level. The office manager builds her annual plan, executes the plan, and delivers the results.

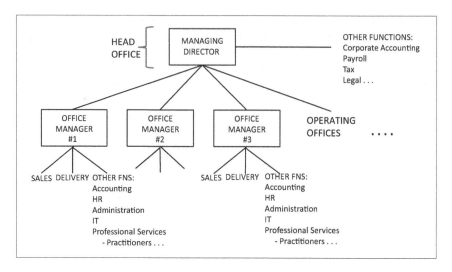

Figure 5.5 Decentralized organizational model

Delivery management is expensive to implement as a specialized function for smaller offices so it is frequently shared between offices with a dotted line responsibility from vendor PMs to DM (matrixed). This is, naturally, a move toward centralization, which tends to promote stronger delivery practices.

If growth continues, then the variability inherent in the decentralized model becomes an impediment to the firm. Another way of expressing this is that the self-interest of the office manager does not now always align with the best interest of the firm as a whole. Size inevitably leads to a requirement for some standardization, and centralization is regarded as an efficient solution.

Centralized model

Centralizing the functions of the firm, as in Figure 5.6, means that each office function does not report to a local boss, but to a functional director in head office. So, all the sales executives report to a sales manager, all vendor PMs report to a delivery manager, and so on. As explained earlier, this is a conceptualization, and in practice, this approach may become complex by the addition of management layers requiring senior sales and delivery managers, or hybrid structures.

The essence of centralization is more management control, more consistency, clear positioning of the firm's interest before that of the office, and stronger delivery practices.

This model, as you might imagine, is less easy to grow, as it removes the entrepreneurial, local boss character that seems to epitomize the successful start-up of an office. Nonetheless, it is a phase that virtually all firms go through because professional services cannot really be franchised, and the only way to ensure long-term success of the firm is to instill standards. The centralized model can do this.

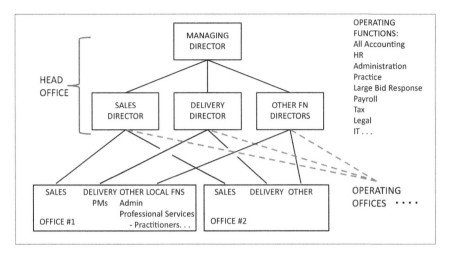

Figure 5.6 Centralized organizational model

Comparison of vendor models

As I am sure the reader has observed, organizations are never static for long, and in practice a pendulum can often be seen at work. If a firm is not growing as expected, or is perceived as becoming too bureaucratic, then there is a push to decentralize and encourage entrepreneurialism. When quality or consistency is seen as an issue, then there is a swing back to centralization.

Table 5.7 Decentralized vs. centralized organization

Strengths and weaknesses of organizational models	
Decentralized	*Centralized*
Autonomous local manager with command.	Weak or no local management (often, an administrative manager is appointed for coordination but not for command).
Entrepreneurial, few growth inhibitors.	Controlling, tends to proceduralization.
Offices can be locations, or can be logical structures that focus on alternative products, different industries, or indeed any opportunity deemed worthwhile.	The complex structures of centralized networks make variants from the norm harder to implement.
Inevitably, functions are duplicated between offices and costs increase. Need for local management and specializations can become expensive.	Centralization improves utilizations and reduces costs overall. Supports specialized functions such as large bid response, practice development, etc.
More difficult to promote delivery management as a separate function from management of practitioners.	Centralized model promotes the development of delivery practices and specialized delivery management.

(Continued)

Strengths and weaknesses of organizational models

Decentralized	Centralized
Manpower flexibility is low as local managers protect their resources.	Manpower flexibility can improve as assignment decisions are centralized.
People join the office. Strong local identification.	People join the firm. Self-identification more varied.
Incentives are locally managed, non-standardized, individualized.	Incentives are formulaic.
Career path appears constrained.	Career path is more open.
Highly responsive to clients and staff.	Less responsive ('have to check with head office').
Idea exchange has to be promoted through other means as offices become silos.	Idea exchange naturally occurs through the management structure.
Inter-office competitiveness naturally occurs.	Less internal competitiveness.

These two models are compared in a summary table in Table 5.7. As the table shows, the type of model strongly influences the strengths of the organization, and the management characteristics that dominate.

6 Risk as a guiding principle for management

Risk management concepts and practices are an integral part of the commercial project environment (CPE) approach. The vendor lifecycle is primarily deployed to mitigate commercial risk, and much of the function of delivery management is a risk management strategy. More than just completing a template, a risk *system* is being proposed that takes a holistic view of the business.

The topic is covered in detail, as risk management is a fascinating but frequently misunderstood and poorly implemented practice. The treatment of risk through all phases of the vendor lifecycle is examined first, followed by the methods of managing overall business risk. Existing models are reviewed, followed by two new models that form the cornerstone of risk management during the bid and execution phases.

A quote from Mario Andretti, the Formula One driver, once caught my attention because he reportedly said, "if things seem under control, you are just not going fast enough." Is this really appropriate when the classic advice on risk is to avoid, mitigate, or transfer—not go faster! Yet, in many ways, Andretti's aphorism neatly sums up the commercial project dilemma. Delivery managers and vendor PMs are faced with these issues at every phase of the vendor lifecycle:

- "There is lots of risk in this RFP, but if we don't respond we won't be seen as a player in this market;
- Risk mitigation and contingency is adding way too much to our costs, we have to reduce it or we simply won't be competitive;
- These terms and conditions that the client is insisting on are adding significantly to our business risk, but if we don't accept them, they have threatened to start negotiations with the second-choice vendor;
- We must find a means to meet the deadline, or the project will be a failure;
- The volume and scope of change requests are threatening project stability; and
- Sign-off has been delayed again, but we must keep going."

Risk management on these terms becomes a balancing act, where the action that might increase risk (going faster) must be assessed against a successful project and happy client (winning the race). This is a model of risk much beloved by the sales executive, as you might imagine, but for the model to have meaning the unfortunate reality is that exceptional skills are needed.

> If you are going to take risks on the racetrack by driving fast, the car had better be driven by Mario!

That is where things come unstuck; many firms have neither the management experience nor the caliber of project management to play this game successfully. There is a fine line between recklessness and a calculated risk. The model must then shift to choosing the track, race, and car so the firm can win on its own terms.

Risk perspective through the vendor lifecycle

During the opportunity phase

In classic risk theory, the view of risk during the opportunity phase is modeled as risk/reward, or risk versus opportunity. Figure 6.1 illustrates the idea of the opportunity being in balance with the risks, perhaps measured by probabilistic techniques such as EMV, but, in this phase, more likely by management judgment. A very preliminary risk screener completed by the sales executive can help that judgment.

Preliminary risk screener

Scoring methods can be devised and a rating inputted to the sales and bid decision process based on only six qualification questions:

1   Anticipated value
2   Type of contract
3   Strength of client relationship
4   Understanding of scope
5   Firm's experience with the solution
6   Availability of required skills

At the macro level, the project itself is seen as the opportunity, and the conditions surrounding its execution represent the risks. Any but the most sophisticated

Figure 6.1 Balancing the opportunity gain against the risk of loss

of firms will balk at the effort of analyzing this equation using probability theory, and such analysis is very prone to the GIGO (Garbage In Garbage Out) effect. It is the role of delivery management to characterize the risks, the role of the sales executive to characterize the opportunity, and the role of business management to make a risk-based decision using their judgment. Using the balancing analogy of Figure 6.1, the opportunity gain from winning the business must be judged to outweigh the possibility of delivery risk costs.

Sometimes, the best way to frame the question is not whether the project should be bid or not, but, given the choice of opportunities before the firm, which is the best to pursue? This allows the risk/reward assessment to be treated relatively rather than as an absolute. Managers usually prefer to make the better of two choices rather than having to choose yes or no. This perspective, and the discipline to weigh alternatives, suggests that occasionally some opportunities will not be bid.

During the bid phase

If the project is to be bid, what is the risk of not being selected? Most aggressive sales managers will take the view that if the firm is going to the cost and trouble of bidding, then they will play to win. Any serious attempt at using probability theory for this scenario is unlikely to succeed because sales executives are unwilling to acknowledge win odds of less than 50%, especially when bid costs of $50K–$100K and more are being incurred. In reality, there are probably at least three or more firms also responding and just as qualified, and so, a priori, it is more realistic to assume win odds of 20–30%. There are only a few actions that the firm can take to improve those odds that can't be replicated by the competition. Unless the firm can submit a demonstrably superior bid, those actions will be based on the existing relationships between individuals in the firm and the buyer. The most significant of those relationships is whether the buyer is an existing client, and a satisfied one. Efficiently exploiting these relationships is far and away the most useful risk mitigation exercise when it comes to winning bids. Selling services is often described as relationship selling and for good reason. When the shoe is on the other foot, and a sales manager sees the competition well-placed to respond to an RFP issued by one of their own clients, a hard-nosed look at the wisdom of bidding is probably the best approach—avoid the risk of not winning by not bidding.

There is another essential view of risk. If the firm is selected for the project, what is the risk of not completing it successfully? This is a forecast of future conditions on the project, and is naturally speculative. It depends upon the eventuality and interaction of complex sets of factors, but at least the use of probability methods is a little more fruitful owing to the volume of projects and randomness. Most readers will be well aware of the myriad of issues that can throw a project off-plan and jeopardize success. The proposed technique looks afresh at these relatively well-known risk facets—such as the team to be used, the type of contract, size and duration of project, etc. These data are then structured into a methodical and easy-to-use questionnaire that generates a risk rank metric for bid phase risk assessment and basic mitigation planning.

A dominant factor in risk ranking has to be a fixed price requirement for the entire project lifecycle to be agreed on concurrently with the hiring of the vendor, requiring the firm to either compress the requirements and general design phases into bid preparation 'for free' or to rely upon their top-down estimating and scope management skills to succeed with the bid. Unless the firm is very familiar with the type of project being tendered, the ideal solution is to negotiate an approach based on the rolling wave.

Another technique that complements overall risk ranking is the use of expected monetary value (EMV) to place a dollar value on a specific risk. This can provide the illusion of precision when values are assigned to risk events, but so long as the reviewers understand GIGO it can be a helpful analysis.

Remember, good project management is by far the best mitigation for everyday risks that can compound on large projects and cause a calamity. Something that confounds many delivery managers is this question—was the project unsuccessful because it was underestimated or because it was poorly managed? To understand whether failure was caused by poor estimation, or by poor management, meticulous recording of scope, risks, and assumptions is essential, followed up by disciplined oversight of project management.

There is no doubt that the larger and riskier a project becomes, the more skilled and experienced the vendor PM must be. The firm must analyze and understand the risk profile of typical projects in the firm's portfolio, then staff and train their PMs accordingly. There is a night-and-day difference between managing a $50,000 three-month time and material engagement, and a $50,000,000 five-year fixed price project.

During the initiation phase

If the firm wins the bid, the initiation phase begins. Signing of a contract creates a commitment for the firm and a potential liability, representing the tangible risk. Careful internal reviews, identification of show-stoppers, and strategic negotiation are the only risk formalities relevant for this phase. There are risk transference terms and conditions that the client may demand (see the discussion in Chapter 3), but these are resolved either by negotiation or are accepted, as they would have been anticipated. If the bid phase risk and bid approval processes have been followed, there should be no surprises sprung on senior management when their contract signature is requested.

During the execution phase

The effectiveness of the preceding risk processes is tested in the execution phase. The view of risk remains concerned for the future, but additionally, the vendor PM must now assess the short-term view. The risk rank assessment and risk register inherited from the bid phase are useful, but only to a point. The mitigation and contingency costs specified by those documents have been budgeted into the bid. Not everything will have been forecast, however, leaving the vendor PM to keep the risk register up-to-date and fund extra risk either from contingency or by eroding the project margin. Support from delivery management is essential when such situations arise. To keep on top of these issues, and mitigate overruns, the concept of a risk alert is introduced. This is derived from a checklist of project risk indicators that typify the status of delivery, the team, and project financials analogous to a project health check. The vendor PM is *not* forecasting when using this checklist, but is reporting current risk alert status, which acts as a leading indicator for probable future difficulties. Based on the checklist responses, the overall risk alert assessment may be taken as a forecast of what could happen if there is no positive intervention.

During the completion phase

During the completion phase, the risk view is highly focused on achieving sign-off. There are no new risk techniques adapted for this phase, but following a prescribed completion phase plan mitigates the risk of delayed sign-off. This means working with the client to draw up a mini-project that delivers sign-off. The firm should be adamant that sign-off is a requirement, specifically for fixed price projects, and should include this obligation of the client in the contract. Without sign-off, the firm faces an unending obligation to investigate real or imagined defects and fix those found.

Overall business view of risk

Keeping a methodical assessment of individual bid and project risk through the lifecycle is a large part of developing successful results for the firm. The models specified are valuable because they yield a set of metrics and can be embedded in the firm's operations. Risk rank conditions the firm's mitigation and bid review strategy. Risk alerts during execution trigger progressive levels of management support, but inevitably some bids are lost, and some projects fail to make profit. The firm needs to know, overall, whether it is on track, or not.

To understand the rationale for the firm's global portfolio management approach, the nature of risk can be thought of simply as uncertainty. That thought leads us to the idea of statistics and the use of statistical theory to stack the odds a little in the firm's favor rather than leaving it all to chance.

Win rate target

The firm's business manager knows that not every expected opportunity will come to the marketplace, and not every bid will be won. There is not much general statistical data that can be accessed for these estimates because so much is dependent upon the niche occupied by the firm, and there are usually idiosyncratic features of the business that make generic data unhelpful. When the firm reaches a statistically valid size, the best advice is to formulate a yearly metric such as a win rate, and to maintain an analysis of the competition. After a period, a benchmark win rate will emerge that represents a healthy annual target.

Project success rate target

The ground is firmer when it comes to forecasting the performance of won projects. To proceed, I must ask the reader to accept a statistical conclusion of contingency estimating, fully explained in Chapter 7, that sets the 70% probability point as the optimum target for executing within the estimate. What does this mean? Estimates subject to risk are an ideal example of uncertainty. Wise estimators add contingency to make success more likely. At one extreme, contingency could be added to achieve 100% probability, meaning certainty, and a very, very expensive bid. The midpoint, 50% probability, suggests a state of unremitting uncertainty, and I, for one, would never bet my project management career on a coin toss. Thus, we arrive at the 70% estimate, which is actually on the knee of the probability curve and represents the minimal increase in contingency for the maximal increase in success probability. If the 70% estimate is consistently exceeded in bids, then too many competitive projects will be lost. If bids are consistently lower, then too many won projects will not deliver profitably.

How can the business manager interpret this? If individual project bids are following an estimating practice based on the 70% estimate point, then the statistical view of the global business would suggest that if 100 fixed price projects are completed in the year, then it is reasonable to expect 70 of them to meet their revenue and margin targets. Of course, the remaining 30 do not fail completely, but deliver results following a frequency profile, down to a few that might lose money—the dreaded 'bleeding project' category.

The wise services firm takes a risk-based view of success. Their financial model is based upon the 70% point, and built into this model is the expectation of the occasional losing project. Otherwise, as Mario might remind us, *we're just not going fast enough!*

Risk models and techniques

Success in risk management means not only following practical risk management practices through the lifecycle, but also adopting and becoming skillful in a handful of techniques. These are the familiar known–unknown and risk event models, the fishbone diagram, and the EMV technique. Then, the particularly valuable new risk factor and the risk alert models are described. These models yield a set of metrics and can be embedded in the firm's operations.

The known–unknown risk model

The Known–Unknown model of risk shown in Figure 6.2 is of interest because it works well if risk is interpreted as implying risk factors as well as risk events. This supports the discussion on risk factor analysis later on.

The model postulates that there are three general sources from which risk (in our case, project risk) can arise. These sources are categorized, rather clumsily, as Known–Knowns, Known–Unknowns, and Unknown–Unknowns. The most helpful definitions are:

Known–Known Risks–These are risks that arise from areas of awareness and where an assessment of the risk level, or impact, can be made. The nature and the likely impact of the risk are known. These risks are naturally based on the firm's experience of the type of project being assessed, and although the model suggests the impact is known, it is just an assessment based on experience.

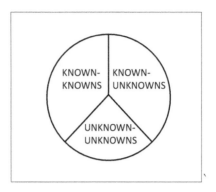

Figure 6.2 The known–unknown universe of risk

Known–Unknown Risks–These are also risks that arise from awareness, but in this case, the risk level that exists is unknown. The nature of the risk is known, but not the level. This might be because the risks are too far in the future, or there are too many other influencing variables, or the project environment for this factor can't be characterized consistently. In risk assessment, these risks are still accounted for, either by making a supporting assumption, or by assigning different probabilities to alternative risk impacts.

Unknown–Unknown Risks–These are risks that exist outside of awareness, and no assessment can be postulated. This knowledge comes only when they occur, thus becoming Knowns and candidates to be added to the checklist for the next project.

Examples of the knowns and unknowns

Example 1. If the project involves landscaping, then wet weather is a risk factor. If the project execution is tomorrow, then this is a Known–Known, based on the short-term weather forecast. Mitigation might be to lay ground covering and dress in rain gear. If execution is planned for a month away, then the risk is a Known–Unknown. In this case the mitigation (and the extra cost) is deferred until needed.

Example 2. If the project involves implementing new software within a recently updated operating system environment, then this is a Known–Unknown, and likely will remain in that category no matter how much research is done. The interesting thing is that even if the guess was a low risk level based on a very low probability, the severity is so high that mitigation, and the costs, might be chosen regardless.

Example 3. If the project is leading edge, in an unfamiliar environment, with a bunch of Unknown–Unknowns, then by definition there can be no specific mitigation plan for this, so this type of risk can only be managed by assignment of contingency.

The risk event model of risk

The classic risk event model is ubiquitous and leads directly leads to development of the risk register. It is comprehensively described in PMBOK® plus many other texts on project management. My purpose is to summarize the features, benefits, and shortcomings to segue later into the risk factor model designed for professional services.

The risk event model is based upon cause and effect analysis and requires the analyst to examine the project asking "what could go wrong?" and "what is the cause?" With those questions answered, it is then possible to either eliminate or deflect the cause, or minimize the impact if the event occurs. In risk parlance, this is called the response strategy. Although centered on mitigation, there are three other strategies identified—transference, avoidance, and acceptance. Figure 6.3 illustrates the model.

Terminology of the risk event model

Risk Event–An uncertain occurrence that will impact project objectives.

Cause–A cause of the risk event.

Triggers–Warning signs, or 'tell-tales', that the risk event is imminent.

Impact–The effect on project objectives, if the risk event occurs. An impact has two aspects: severity and probability.

Severity–The degree of impact on objectives, from minor to major.

Probability–The likelihood that the event will occur with the severity anticipated.

Root cause analysis

This model is used to determine response strategy. If the impact on project objectives is low, then the risk event may be accepted—no further effort is required. If, on the other hand, the impact is significant then the cause and effect model encourages root cause analysis. Similar to the traditional Russian doll where layers are opened successively until the final layer is discovered,

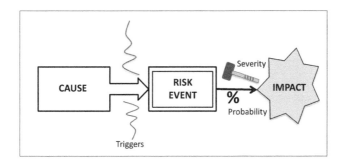

Figure 6.3 Risk event model

the root cause can be revealed. It must be sufficiently deep as to be clearly causative, but not so deep that there is nothing to be done about it. Herein lies the art of effective mitigation planning.

A useful technique is to express root cause analysis in terms of a semantic model that, if properly done, immediately suggests mitigation.

"Because <of cause> then <risk event> may occur {repeat to root cause}, causing <impact on project objectives>."

Example of root cause analysis

Consider a large project where a high volume of change requests is causing work slowdown, loss of control, and high team frustration. Using the discipline of the semantic model: "Because of a high volume of change requests, then control of the configuration may be lost, causing delay in work and probable cost increase."

A moment's thought suggests the analysis is incomplete. The statement must be refined to reveal another layer: "*Because many user departments were not consulted*, then a high volume of change requests may be experienced, then control of the configuration may be lost, causing delay in work and probable cost increase." Now the mitigation actions are revealed.

Example of the risk register

The deliverable from risk event analysis is the risk register; this terminology is now almost universal and the basic process widely understood. The results achieved are exemplified in Table 6.1.

All elements of the risk event model are covered, and the attributes of severity and probability have been factored to yield an overall risk rank to help prioritize mitigation (5 very high, 1 very low). Creating a risk register as a workshop exercise forces analytical thinking and the development of mitigating actions. It also serves as a potent team building exercise when undertaken as a joint client/vendor endeavor.

Table 6.1 Risk register example

Risk register example				
Risk events and impact	Severity *L M H*	Probty *L M H*	Risk rank	Mitigation plan
1. Possible department reorganization, client project staff reassigned, will cause delay.	M	H	4	• Initiate project as early as possible. • Front load much of the test plan development and client tasks. • Increase time of key resources on site to assist client. • Lobby sponsor to defer reorganization.

Limitations

When done conscientiously during bid, initiation, and execution, the risk register is a key element of the risk management process. However, despite its value to project management, I have discovered some drawbacks with the risk event model and its companion, the risk register, during the bid phase.

A big problem is lack of time. During the bid phase, the firm needs something quick, relatively accurate, and applicable to building the bid strategy and approval process. Unfortunately, although the risk event method works well for detailed analysis, it is not 'quick and easy' and is not designed for overall risk metrics such as project risk rank.

There are other drawbacks with risk event analysis:

- The method requires an experienced analyst. The method itself is simple, but providing a genuinely useful analysis and mitigation plan is not for beginners.
- The method starts with a blank risk register. Although a checklist of risk categories can help with a quick start, there is little enthusiasm for a risk workshop during the haste of bid preparation.
- The method can be repetitive. A large project can easily generate a list of 20 risk events and causes, many of which have similar mitigation actions.

An observation from my career is that very few projects have failed identifiably from one significant risk event. I can think of a few cases—a project whose irreplaceable technical architect left half way through; a project manager who suffered a nervous breakdown; cancellation of a program due to funding cuts; a project cancelled as a result of due diligence auditing during an unexpected company merger—and I am sure there have been a few more. The conclusion I have reached, however, is that the overwhelming majority of project failures occur either from negligence in recognizing risk factors in the environment while the project just keeps going till it drops off the cliff, or the project becomes victim to long sequences of incessant small failures—death by a thousand cuts.

Project death by a thousand cuts—the result of unmitigated risk factors that accumulate over time.

The fishbone diagram

Another useful method for cause and effect analysis is the fishbone diagram (or Ishikawa diagram) shown in Figure 6.4. This is a visual technique and works well with teams in a workshop setting. To assist in a comprehensive analysis, especially for beginning practitioners, it is helpful to pre-populate the ribs with common areas of risk for the project family. Figure 6.4 shows risk categories often seen in the literature, but one could also use the risk facets discussed later.

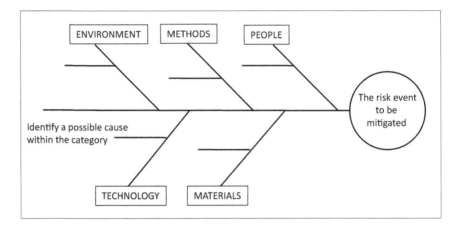

Figure 6.4 The fishbone diagram

The facilitator draws the diagram in front of the group, writing the risk event they wish to avoid in the 'head'. Each one of the ribs is then examined in turn to determine any causation. If a cause is drawn in, the analysis continues, analogous to the Russian doll, until a consensus root cause is established. As a separate exercise, this can then be mitigated.

Expected monetary value

In some organizations, there is a desire to supplement risk assessments that typically deal in high, moderate, and low rankings with a more tangible rating. The ideal solution to this requirement is the EMV technique. EMV can be used to express risk as a monetary loss. The formula is:

EMV (\$) = $\sum$ Financial value of loss (\$) × Probability of loss (%).

The strength of this method is that multiple risk outcomes, each with a different probability, can be expressed in one EMV number.

A typical example might be the need to assess the impact of late delivery, which will incur a sliding scale of penalty payments. A table can easily be built to express the EMV for this risk, as shown in Table 6.2. In this example, EMV is calculated as \$7500.

Users must be aware of the limitations of this technique. The penalties are concrete, coming from the proposed contract, but the probabilities are not. GIGO applies. The assumption must be that the expert supplying that data has experience in similar projects and a delivery track record that mirrors the probabilities. Additionally, the \$7500 result is highly conceptual, as it is only a statistical average. Only if the firm ran this project many, many times would the penalties average to \$7500 per project! So, for the statistics to work for just one project, there

Table 6.2 EMV used to assess risk impact

	EMV used to assess risk impact of late delivery penalty		
Condition	*Penalty ($)*	*Probability (%)*	*EMV ($)*
On time	0	50	0
1 week late	10,000	30	3000
2 weeks late	20,000	15	3000
3 weeks late	30,000	5	1500
Total		100	7500

would need to be many other risks each assessed using the same methodology so that the overall project would be assessed a total EMV with many components.

Assuming the project is indeed large and complex and with 10–20 risks, then risk loss might be assessed a total EMV of, say, $100,000. What is to be done with this information?

The first use is for pricing. The expectation is now monetized—this project must expect to lose $100,000 to risk if nothing is done. If this were a $1M bid, a financially responsible approach would be to add 10% for risk coverage. Of course, the second application is for mitigation justification. If mitigations can be designed to cover these identified and quantified risks for only $50,000, that might be a better way to go. Remember, other risks may also exist outside this analysis and must be handled using other methods.

The risk factor model of risk

The limitations of the risk event model, specifically as a practical tool for supporting bid preparation, have led to a formalized but more efficient methodology based not on risk events, but on risk factors. Risk factors are numerous and specific and exist on all projects. They are generated by project risk facets, which are fewer and generic. They are the foundation of an alternative model of risk. Figure 6.5 is a representation of this model, and the graphic emphasizes that the risk factors attack the links established between the work of the project (activities) and the objectives. This model provides the means to standardize risk analysis and select common mitigation strategies for a family of projects.

Terminology of the risk factor model

Risk Facet–A generic aspect of the project, or family of projects, that generates risk.

Risk Factor–A characteristic of a risk facet that has a detriment on project activities.

Risk Rank Assessment–An instrument that processes responses to 20 or so questions based on the risk factor checklist to generate a risk score.

Risk Rank–A standardized metric for characterizing the risk inherent in a planned project, usually 1 to 5, mapped from the risk score.

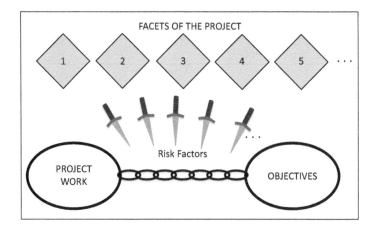

Figure 6.5 The risk factor model of risk

Example of risk facets and factors

I have observed that there are really only six basic facets that generate 99% of the risk factors for the family of projects with which I am familiar:

1   Team–The people doing the work, skills, experience, culture.
2   Contract–The terms and conditions, penalties, contract type, and constraints under which the vendor PM must deliver the project.
3   Size–Includes the number of active team members, the duration, and the costs.
4   Solution–The nature of the business solution itself, the scope, clarity of requirements, and the stakeholders affected.
5   Technology–The means chosen to implement the solution, novelty, complexity, ease of use.
6   Customer–Partner in the delivery but answers to a separate authority and has different priorities and culture than the firm.

This is not a universal list. Implementing the risk factor model starts with analysis of the firm's application area and the project portfolio. Facets are a step towards identification of risk factors. The goal is a standardized checklist of factors that can be used for risk assessment, ranking and mitigation planning.

Types of risk factors

There are three types of factors: base, compounding, and mitigating. These different types affect the project risk in different ways and so are treated differently in the assessment model.

Base factors

These are the inherent risks found in all projects, each one of which is contributing an additional element of risk. They are 'known–knowns' and can be readily assessed. Checklists might include: fixed price, time and material, specified deliverables, rolling wave, big bang, type of approach, duration, fixed deadline, team size, team experience, customer relationship, customer reliability, technology maturity, solution fit, and more.

Compounding factors

These are factors that might be present. If so, they do not just add themselves into the existing base factors; instead, they tend to magnify the risks already present. They can be knowns, but are likely to be 'known–unknowns' and require assumptions to be made in order to make an assessment. Examples of compounding factors might include delivery penalties, clarity of requirements, multiple departments (stakeholders), dependency on third parties, and so forth. I can take one of these—clarity of requirements—to explain a little more. Consider two extremes of project: one with a small, experienced team, excellent customer relations, and a phased contract structure; and a second with a two-year duration, very large team, poor customer relations, and a 'big bang' contract. It is wrong to say that unclear requirements add the same risk to both projects. To the first, it adds virtually nothing, and to the second, it probably doubles the risk, or more.

Mitigating factors

Mitigating factors are the reverse of compounding factors. If present, they tend to reduce the base risk of the project and no matter how they are assessed they don't make things worse. A valuable attribute of mitigating factors is that they point the way to standardized risk mitigation and can force project decisions during the bid stage to reduce risk to an acceptable level. Some examples of mitigating factors include force of the business case, adequacy of contingency, seniority of project manager, and mutual quality planning.

The analysis to derive a starter set of factors for the firm involves some effort, but it is a once-off task. The work surrounding the old risk event model is being inverted from a simple model but hard to use, to a more complex model that requires development effort but is simple to use and immediately adds value.

Metrics for risk factors

The development of risk factor checklists for each facet is now complete. The requirement is for useful and comparable metrics, like a risk score or a risk rank, so there are further steps of analysis to be taken.

Normalization

The recommended approach is to normalize by weighting each facet by allocating risk points out of 100. Start by identifying the facets for the project family under analysis. Then assess the relative impact on project risk for each of the facets expressed as points out of 100. For example, the facet 'Team' might be considered the source of 15% of the risk, so it would be given a weight of 15 points. And so on for each facet. This requires some thought, but it is easy to tune the model as experience is gained. Should facets be added later to the basic list, the percentages must be rebalanced so the new total potential base risk still adds to 100. After such a change, risk scores of different projects can only be compared in absolute terms if they are using the same facet list.

Scoring

How do we decide whether a facet, like Team, gets the full 15 risk points, or less? Turn to the checklist of base factors for each facet and create a question for each factor with a response that can be graded from low risk to high risk. The maximum risk points for all factors from the facet will add up to the total points for the facet. Lower risk answers will score fewer points. Table 6.3 is an example of questions for the Team facet.

Each response must be designed for grading. So, for Q1, the 'no' response earns the full four risk points. A 'yes' (low risk) response earns one, and if the team is partially skilled, then two or three points are awarded as judged.

The compounding factors must now be designed for scoring. Again, each compound factor is turned into a question with a gradable answer. A multiplier is chosen that will increase the base score. A multiplier of 1 has no effect. A multiplier of 1.2 will increase the base risk by 20%. A typical compounding factor question might be, "Are there multiple departments involved in determining requirements?" 'No' scores 1, 'yes' scores the max assigned multiplier, with gradations chosen between for partial answers.

The mitigating factors follow exactly the same logic, though in this case, the maximum risk multiplier is 1 (no impact) and lesser risk scores are below 1. A multiplier of 0.80 will reduce the base risk by 20%. A typical mitigating factor question might be, "Will a senior project manager be assigned?" 'No' scores 1, 'yes' scores the minimum multiplier, with gradations chosen between for partial answers.

Table 6.3 Example of four risk factor questions

	Example of four risk factor questions to score the team facet		
Team	*Risk factor question*	*Response*	*Max points*
Q1	Are the skills available in-house?	No	4
Q2	Will the team be co-located?	No	4
Q3	Are there cultural dissimilarities?	Yes	3
Q4	Has the team worked together before?	No	4
Total risk points			15

Use of the risk rank assessment

The development of the risk rank assessment requires some investment of time, and leverages the firm's experienced and senior practitioners. But, as a result, the firm now has an assessment instrument that is totally reusable and can be completed by a sales executive and a professional services manager (PSM) in 20 minutes.

A word of caution: remember that useful rule of project management, the 80/20 rule. Applied to this case, 80% of the value can probably be achieved with 20% of the development effort. So long as key risk facets that have a real impact are included, resist the temptation to generate long lists of questions in the hope of getting more accuracy. Risk analysis is still an art, not a science. Do not make gross changes (unless it's really wrong) as that slows down the process of assimilating the model and getting a feel for risk. It is easy to add compounding and mitigating factors, less so to add base facets/factors because weightings have to be revised. Try and get the base stabilized early. Incidentally, if the firm cannot agree on a universal base because they specialize in two or more different families of projects, then simply create a different base for each, being careful to use the correct template during risk rank assessment.

Designing the risk rank

A good definition of project risk is 'the degree to which the business has accepted uncertainty'. The risk assessment instrument based on risk factors is an excellent tool for assessing overall risk during the bid phase. The risk score from the answers to the assessment can easily be translated into a risk rank for the project.

Risk rank is a forecast, based on conditions seen at bid time, and is used to make the firm's bid more effective. That is its sole purpose; it is not maintained into execution if the bid is won. As the project proceeds, risk factors cause a drag on the project and risk events occur, requiring a new metric to measure execution risk called the risk alert, discussed later.

The risk score from the assessment can be calibrated into a risk rank. A five-point scale is adequate for ranking risk. A three-point scale is too coarse, and granularity in excess of five points has never been found to add any particular value. Each of the risk ranks must be defined, as shown in Table 6.4, and then mapped to the score from the risk assessment instrument. In general terms, a high-risk project is one that exhibits a high degree of uncertainty regarding the outcome (schedule, cost, or customer satisfaction) and a low risk project is one that is expected to meet objectives with some certainty.

Approach to risk rank implementation

Tagging a project bid with a credible risk rank allows efficient standard operating procedures and authority levels to be followed. This avoids the fatal

Table 6.4 Risk rank definitions

	Definitions and descriptions for risk ranks 1 to 5	
Rank	Definition	Definition guidance
#5	Very high	Very high risk. This rank is reserved for situations where the outcomes will almost certainly deviate from plan. (Only 1 PM out of 10 forecasts good outcome, or 10% positive/90% negative.) Mitigations and contingency are either inadequate, or the nature of the risk being assumed cannot be handled using normal risk management techniques.
#4	High	High risk. This rank suggests outcomes may or may not be favorable (50%/50%). Mitigation and contingency have been brought to bear, and are just sufficient to make the project feasible as a business proposition.
#3	Moderate	Moderate risk. This rank indicates risk exists, but outcomes should be favorable (70%/30%). Mitigation and contingency have been applied as required and the project is feasible.
#2	Low	Low risk. There remains a quantifiable business risk, but outcomes are expected to be favorable. Mitigation and contingency have either been well applied, or are irrelevant.
#1	Very low	Very low risk. No significant risk.

'one-size-fits-all' process trap that so many firms can fall into. Here are examples of how process engineering can be used to effectively manage risk based purely on the risk rank metric:

Bid Approval–Sales executive and professional services manager approve rank 1 and 2. Sales manager and delivery manager approve rank 3. Vice president approves rank 4. President approves rank 5.

Documentation Requirements–Risk register not required for rank 1 and 2. May be required for rank 3 as determined by delivery manager. Required for rank 4 and 5.

Executive Reporting–Rank 4 and 5 projects must be reported on a monthly executive dashboard.

When risk rank assessment has been established, another global business risk metric can be derived allowing the firm to characterize their portfolio of booked projects in terms of risk. At the portfolio level, an aggregate risk of 3.0 or less should keep the firm in business. This metric must be supplemented by knowledge of the percentage of projects at each risk rank. (An average of 3 can be constituted in many ways.) From that perspective, more than one project at rank 5 might be cause for alarm. The sum by value of projects of rank 5 and 4 should target less than 30% of portfolio value.

> Use risk rank to characterize project and business risk and to prescribe
> a progressive response to increased risk.

Benefits of the risk factor approach

Risk assessments yielding a risk rank can now be done quickly and reliably
in a standard format that can be reviewed and critiqued. The major work of
analysis is done once, in thinking out the facets and risk factors that might
come into play. The risk rank assessment does not start with a blank sheet of
paper and can be performed by a non-expert.

The second benefit is that by using mitigating risk factors, mitigation automatically emerges from the assessment for agreement by management. This
provides excellent leverage for the assigned vendor PM when it comes to
execution. It is certainly a more efficient mitigating process for medium risk
projects. For higher risk projects, risk rank assessment supplements conventional risk event analysis and the risk register.

Thirdly, the risk rank assessment lends itself to metrics. Instruments can be
designed and built using interactive online technology, or MS Excel spread-
sheets. These tools not only facilitate analysis, but also automatically compute
the score and rank, and 'next-steps' in the process conditioned by the result.
Designed correctly, these models are easy to tune and their ability to forecast
project results can be continually improved.

Finally, the biggest benefit of all is that the risk factor model integrates risk
thinking into the planning process. It moves from a fringe technique that
practitioners feel they should do but rarely has any impact, to an integral part
of building a bid response. It eventually changes the culture of the organization as illustrated in these case histories:

- One firm became sensitized to the fact that they were accepting too
  many fixed price projects, in some cases unnecessarily. Alternatives were
  accepted by clients as reasonable when they were explained.
- Another firm adopted rolling wave contracts which became an intuitive
  initial response, whereas previously the big bang was proposed because
  "it's what the client wants."
- The same firm also learned to embed key mitigation tactics into their
  responses, e.g., early agreement on acceptance criteria, a standard
  method for document approvals, a standard method for issue escalation, etc.
- Still another firm simply established a rule, with criteria, that meant low
  payback, high-risk projects were avoided.

The bottom line benefit—the firm makes more profit.

The risk alert model of risk

When a project starts executing, everything changes. Things that were thought of hypothetically during the bid now become reality. Project experience rapidly gains currency and the risk rank, whether experience proves it correct or not, loses relevance as a management tool. It is not worth maintaining. The risk register, on the other hand, increases in relevance. On large projects the register will be informally reviewed every month, and formally updated in a workshop and integrated into plans about every three months. The register is now the project's primary future-focused risk tool.

To supplement forward looking processes based on the risk register, a more responsive model is needed that looks at the reality of the project as it now exists, not as it might exist in the future. With this model in play, a new metric can be generated that gives management an objective 'trouble' rating. The metric is called the risk alert and indicates whether project support is needed.

The risk alert can be modeled by redeveloping the risk factor model. As the project is now executing, concern turns to the current strength of the links between work and objectives. How many chains are there, relevant to project performance, and how strong are they? The resultant risk alert model is shown in Figure 6.6.

The linkage between the work of the project and the firm's objectives derive from the success criteria discussed in Chapter 3. These criteria help define the performance chains it pays to monitor. To determine how well the work is going the state of health of each link, or risk indicator, in the performance chain is interrogated.

Terminology of the risk alert model

Performance Chain–An aspect of project performance that is moving the project work toward the project objectives.

Risk Indicator–A risk metric that assesses the status, or health, of a link in the performance chain. There can be many risk indicators for each chain.

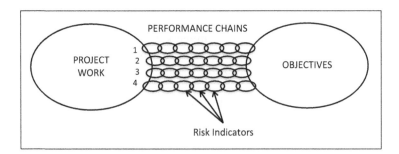

Figure 6.6 The risk alert model

Risk Alert Assessment–An instrument that processes responses to 20 or so questions based on the risk indicator checklist to generate a risk score.

Risk Alert–A standardized metric for characterizing the risk immediately present in an executing project, usually green (low) to red (high), mapped from the risk score. Risk alert is interpreted as a leading indicator of failure to meet one or more project objectives.

Example of performance chains and indicators

An analysis of the common success criteria for professional services firms strongly suggests that projects can be accurately assessed during project execution by monitoring just four standard performance chains:

1   Delivery Achievement–Demonstrable progress is fundamental to a project. As an example, the kind of risk indicators that might be specified include: missed milestones, level of unresolved technical problems, external dependency delays, and anything specifically called for in the contract that is not being delivered.
2   Financial Integrity–The financials of the project must remain whole. Costs must be in balance with revenue, additional work must be funded, contingency must not be over-consumed, and forecast costs must not exceed budget.
3   Team Efficiency–The assembled team must be capable of doing the work and aligned with the agreed resource plan. Another risk indicator is the level of unplanned resource changes.
4   Client Relationship–The client partnership must support collaboration on project procedures and mutual commitments. Approvals must be granted within the agreed period, issues resolved, and resource commitments acted on.

These performance chains are not the same as risk facets, which are defined as areas of the project that generate risk. A performance chain is concerned about how well the work is going. It is quite consistent for a project to be performing very well and also rank as a high-risk project.

Types of risk indicators

Risk indicators range from objective to subjective and can be chosen from these categories:

Published Accounting Results–This takes care of most of the financial indicators.

Countable Items–Indicators based on counting. For example, events that occurred, issues or trouble reports open versus closed, rate of change requests and so on.

Happened vs. Didn't Happen–A target achieved, like a review meeting, might seem objective, though opinions can differ on other targets like obligations agreed, commitments met, and plans completed.

Satisfaction–Measuring satisfaction is always problematic until someone invents a satisfaction meter, and it might change tomorrow.

These categories start objective and become more subjective. Human nature usually paints subjective indicators rosier than they are, so I prefer objective indicators. It is easier to assess an indicator if it consists of defined numeric data than if it depends upon opinion and judgment.

A risk indicator is not an issue

Accounting numbers, item counts, and checking off what happened and what didn't are not issues. They are facts that point to status, and doubtless, the astute PM will uncover an issue or two underlying that status and get them resolved. Issues in the project context are defined as 'impediments to achieving an objective'. An impediment requires action or decision, pending which the project will suffer delay, cost, loss of function, lower quality, etc. I think of issues as risk events that have actually happened and need a response, though they can arise from other sources.

Metrics for risk indicators

Once performance chains and the associated risk indicators have been identified, work can proceed on designing the metrics. First, weighted points are allocated to each performance chain. For example, Team Efficiency may be rated as 15% of the firm's project objectives, and can be awarded a maximum of 15 points out of 100.

In order to score each performance chain, the identified risk indicators must be framed as questions. Each question is designed with a gradable outcome and each response will be awarded low points for a low risk response, and higher points for the high risk answer. Table 6.5 is an example of questions for the Team Efficiency performance chain.

Table 6.5 Example of three risk indicator questions

Example of three risk indicator questions to score team efficiency			
Team efficiency	*Risk indicator question*	*Response*	*Max points*
Q1	Is the resourcing plan being followed?	No	5
Q2	Is the team working overtime consistently?	Yes	5
Q3	Are unplanned staff changes occurring?	Yes	5
Total risk points			15

Each response must be designed for grading. So, for Q1, the 'no' response earns the full five risk points. A 'yes' (low risk) response earns only 1, and if the plan is only being partially followed, then 2, 3, or 4 points are awarded as judged.

This is the same method explained for facets and risk factors. The result is a system that will score risk indicators for each of the four performance chains and cumulate a project risk score, which can be mapped and reported as a risk alert.

Designing the risk alert

The industry standard method for executive highlighting is the RED/YELLOW/GREEN flag system, and this is a reasonable starting point in design. The main problems are detailing the definitions, and designing the implementation. Workable definitions are proposed in Table 6.6.

Risk alert is formally assessed using a risk instrument based on the risk indicator checklist. This comprises a set of questions that automatically yield a risk score. The questions deal with current project performance for delivery, financial, team, and client. Using calculation, judgment, rules, or a combination of all three, the questionnaire results are converted into a risk alert. Exactly how this is done is an implementation question. Is it wise to rely on a dispassionate algorithm? Is it better to rely on the judgment of the vendor

Table 6.6 Risk alert definitions

Definitions and descriptions for red/yellow/green risk alert		
Alert	*Definition*	*Definition guidance*
Red	Severe	Severe alert. The project situation is negative, outcomes are deviating significantly from plan and the project is not stable. Recovery actions are mainly outside the scope of the project manager and the project has the attention of senior management who are providing active assistance.
Yellow	Warning	Warning alert. The project situation is trending negative, some outcomes are showing signs of deviation, and indeed minor outcomes may already be negative. The project is not yet unstable, but action by the project manager is probably required to retain stability and reverse any negative outcomes. Management should actively monitor this situation and provide assistance as requested.
Green	Normal	Normal alert. No unexpected events or issues are threatening the stability of the project. The project manager works actively to maintain risk control and the project is subject to regular management monitoring.

PM? There are consequences of red status, otherwise why bother, and no matter how it is presented, the PM will tend to interpret this as a stain on his record. It can become a delicate issue and create other problems.

Approach to risk alert implementation

The best solution is dependent upon the organization and culture of the firm, but the following approach is usually practical:

- The score that results from the risk alert assessment automatically calculates an R/Y/G for each performance chain based on an algorithm.
- The vendor PM uses judgment to declare the overall project R/Y/G. The delivery manager reviews this rating with the PM and confirms or modifies the rating.
- Action plans are developed and implemented as agreed. For example, if the project is red, then a red review is scheduled.

The value of risk alerts lies in objectively assessing current performance and in responding to it. The alert assessment is usually done concurrently with the project status report and can be quite dynamic, changing from period to period. The assessment tends to focus upon stability rather than adherence to plan. Loss of stability is a leading indicator for going off-plan and the risk alert assessment provides the possibility of fixing an off-plan condition before it occurs.

> The risk alert signals if present conditions are trending off-plan and can trigger progressive management support.

Benefits of the risk alert approach

There must be a tracking system for projects, and a way of summarizing status for senior management. Alert flags are a well-known system of summarization and can easily be displayed on an executive dashboard alongside standard financials. If a probe is requested, the next level of interesting executive information is the risk trend line, showing the value of the risk alert score for a project since inception.

The drawbacks encountered with previous risk tracking systems lie first in developing definitions that are practical, reasonably objective, accepted by all stakeholders, and prove useful; and second, in gaining the support and engagement of vendor PMs who may see little value doing this for their projects.

The risk alert system attempts to resolve these drawbacks. The use of risk indicators to assess performance chains enables objectivity. The alert definitions go a long way to removing the mystery of ratings. If the system is open and objective the vendor PM will be more positive if project restructuring is needed. In many cases, the PM values the risk indicator checklist as exactly that—a useful checklist of project health that can play a role in project management. After considerable customization, it is also possible to use this system of risk assessment in joint meetings of the vendor and client PMs, with the results presented to the steering committee. This helps focus on the red issues and promotes a teamwork approach.

The final point is the trigger for action. Obviously, performance chains showing red galvanize corrective action from the PM as part of the day-to-day job, but when the project overall is rated as red, then a red review must be scheduled under the auspices of the delivery manager. She works with the vendor PM and account team to stabilize the project, get to the root cause, and restructure as necessary.

7 Overcoming estimating anxieties

The ability to estimate is a learned skill that requires experience and the relevant technical and business knowledge. This must be coupled with a proven process and the discipline to practice it. A practitioner who combines these attributes is a rarity, making such people a valuable asset to the firm. A result of this scarcity of estimating skill, and frequently a lack of clarity in the estimating process, is doubt and anxiety about the reliability of the estimate, which can easily lead to a loss of credibility in the bid preparation process and unwelcome management criticism.

The firm therefore needs a formal estimation practice, defined accountabilities, and a supportive environment. All too often, estimating is a poorly documented ad hoc process with the sources of the estimating data obscured and the location of the estimates file a mystery. The vendor PM should possess an intimate knowledge of the estimate, but often cannot locate a single document showing how project costs were derived. Arguably, the success of the entire bid can turn upon the quality of the estimating practice. It should be treated accordingly.

A first step is to acknowledge the anxieties that accompany the preparation of an estimate. This challenges the firm to build a culture that respects a professional approach. The approach includes top-down and bottom-up methods and 'rule of thumb' (ROT) estimating and deals explicitly with uncertainty. This material is not a silver bullet for project estimating but will, if put into practice, steadily improve the firm's estimating judgments and hence their project margins.

Many PMs are familiar with the trials of coaxing an estimate from a reluctant practitioner. Often, the requester is made to feel like he is totally unreasonable, even borderline imbecilic, to think that the practitioner's complex and unpredictable activity can be reduced to something as specific as an estimate. The response ranges from the non-negotiable "it'll be finished when it's finished" to the passive and equally unhelpful "it's hard to say."

The vendor PM needs patience, techniques knowledge, and considerable facilitation skills to move beyond these roadblock comments to get what's needed. She must support and coach a reluctant estimator without taking primary ownership of the estimate—a deadly mistake, and unfortunately an unconscious objective of the putative estimator.

The foundation of professional estimating

Recognize negative pressures

The perspectives of the estimator and the sales executive provide some insights for the services firm wishing to build an effective estimation practice.

Pressures on the estimator

First, these are some of the anxieties, difficulties, and challenges faced by an estimator:

* A lack of full understanding about the work to be done;
* Choices and decisions yet to be made that will impact the estimate;
* Unfamiliarity with the technology, work processes, or methodology to be used;
* A lack of fluency in the essential skill of decomposing a large, complex activity into multiple smaller, simpler activities;
* A tendency to focus on side issues not integral to the task at hand, such as resource availability;
* Concerns that the estimate will be misused or misinterpreted, and if the bid or project fails, the estimator will be set up as a scapegoat;
* Anxiety that the result will not be the 'right answer'; and
* Lack of organizational support.

These concerns are a factor in all phases of the vendor lifecycle, but they have a special influence during the bid phase, when the vendor PM has not yet assumed control of the project and the estimator may be seen as working for the sales team. This creates a pressure point that can exacerbate the estimator's anxieties.

Pressures on the sales executive

During the bid phase, the business management and especially the sales executive must deal with their share of anxieties as well:

* The dominant question is always "What is the customer's budget?" If known, there is pressure to come up with the same 'right answer'. If not known, that becomes an anxiety in its own right.
* If the firm is working with the customer on precedent projects, that means they have knowledge of complexity that the competition doesn't. This creates the fear that the competition will undercut the firm's bid. On the other hand, if the competition is working with the customer, the firm may fear that they won't be able to overcome the competition's credibility, even though they can offer a superior product.

- The expectations of the customer must be met, but sometimes they are unrealistic given the features of the product driving the bid or the available budget.
- The sales team naturally wants to see costs kept as low as possible, and any distrust between the sales and estimating teams can give rise to a suspicion that 'padding' is inflating the cost estimates.

These are human, perhaps emotional, impediments to good unbiased estimating. How management behaves influences success with estimating as much as good technical knowledge. Positive behavior is the key to building a positive corporate culture, and in the case of estimating, it should be made explicit in a written practice guide. This provides a clear understanding by all employees of 'the way we do things around here'.

Guidelines for a positive culture

The observed behavior of senior management must be consistent and supportive. Don't confuse promotion of culture with simplistic slogans such as 'The Customer is King', or 'People are our most Valuable Asset', or my favorite 'Quality is Job 1'. Managers build the culture of the firm by supporting the following principles, reiterating how things are done, and modeling the behavior where possible.

Clarify and manage accountability

Estimating is a serious and highly responsible task. Practitioners who are estimators should understand both the responsibility and to whom they are accountable. That manager needs a process to track, evaluate, and provide feedback on the success of estimates. This must not be treated as a blame game, but as follow-up to ensure that everything was done that should have been done, and make sure any deficiency is fixed. This might include: Did the estimator have the skills and experience required? Was the estimator provided with the input information needed to perform the estimate? Was the estimating procedure followed? Were the assumptions valid?

Practice continuous improvement

The firm who embeds continuous improvement into their culture will win the game. This means the feedback process, but also allows standard estimates, productivity rates, rules of thumb, and so forth to be treated as tunable and not cast in concrete. A period (say, annually) should be chosen for review and update of standards. Standard lists of assumptions and risks can be subject to a similar process. Project methodologies often require an end-of-project analysis called 'lessons-learned', and these templates can be used to feedback estimating improvements.

Explicit contingency

Contingency obliges the estimator to think about risk, and gives him a mechanism to deal with it. Risk management can only be delegated to the vendor PM if he has a spending account to deal with it. With the right process, making all contingency (wrongly called padding) explicit can build trust between the sales and delivery teams, and can play a role in devising alternative approaches for the project. As an example, a customer faced with a fixed price bid with a very large built-in contingency may be persuaded that a time and material contract is a better option for all parties.

Estimates aren't negotiated

This is one of those principles that every estimator breaks and wishes she hadn't. Don't interpret this as license for stubbornness. Estimates of effort must be in balance with scope of work, assumptions, and required risk mitigation. Clearly, if those change, it is reasonable to change the estimate. Agreeing to a lower number without matching new information gives zero credibility to the original estimate and will not position the estimator favorably in the future. Don't do it. Two things can be done if the deliverable is too expensive after all clarifications and options have been exhausted. First, look at the allocated contingency. This can be negotiated, to a reasonable limit, so long as all parties fully understand that as contingency reduces, project risk increases. Second, reduce prices or practitioner rates, which also reduces margin. This is not a practitioner responsibility, but a business decision, usually not an easy one and the last one remaining.

Separate the sales process from the estimating process

Separation keeps accountabilities focused, and avoids potentially disadvantageous situations arising if both parties are dealing with the customer in an uncoordinated manner. The sales job is to discover the customer's wants, the requirements priorities, and the opportunities for innovation. After the estimate has been prepared, the job of the sales executive is to close the sale at a price that generates the desired margin. As sales managers say about sales executives who are always seeking discounts, anyone can sell if the price is reduced. To be worth a sales commission, the customer should be persuaded that the deal on offer is the best value available.

Support the estimators

If management wants to bring accountability to the estimating process, part of the bargain must be true support and appreciation. Start by identifying who the firm's estimators are. It is likely that each specialization has its own senior estimator and an apprentice who can estimate smaller jobs. They should be regarded as highly valuable employees (they are) and treated accordingly. This can mean training, exposure to advances in their field, recognition for their successes, and formalization of estimating skills and experience into the firm's career path definitions. With this will come a reasonable expectation that extra time to prepare and defend estimates may be needed in addition to normal billable work.

The other more prosaic area of support is provision of useful processes, templates, standards and checklists. In some firms a project management office (PMO) develops and maintains these. Without the support of the firm, then the estimator must build and maintain her own toolkit, log of estimates and results.

Everything is reviewed

Most successful firms come to the realization that deliverables are improved if they are reviewed. This definitely applies to the project estimate. Negative sentiments and behaviors from either the reviewer or reviewee do not build a supportive culture. Guidance is particularly important for the reviewer, as nothing is more demoralizing than to suffer at the hands of a reviewer (especially a superior) who is untrained in the skills of constructive criticism, making improvement suggestions, and general coaching. The intent of a review culture is to build an environment epitomized by 'trust, but verify'. This means practitioners are given the training, opportunity and support to develop their estimation skills, and at the same time expect to have their work reviewed. This is accepted as a normal part of a formal quality procedure, and not as someone looking over their shoulder. Occasionally, if someone takes a quick look at a deliverable to provide help and guidance, don't discredit the formal procedure by calling this a review. Give it another name—sanity check, completeness check, or quality check.

Develop a corporate memory

Is there a 25-year man on the project? This provides quick access to memories of how the firm coped with a similar situation many years ago, or what outcomes were experienced with a similar scenario. Obviously, this is not a long-term solution. There are two ways of reliably building a corporate memory. One is to maintain a personal documentation discipline. The other is to maintain a PMO function. A PMO job is to specify and maintain the documentation standards, in this case, the estimating guidelines and consolidation of project learnings. They also ensure that new information is integrated into the practice and disseminated to the firm.

Maintain a documentation discipline

When this cultural norm is in place, complaints and excuses such as "I didn't think you would want that," or "I will have to go back and prepare that specially," or "We didn't keep that data" should disappear. When it comes to estimates, the provision of a predefined template is the best way to clearly set the expectation for what must be documented. The main components of a work effort estimate template should include deliverables, activities, effort estimate, overhead, cost estimate, contingency, assumptions, adjustments, and sign-off.

The easiest and best time to build the firm's culture is when the firm is founded. Culture change in a large, established company is a protracted, expensive, and not always successful exercise. The young firm can review the above points and translate each into action items that become a part of the firm's early development plan.

Preliminaries to the estimate

Before considering the techniques of estimating, these are the three prerequisites to excellent estimating that the estimator must establish:

1   The estimating principles hard won from experience;
2   Understanding exactly the expectations for the estimate;
3   A significant amount of project planning.

Principles for estimating

Use Past Experience–The key to realistic estimates is the ability to relate past experience and results to the subject project.

Decompose the Project–Experience from the past cannot be reused reliably until it has been broken down into smaller parts. For most projects, this means decomposition using a work breakdown structure (WBS), or applying methodologies with consistent phases and deliverables.

Limit the Project Duration–Projects have a much better chance of being completed on time and on budget, and meeting customer requirements, if they can be kept under duration of a year. This usually means defining a program of projects in which each project is designed to meet the one-year duration criterion, though the program itself may go on for several years.

Keep Records–Unremembered experience has no value, and for most of us that means creating and retaining written records. Such records should be set up in a consistent fashion, recording information such as estimate versus actuals and data that characterizes the size and complexity of the project.

Involve the Responsible Practitioner–Those who will be doing the work should participate in the estimating process.

Review and Revise–Estimates should not be done in isolation, but should follow a process that includes steps to review and make revisions. This applies not just to estimates at the bid phase, but at all phase-end checkpoints where existing phase estimates are reviewed based on new and improved data from the previous phase.

Avoid Single-Point Estimates–Generally speaking, at the early stages of most projects, there is insufficient information to commit to a single number for expected project cost. Methods of dealing with this dilemma are discussed later.

Expectations for the estimate

The estimator must understand the deliverables expected from the estimating process. To what use will the estimate be put and what are the requirements?

There are three standard outputs required to build a standard project bid—effort by resource, duration, and cost. Support for the estimate is also usually required in terms of assumptions, risk, and contingency. Finally, the estimator should be given some guidance for the priorities of the project that influence the approach and estimate—for example, does the client wish to minimize duration, minimize cost, or maximize quality?

Planning methodology

If rolling wave theory is being applied, then the estimate is as far as the next visible peak. What lies beyond is an educated guess and details will inevitably change by the time you get there. A peak we can 'see' means a scope that can be described and a set of answers (or reliable assumptions) for the following planning items:

> Business Purpose–This positions the project in terms of its benefit to the sponsor, and perhaps its fit within a program of projects, some accomplished, some still planned. This gives a high-level boundary of project scope.

> Project Objectives–Objectives are a measure of project success. Experienced estimators consider these carefully as they can have a strong influence on the estimate. Table 3.7 provides a checklist.

> Project Lifecycle Phases–In the planning for lifecycle mapping, the client and vendor PMs agreed on the project lifecycle to be used, and the phases to be included within the current contract.

> Product Requirements–This further narrows the scope and elucidates the customer's needs and wants. Product requirements are usually expressed as functional, technical, or usage requirements, often listed in the RFP. Non-functional requirements might include elements such as: level of service, performance, safety, security, standards compliance, maintainability, durability and so forth. Requirements can be a source of project risk.

> Project Requirements–These embrace attributes, constraints, success factors, or prerequisites necessary to meet project objectives. As an example, a project with a very tight, inflexible schedule could adopt the following project requirements sometimes referred to as critical success factors:

> - Prioritization of functions into 'need, want, wish'
> - Time limits on approvals
> - Skilled resources
> - Identification of quality trade-offs
> - Readiness to work overtime
> - Accurate progress reporting
> - Early detection and response to variances.

Deliverables—Most estimators consider a defined set of deliverables as a solid base for the estimate. Some attributes to consider when defining deliverables:

- Tangible, including either interim or final, documentation or product
- May be hierarchically structured into work packets
- Deliverables and work packets are created by activities
- Essential for accurate estimates
- Predefined by most methodologies
- Invaluable for progress monitoring.

WBS—The work breakdown structure (WBS) is the traditional culmination of the scoping process and serves as the ultimate documentation of the scope baseline. It decomposes the project into deliverables and work packets, plus support activities that don't easily express as deliverables. Support includes project management, technical assistance, and project administration. The key issue is that the WBS completely expresses the project work, and can be estimated.

Activities—The further decomposition of a solid WBS into activities may not be necessary for the purpose of effort estimating. It depends on project complexity and estimator experience. Firms that specialize in repetitive projects of a specific type will not gain significant benefit in breakout to activities. On the other hand, an innovative, complex project can only be properly understood by developing a set of activities for each work packet or deliverable.

Dependencies—Dependencies between activities must be identified in order to create the network diagram. The network diagram illustrates the sequence of activities and what can be done in parallel. It is required for a schedule to be estimated.

Estimating techniques

Although estimating cannot be taught, in the sense that someone can be taught how to tie their shoelaces, there are some valuable techniques that can be learned. They allow a practitioner to develop and apply expertise more effectively and gain proficiency sooner, though there is no substitute for time and experience, usually measured in years.

Once the preliminary planning information has been gathered and the scope understood, an estimate can be prepared. A model that reminds the estimator of the interacting parts of the estimate is shown in Figure 7.1, the estimating triangle.

The basic scope is the work to be done, represented by the triangle. This is not enough, however, upon which to base an estimate—assumptions and risks must also be considered, and if they change, then the scope of work changes, too, along with the estimate.

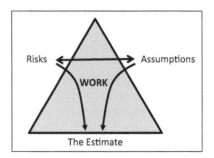

Figure 7.1 The estimating triangle

There are fundamentally two methods of estimating, although they can be combined to create hybrid methods. These methods are called top-down, or expert, estimating and bottom-up, or methodical, estimating. Top-down or expert estimating is a quicker method but can only be done by a practitioner with previous experience in similar projects. Top-down estimates can be used to give an early estimate, and can also be used as a sanity check when the bottom-up result is available. Bottom-up or methodical estimating requires the decomposition of the work into work packets, and perhaps activities. Methodical estimating methods fall into two categories—activity list estimates, and standardized grid estimates.

The accuracy of both top-down and bottom-up estimates is enhanced by use of an application methodology. The project lifecycle is often expanded into a full-blown methodology, or commercially available products are adopted. Mature methodologies will usually include estimating guidelines as part of their support documentation, and this can be tapped to help develop a reasonable top-down estimate.

> Every project needs two estimates—top-down and bottom-up.

Expert (top-down) estimating

Experts use a number of related techniques for top-down project estimating:

Comparison with Similar Projects. Projects must have broadly similar objectives, develop equivalent deliverables, and be subject to similar requirements. The number of stakeholders or departments must be assessed, as that can impact on the estimate. Experts do not rely on their memory for this task, but refer to their personal database of actuals by deliverable and influencing project variables. Possibly, a PMO might be able to provide this information. Ultimately, the best advice is to keep your own records, including experiences at previous companies and results from other reliable project managers.

Comparison with Analogous Projects. Some projects can have large parts of their functionality comparable, without the projects as a whole being the same. The analogous project can be compared in terms of effort, duration, and complexity, with scaling factors applied as appropriate. For example, it may be that a rail scheduling system and a truck scheduling system have points of commonality that make estimates transferable.

Ratio Estimating. This method extrapolates from the expended effort to-date to estimate the next phase and possibly the entire project. Success with this method requires the use of a consistent project lifecycle, lots of results in the database, and confidence in a statistical approach. If historical results show on average 15% of effort is spent on requirements and general design, then if a project has spent 1500 h on those phases it could be extrapolated that the total project is 10,000 h.

Duration-Based Estimates. Some phases of a project are best estimated by starting with duration. For example, the test phase may range from 2 to 12 weeks. This would then drive the effort requirement. A 10-week test period supported by two full-time testers and 1.5 staff for rework has an effort estimate of 1225 h. Warranty, always quoted in terms of duration, can be estimated the same way.

Delphi Technique. This costly technique is used for general purpose problem-solving but is particularly suitable for estimating because the answer is numeric and differences between experts are logically discussed. A group of experts is used, under the guidance of a facilitator. Each expert, working independently, develops an estimate. They are submitted to the facilitator who takes the average of the group after discarding the extreme high and low and then conducts a meeting to discuss the results. This process represents one 'round'. The experts then redo their estimate to begin round two. If necessary, the process can go to a third round. The result should be a convergence of individual estimates with the average of the group, giving a high degree of confidence in the result.

Formulae. Using formulae for estimating requires belief that projects can be mathematically modeled. In software development, for example, the method is typified by Barry Boehm's COCOMO (Constructive Cost Model) or one of its derivatives. Boehm first published this algorithmic approach in 1981 (*Software Engineering Economics*). Founded on the principle that software development can be modeled using equations, users specify their assumptions and project sizing parameters, whereupon the model outputs a cost. Of course, GIGO applies, and considerable effort must be spent calibrating the model, which typically means selecting the best assumptions. A veritable industry has developed around these ideas, offering a wide choice of software packages and consulting services to implement them. Boehm updated his theories in 2000 by publishing *Software Cost Estimation with COCOMO II*.

As a broad generalization, top-down estimates tend to *underestimate* the final results.

Methodical (bottom-up) estimating

Methodical estimating can be tackled in one of two ways: using an activity list or a standard grid. Activity list estimating is commonplace and is based upon the decomposition of deliverables into work packets and activities. Familiar projects need breakdown only to the work packet level. Standard grid estimating is less common and requires a good database of results to apply effectively. It relies on assessing the project effort in terms of functional elements rather than deliverables and activities, and then applying a standard estimate based on the complexity of the element.

Activity list estimating

Activity list estimating picks up where the planning methodology outlined earlier leaves off. The estimator must fully understand the scope of the project and have developed a solid list of activities needed to build the deliverables. The estimating steps, which can be iterative, are as follows:

Assumptions. An assumption is a simplifying mechanism that takes something as true though the facts may be in doubt. Assumptions may address client issues, specific requirements, critical success factors (CSFs), resources, adequacy of third party equipment, methodology, risks, etc. More detailed assumptions concern complexities, interactions, interfaces, and stability. One way for the estimator to grasp assumptions is to ask, "What conditions must apply to the likely estimate, and what less favorable conditions apply to the higher or more pessimistic estimate?" Beware of an estimate presented with no accompanying assumptions.

Risks. Study the existing risk assessment and risk register. Consider the activity being estimated—is mitigation included in the estimate? Are there specific unmitigated risks that could increase the estimate? Document the level of risk associated with the estimate.

Resources. Assign a resource category to the activity. Assign the right category of generic resource to the activity to ensure a representative estimate of cost.

Work Estimate. Apply an estimate of work effort to the activity using the estimator's experience and judgment. Technically, effort is best estimated in hours because an hour of effort is totally unambiguous. To be pragmatic, large projects sometimes use a unit of workdays and document an assumption regarding hours in the day.

Complete and Review. With the work effort established, the estimate can be completed as needed: duration, schedule, support, contingency, and cost. The estimating package can then be submitted for review.

By its nature, activity list estimating tends to ignore overlaps and synergies that can reduce detailed estimates, so this type of estimate can be *overly pessimistic*. Comparison with estimates derived from other methods is advised.

Standard grid estimating

In well-established disciplines such as engineering and construction, a cost estimate does not require the complete development of a project plan, but merely the specification of parameters governing the function, size, and grade of the product. Given these parameters, engineers use tables, suppliers' cost sheets, etc. to develop a cost estimate based on client requirements. This is called standard cost estimating, and may be considered a top-down method, but is really a highly matured form of the standard grid estimating method summarized here:

1   In standard grid estimating, the first step is to build a grid or table of the standard estimates for the elements to be constructed, categorized by degree of complexity. These standard estimates are ideally taken from previous experience, adjusted to equate to an average skill set, and are accepted as applicable to the project being estimated, though the standard can be adjusted if appropriate. Five levels of complexity are usually adequate.
2   Estimate the total number of elements to be built and, based on the assessed complexity, allocate each of them to one of the five complexity levels. With a statistically sufficient quantity of elements, the standard estimates are more likely to prove valid for each level.
3   Apply the standard estimate to each of the elements at each level of complexity. The total of elements is multiplied by the standard estimate for that complexity level in the grid. The results for each level in the grid are then summed to give an estimate for all elements. Table 7.1 shows the components of a 3810 h effort estimate.

Finally, because the standard grid only estimates the effort to build, estimates for project management, administration, technical support, and contingency must be added.

Table 7.1 Completed standard grid estimate

	Completed standard grid estimate for a project			
Ref.	*Complexity level*	*Standard estimate (h)*	*Number of elements*	*Estimate (h) for complexity level*
1	Very simple	10	24	240
2	Simple	20	31	620
3	Moderate	30	25	750
4	Complex	60	25	1500
5	Very complex	100	7	700
Total				3810

Cautions with grid estimating

The accuracy of grid estimating relies heavily on statistical validity; if there are a large number of elements, those underestimated are compensated by those overestimated. Smaller projects with fewer functions cannot rely on statistical averaging. In such cases, the estimator should use estimating grids with care, and might be advised to rely on activity list estimates instead.

The completeness of element decomposition is the other big factor in successfully using standard estimates. Missing elements will obviously not be estimated. Reliance on statistical averaging to compensate between under- and over-estimated elements won't compensate for that error and this is clearly a role for contingency.

A complexity baseline

The grid estimating method is an excellent discipline for the estimating team and forces them to make estimating assumptions within a working framework. The ability to frame complexity is often a challenge. Solving it is a big step forward, and the grid estimate integrates the estimate and the complexity assumption in a very satisfying manner. The count of elements at each complexity level is in itself a set of project assumptions to be either challenged or proven at completion.

The grid estimate yields the closest thing that can be devised as a baseline for project complexity. If more information becomes available about the complexity of project elements, then the estimate can be changed based on logic in the estimating grids. This is an important and credible adjustment. Many projects are underestimated because of erroneous complexity assessments, as well as misjudged scope.

> Complexity as well as scope must be baselined, and the standard grid estimate provides a credible method.

Rule of thumb estimating

A rule of thumb (ROT) is an experience-based rule, metric, or ratio used in the estimating process. It has much in common with an expert estimate, as it requires a good grounding in experience and an appreciation for the implicit assumptions.

ROTs are very useful for estimating work that does not directly produce a deliverable. Non-deliverable work can be difficult or tedious to estimate using bottom-up techniques. ROTs are also invaluable in tight estimating timeframes, like responding to RFP deadlines. The development of ROTs is a good fit with a services firm because they have the technology and disciplines in place to capture the data, and a large number of project results from a limited set of project families. This is an ideal task for the firm's PMO, though there is no substitute for personal experience and every PM should develop their own ROTs. The following ROTs are drawn from my own experience and may not apply in other circumstances.

Project management estimate

Three typical techniques include:

1   Estimate Based on Team Size–Allocate 1 full-time equivalent (FTE) management resource for every 7–10 team members. Useful on large teams and as a cross-check on the percent of effort method.
2   Percent of Effort–Assess PM effort based on the total project effort estimated. Small simple projects 3–5%, moderately complex projects 5–15%, and large complex projects 15–25% (this would include a full-time vendor PM and a percentage of team lead time).
3   Percent of Duration–Assess PM effort as a percent of the project duration. Useful as a cross-check for smaller projects using a part-time vendor PM. For example, a 6-month project may need 30 h/month of PM effort, for a total of 180 h.

Technical and project administrative support

Support in its various forms is often overlooked, but even small percentages can add up for large projects. The most common areas are administration, either performed by the team themselves or by admin staff, and technical support. Admin support tends to range from 1% to 3% of project estimate. Technical support is more variable, and can run from 3% to 10% of deliverable estimate. Complex, technically innovative, or performance-oriented projects tend to require more.

Other non-deliverable work

In addition to the previous categories, time may also be leaked to other areas. If not identified and estimated, a cost overrun can be anticipated. These areas include: client assistance, project meetings, coaching, travel, reviews, and rework.

Caution on productivity

For project work, output per person is not the same. It varies based on their experience and knowledge of project technologies. Training can be used, sometimes, to boost individual productivity but at additional cost and lost time to the project. Time for project familiarization also reduces the productivity of new team members as they adapt to the project and meld with the existing group. An ROT can provide a productivity factor (e.g., factor the standard effort by 1.1) for staff not meeting the average criteria.

Project duration estimating

Although this chapter is primarily focused on estimation of effort, as duration and effort enjoy a mutual interaction, this section also covers a few additional rules that apply specifically to duration.

Classic scheduling

Classic project scheduling relies on developing an initial activity effort estimate (E), then allocating resources (R). Activity duration (D) is then given by the formula:

$$D = E/R.$$

The schedule is developed by mapping activities onto a calendar, whilst adhering to activity dependencies defined in the network diagram. Resources are not infinite, and so a process called resource leveling resolves instances of resource overload. This process leads to the critical path.

In practice this approach is too theoretical for projects that operate in an unpredictable client environment. Projects can operate along a critical path under the firm's control for a period, but these periods can be interrupted by client-controlled situations where the firm's resource utilization can fluctuate unpredictably and classic schedule management breaks down.

Most vendor PMs deal with this reality by applying an experience-based 'model schedule' that attempts to account for planned and unplanned durations. Thus, although $D=E/R$ might apply to a vendor's specific planned activity durations, it is definitely not applied to the project as a whole.

To reiterate, the client has an impact on duration over which the firm has little control. It is also hard to make an ROT, as clients are not standard. However, if the contract has stated the need for client responsibilities, then they can be held accountable.

Crashing the schedule

There are situations when the overall schedule is highly dependent on large and significant activity. $D = E/R$ applies, and crashing the schedule to advance the completion date is feasible. This means applying increased resource levels either through adding team members or working overtime. Three points must be observed to maintain control in this situation:

1   There must be a reliable estimate of effort available at the outset. The assumptions that underpin this estimate must be reviewed for applicability and, if necessary, the estimate updated.
2   The nature of the activity, and the current and planned additional resources must be reviewed to assess whether linearity continues to apply to the formula $D=E/R$. For example, an activity to build four units, with three staff applied, is probably linear and an additional resource could be

added to reduce duration by 25%. Activities that are not partitionable will not yield linear improvement.

3   In cases of poorly partitionable activities, a ROT factor is applied to the original estimate (e.g., 1.1) to acknowledge the non-linearity caused by the need for additional overhead, meeting time, communications, and potential work overlap when more resource is added.

Generally, most vendor PMs prefer to increase resource level by overtime work as being the most efficient of the options. This acknowledges that new resources require assimilation and training, and sometimes are just not available.

Unplanned resource reductions

In practice, there are distractions that can remove team members from the project, and ROTs can be applied during project scheduling to take these into account. These items do not necessarily add to the project effort, but because resource is reduced, they can affect duration. Items that are not charged to a project but can increase duration include assistance to other projects, training, sales support, office administration, vacation, other absences, and firm's business meetings.

The horizon effect

Resource availability for project work represents an estimating challenge. Even a resource designated 100% does not spend all available time on the project as noted above. Additionally, the duration of the project itself dictates the reasonableness of availability assumptions. I call this the horizon effect— if the project horizon is visible, then higher availabilities can be assumed or negotiated. Otherwise, availability assumptions must be lowered. For example, it is probably safe to assume that resources for a one-week project are actually close to 100% available (ask them). For a 3-year project, however, the vendor PM cannot rely on this, because lost availability is a certainty. Some duration-based ROT based on increasing time horizons are as follows:

*   Subtract 5–6 h of availability from an average 37.5-h week.
*   Subtract 1–2 days of availability from an average 21-day month.
*   Subtract 40 days or more from an average 250-day year.

These ROTs are statistically based and subject to further validation by the PM as data and experience are gathered.

Managing uncertainty

The guiding principle when dealing with uncertainty is to avoid single-point estimates. There are a number of simple techniques, like estimate ranges, which avoid single-point estimates, each with their own applicability, and these are discussed first before explaining contingency methods.

How to avoid a single-point estimate

The following methods apply to estimates of effort or cost, and care should be taken when extrapolating to duration, as discussed later.

Quote a Confidence Factor–An example of this method is, "Based on my current understanding and investigation of the issues, I have a 40% confidence that your available budget of $150,000 will be adequate." As implied by the example, this technique is useful when the estimator is confronted with a pre-existing budget that he was asked to validate. This method offers little help in developing a better estimate, and is just a critique of what is there already.

Quote the Estimate, Plus/Minus a Percent–Using the plus/minus percent method is widespread; an example might be: "Based on the factors we've had time to examine, I'd estimate your project at $150,000 plus 50%, minus 10%." This methodology yields a three-point estimate, usually referred to as the optimistic, most likely, and pessimistic values. These are sometimes called PERT estimates. Applied to the activity estimates using a bottom-up approach, this method generates lots of data and, with the help of statistics, can be used to supply reasonable budget estimates.

Quote the Estimate, Plus/Minus a Percent based on Phase–A top-down ROT version of the plus/minus percent method can be applied to phases of the lifecycle model. These ROTs are examples only:

1   Planning phase estimate is plus/minus 50%.
2   Requirements phase estimate is plus/minus 30%.
3   Design phase estimate is plus/minus 15%.

The estimate for the balance of the project thus increases in accuracy as a phase is completed, which is common sense.

Use an Estimate Range–The estimate range is an alternative to the plus/minus percentage method. For example, "I'd say we could get this project done for somewhere between $140,000 and $160,000." This can be taken as a negotiating ploy leading to a budget of $150,000. It's hard to tell if this is satisfactory because the range omits the notion of any kind of target value, and the probabilities of the extreme values are simply unknown. Be cautious about using estimating ranges without an explicit target because more data is needed to make a meaningful interpretation.

Run a Monte Carlo Analysis–This method requires computerized, multi-point activity estimates and an assumed probability curve for each estimate. The computer runs a set of simulations; the output is a probability curve for the project, showing the probability of each project estimate. This approach is prone to GIGO. There is also an unfortunate propensity for managers to regard a computer output with more respect than it deserves.

Variable Scope–It might sound like an improper way to deal with estimating uncertainty and not something to take into a certification exam, but fixing the estimate and varying the scope is increasingly accepted as a valid approach. It is acknowledged in modern systems development methodologies (e.g., Xtreme Programming, Dynamic Systems Development Method, and Agile). Faced with a budget that seems insufficient, it may be a valid strategy to declare scope as a variable. In other words, "We'll do what we can with the money available." This technique can only be successful with certain types of projects, and can involve contractual challenges.

Quote a Target and a Budget–This is the generally preferred, formal method and is discussed next in detail. The concept is to take the most likely estimate and declare that the 'target'. Then, calculate a contingency. The official budget for the project is the sum of both.

$$\text{Budget} = \text{Target} + \text{Contingency}.$$

Always quote contingency to avoid a single point estimate.

A statistical method for contingency

This method capitalizes on the statistical connection between a project estimate and the level of project risk. From the firm's point of view, the aim is to avoid losing the bid with an over-cautious (too high) estimate, but also to give the project a positive chance of succeeding if the bid is won. A large inventory of active projects using a statistical approach with the right parameters ensures that the majority of projects, though perhaps not all, will succeed.

Regardless of how it is calculated, the contingency is always aggregated and preserved as a single value of effort, or cost. It is drawn down by the vendor PM when needed. This method is simple, creates the concept of a planned target for each deliverable (the likely estimate), and helps avoid the phenomenon of work expanding to fill the maximum effort allowed.

Accuracy of estimate related to risk

Looking into the future, uncertainties arise that may cause actual events to deviate from forecasts. These uncertainties are called risks—as risks increase, so too will deviation from forecasts.

Figure 7.2 illustrates a low-risk and high-risk project, and the probability of completing the project for any given estimate of effort. The most likely estimate is the peak of the curve—the most probable. Estimates higher and lower than the most likely show decreasing probability, but, of course, still have a chance of occurring. The low-risk project is, by definition, less uncertain, and so the range of estimates is closely bunched around the most likely value showing little variation. In statistical terms, the project has a low standard deviation. Conversely, the high-risk project, loaded with uncertainties, demonstrates

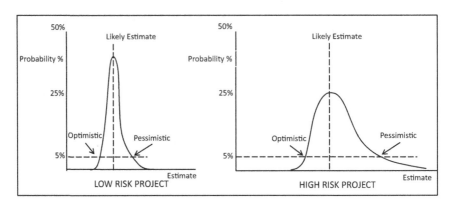

Figure 7.2 Probabilities for low-risk and high-risk projects

a high standard deviation and a broad range of possible estimates that could occur. Significantly, the higher end of the estimate range shows probabilities of occurrence that can't be ignored—experienced by all as project overruns. Intuitively, the higher-risk project warrants higher contingency and probability theory seems the most likely tool for establishing a practical link.

Using probability theory for contingency

The question now arises—what is the basis for determining the amount of contingency? To answer this, think about estimate probabilities from a cumulative perspective. It's not important that the project cost exactly meets a specific estimate, but that it completes *within* the planned estimate—any value below the budget is perfectly acceptable. Figure 7.3 shows cumulative probability of finishing within the estimate, shown on the *x*-axis, for a moderately risky project. This is an example of an S-curve, and has certain interesting characteristics.

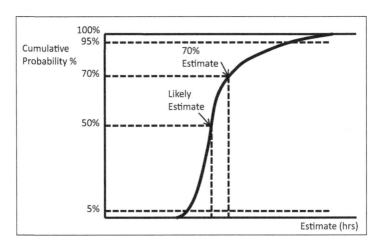

Figure 7.3 Project S-curve showing cumulative probability

The S-curve plots the probabilities on a cumulative basis, so at the 50% point on the *y*-axis, the project has a 50% chance of finishing at the estimate shown on the *x*-axis, *or less*. Of course, it also has a 50% chance of finishing over that estimate. The 50%, or median point is the steepest part of the curve—a small change in the *x*-axis value (estimate) gives a proportionately larger change in the cumulative probability. This phenomenon continues for a short while until the 'knee of the curve' occurs and now increasing the estimate has proportionately less effect on the cumulative probability, which is already at a fairly high value. Here is the clue to how to use cumulative probabilities to establish contingency. Take the median estimate and add to it a relatively small amount, the contingency, to achieve a significant increase in probability until the knee of the curve is approached. It turns out that a 70% probability is around the optimum. (Statisticians will point out that the median estimate is not quite the same as the most likely estimate—I ignore that difference in this argument.)

Think of the most likely estimate from this perspective: there is a 50% chance of meeting a 'likely' estimate, and a 50% chance of exceeding it.

Would you bet your job on the toss of a coin?

Incredibly, clients demand estimates that only have a 50/50 chance and discard higher numbers as being 'padded'. Even more amazingly, vendor PMs keep providing them! Now assume a calculated contingency is added that moves the probability to 70%. Not a sure thing, but a good chance, and the small contingency should be affordable and competitive. Following this logic, why not increase the odds—say a 95% chance? Unfortunately, the estimate would be so high that the project would never be considered, or the client would go elsewhere.

Figure 7.4 shows cumulative probabilities for a sample project. To make the explanation less theoretical, contemplate the model from a different angle.

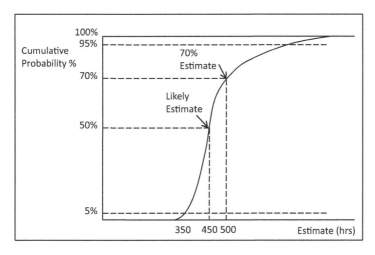

Figure 7.4 Sample project showing small increase to give 70% estimate

Consider this sample project being executed 100 times, each time completing within an estimate driven by the probabilities. On average, 50 executions will succeed in meeting the target of 450 h or will do better. Fifty executions will exceed it. That's the coin toss at work. Five executions will complete within 350 h. Would you quote 350 h? With a 5% chance of success, probably not. Interestingly, 70 executions will complete within 500 h. Quoting 500 h is a definite option. A budget of 500 h is only 10% over the target, and gives the team a 70% chance of success. Not the sure thing, but a good chance.

Applying contingency methods

The statistical approach to contingency can be applied either bottom-up or top-down.

Bottom-up method

The bottom-up method uses the cumulative probability model (Figure 7.3) for each activity of the project. As proven below, a good approximation to the 70% estimate is given by:

Activity Budget = Activity Target + (Pessimistic − Target)/4 h Effort.

Using this model, effort contingency is calculated bottom-up for each activity and summed.

Statistical theory

For readers with an interest in statistics, here are the statistical assumptions behind this technique.

First, assume the pessimistic estimate equates to the 95% confidence level. Then, assume the frequency distribution of possible estimates is normal (bell curve). Thus, the likely estimate equals the median and becomes the target estimate—the 50% point. Given these assumptions, statistical theory tells us the standard deviation is equal to 0.5 of the difference between the mean and 95% value. Statistical tables can be consulted to show that a 70% confident estimate can be achieved by adding 0.52 of the standard deviation to the mean. Therefore,

70% Estimate = Target + 0.52 × 0.5 × (Pessimistic − Target).

Assuming that for most projects, the 70% value is the knee of the curve (the best compromise between affordability and the coin toss) and becomes the budget, then rounding out the arithmetic gives:

Contingency = (Pessimistic − Target)/4.

Table 7.2 Bottom-up estimates for target and contingency

	Completed deliverable estimate for a project showing contingency				
Phase	Deliverable	Likely hours	Pessimistic hours	Pessimistic— likely hours	(Pessimistic— likely)/4 hours
Reqts	Charter and Scope	20	25	5	1.25
Design	Proj Plan	40	48	8	2.00
	Design Spec	55	65	10	2.50
	Test Plan	15	20	5	1.25
Build/test	Tested Code	120	160	40	10.00
	Converted Data	65	90	25	6.25
	Training Material	20	23	3	0.75
	Delivered Course	10	12	2	0.50
Implement	Accepted System	30	45	15	3.75
Totals		375	488	113	28.25

Calculation:
  Budget defined as = Target (Likely) + Contingency (Pessimistic − Likely)/4
  Budget = 375 + 28.25 = 403.25 h
  Consolidated contingency as a percent = 28.25/403.25 = 7%

This is a highly applicable ROT for determining a defensible contingency, better than an arbitrary 'add 10% for contingency', and almost as easy to calculate. Critics who disparage this as an over-simplifying approximation should remember this is project estimating, not microsurgery, and it is better than plucking a number from thin air.

Although the derivation is at the activity level, contingency is consolidated into a single bucket, not allocated to specific activities or deliverables. Refer to Table 7.2 for a simple worked example of a project estimate (based on deliverable, not activity) to demonstrate the steps taken to estimate the contingency.

Top-down method

Although contingency assessment at the activity level is the recommended method, there is an opportunity for top-down assessment to provide either a quick 'first-cut' or to validate the bottom-up results. The top-down estimate is based on the project risk rank.

Observation, supported by common sense, suggests that contingency should be increased as risk rank increases. Table 7.3 presents some estimating ROTs based on a specific family of projects.

In most firms, very high-risk projects are unlikely to be bid, not least because the contingency requirements become uncompetitive. Even so, I have seen software development bids succeed with contingency as high as 35%, under some unique circumstances.

Whether the firm selects the 70% method for contingency assessment or some other method, single point estimates should never be quoted and project budgets should always be defined as comprising the target plus the contingency.

Table 7.3 Top-down estimate for contingency

Correlation between risk rank and contingency range		
Risk rank	Description	Suggested contingency range
#1	Very low risk	Usually not required
#2	Low risk	3–5%
#3	Moderate risk	6–12%
#4	High risk	13–25%
#5	Very high risk	>25%

These contingency guidelines are intended to assist in the process of building a sound bid and a successful execution. They should lead to a reasonable solution. If, in your judgment, the result does not conform to common sense, then common sense must prevail.

Change request contingency

The methods being discussed only apply to contingency arising from uncertainty in the estimates based on the current scope. Clients sometimes think of contingency as referring to a fund for scope changes. A separate exercise is required to persuade the sponsor to budget an allowance for change requests to be applied to approved scope changes. This amount is managed separately from the risk contingency and is probably kept under the sponsor's control for the duration of the project. An ROT can be developed for change request contingency, and 15–20% seems reasonable for projects with uncertain requirements.

Duration contingency

In a simple world, there is a direct relationship between effort and duration, usually making duration a derived estimate ($D=E/R$). The exception is for activities such as testing, which tend to be duration-driven ($E=D×R$). Then things get more complicated when dealing with activities that are partially partitionable. The linkage between schedule and effort becomes distinctly problematic when contingency enters the picture. It is rarely wise to add schedule contingency to every single activity and then build a project schedule on the assumption that contingency is automatically taken care of. Schedule uncertainty tends to arise from different sources than effort uncertainty (e.g., risk to external milestones, such as delivery delays from a supplier).

This suggests that apart from situations where duration overrun can be traced to effort overrun, use of calculation or ROT techniques are unhelpful when it comes to duration contingency. Effort should be allocated to activities using target estimates, then the activities scheduled, and then a duration contingency added as an additional manual step using project management judgment. Expert project managers may use an advanced technique to deal with duration risks, such as Critical Chain Scheduling buffers.

Schedule contingency is a thorny issue. Unlike effort contingency buried in an FP bid, duration buffers stare the client in the face when he first scans the Gantt chart. Unless there has been an opportunity to review the matter openly and for both parties to understand the need, this can create a negative reaction. RFPs commonly state required completion dates that cannot be demonstrated when a gap is deliberately drawn in the schedule. The unstated RFP assumption is that time can be made up through overtime, crashing the schedule, or other techniques, as an alternative to building some float into the schedule. In reality, it often turns out that client deadlines are not always mandatory and are frequently deferred for client reasons, to be taken care of through the change control process.

Business considerations

To this point, contingency has been regarded mainly from the perspective of the need to protect the project from risk and to deliver successfully. However, contingency is far from just a project management nicety and, along with estimating in general, should be regarded as a success factor for the firm. These business-related topics are covered in this concluding section.

Management reserve

Some firms bolster their management of project risk by introducing a management reserve—similar to contingency, but with a slightly different definition. Like contingency, management reserve burdens the project with additional costs, lowering the margin, but the usage and allocation of those costs remains at the discretion of Finance management. This is distinct from contingency, which remains under the control of the vendor PM. After all, without access to a risk fund such as contingency, is it fair to ask a PM to be accountable for a project with known risk? If contingency is depleted, and if a management reserve was set aside, then after reviews and project resets the reserve may be used to renew contingency. The benefit of this approach is that if these maneuvers are done correctly, financial results can be stabilized.

The dynamics of contingency management, given these definitions, are quite important. The delivery manager and Finance share authority for both contingency and reserve management, with the DM (delegating responsibility to the PM) taking the lead on the former, and Finance on the latter. These values are ideally established, based on bid data, at the start of the project, though management reserves are sometimes taken during execution if the project unexpectedly deteriorates. In that case, there will be a hit on margin. For large, risky projects, both contingency and reserves will be in place, though for the vast majority of projects, only contingency is required.

At initiation review, allocated contingency is discussed. All financial forecasts are based on the cost budget (target + contingency), and so they presume a worst-case consumption of contingency. Nonetheless the expectation is that the PM will return at least some of the contingency to the firm at the end of the project. The corollary of this expectation is that contingency usage, although controlled by the PM, must be justified, and he can expect to be held to account during management reviews of the project. This disciplined stance helps avoid the 'work expands to meet budget available' syndrome.

> Give PMs contingency, but tell them the business would really like it back at the end of the project.

Impact on revenue recognition

Finance takes a conservative view of revenue recognition with respect to contingency. The vendor PM calculates percent of completion (POC=AC/EAC) to include unused contingency. This means that the EAC (denominator) in the POC equation includes contingency and thus reduces POC from what it would be without contingency. This philosophy also acts to stabilize margin. When the project completes, or when the PM determines that contingency is no longer needed, the POC and margin experience a boost as the EAC takes a sudden reduction.

Summary of the firm's support

These points summarize the actions by the firm to support their estimators:

Culture of the Firm—The topic of estimating was introduced by recapping on some of the impediments faced by estimators if inappropriate pressure is allowed to apply. The firm must make it a priority to build a positive and supportive corporate culture.

Estimator Recognition—The term 'estimator' has naturally been used a lot. This emphatically does not imply a remote specialist who does nothing but estimate. An estimator is an adopted role and can be taken by any skilled practitioner who also has a regular job, such as project engineer, analyst, or even project manager. The firm needs to properly recognize the extra time and skills of these individuals who are taking on an important temporary role in addition to their regular responsibilities.

Information Repository—Either through a PMO, or other means, the firm must establish a reference repository of categorized project results. When sufficient data are available, then publish standard estimates for the firm's project families.

Policy and Procedures— Set policy and guidelines for responding to challenging RFP estimating requirements (e.g., big bang). Establish and monitor the risk rank profile of the project portfolio and the observed relationship between contingency allocation and the desired 70% success rate. Document a guide to the estimating practice and set policy on use of templates.

Technology–Provide and support the best possible, affordable technology infrastructure and include a PM tool. Construct templates for the automated development of estimates and contingency. Two distinct templates are required—a work estimate and a bid estimate. Use a bid estimate template for financials, and a work estimate template for effort.

It is hard to imagine a more significant success factor for project delivery than an efficient, accurate, and professionally managed estimating practice. The firm that invests wisely in developing their capabilities in this practice will surely reap a reward.

8   Solving the quality conundrum

During a difficult conversation about project quality with a client at the start of a project, I experienced a sudden flash of understanding. At issue was how much emphasis the client wished to place on quality, as this would significantly influence the project costs. Soon the exasperated client stopped the conversation, looked at me and said, "Hornby, the reason we hired your firm was because you do high-quality work—that's right, isn't it? So let's just get on with it." In this case, I had committed two serious gaffes: one, having this conversion *after* signing the contract, and not before; and two, presuming that anyone would be prepared to answer thoughtless questions about quality.

Henry Ford reportedly said that quality means, "doing it right when no one is looking." My client, like Henry Ford before him, obviously felt that quality was simply a natural way of working, an exclusive focus on doing the right thing. Proponents of this view might be carpenters who use a 2×6 behind the wallboard when 2×4 might be adequate, or dressmakers who line the entire garment even when wear or comfort does not demand it. If challenged, the response may be, "aah, but the gods see everywhere!"

The unfortunate fact of modern, complex projects is that doing it right is not always self-evident, and the gods of commerce and not just craftsmanship are peering into the hidden corners. These realizations precipitated a serious attempt on my part to structure useful conversations, models, and frameworks for quality planning that continues to this day. The commercial environment complicates an already complex topic and the purpose of this chapter is to clarify the issues and propose solutions.

In some cases, the quality conversation is straightforward, but for many projects it is not. In application areas where quality is defined in terms of defects, like the number of failed welds on a pipeline, there is a reasonable expectation that the vendor PM and sponsor will enjoy strong communication. In multifaceted developments, like custom software, communication is more ambiguous. In any event, either competitive pressure or client curiosity can provoke the firm to establish a position on quality. But, what is the most cost-effective solution? It lies somewhere between the firm's executive issuing a generic policy statement saying they are unanimously in favor of quality and a full-blown implementation of ISO9000.

The meaning of quality

Philosopher and author Robert Pirsig concluded that quality couldn't be defined. Pirsig spends much of his cult book *Zen and the Art of Motorcycle Maintenance* agonizing over this question. The clearest take-away from the hours I spent reading and interpreting his complex thought was the possibility that quality cannot be regarded as an intrinsic characteristic of a product, or a project, but an indefinable and highly personal assessment by an individual based on integrating all that is important to the individual at the time. In other words, quality, like beauty, is in the eye of the beholder.

Students in a class I teach on quality management demonstrate this conundrum by answering an open-ended question that asks what quality actually means to each of them personally. Table 8.1 shows the wide range of responses.

The answers are placed into one of two columns. The left hand corresponds to inherent or intrinsic characteristics of the project or product that are relatively self-defining, specific, and easy to measure. These are the objective views of quality. The right hand column lists the intangible, much harder to measure subjective factors. It is interesting to note the responses that, on the surface, appear to have nothing to do with the topic of quality—timely, on budget, efficient, value—might be examples. There is something happening when people think about quality that creates a multidimensional reaction, and that makes a definition rather problematic.

Table 8.1 Responses to the question of quality

"What does quality mean to you...?"	
Objective views	*Subjective views*
Defect free	Craftsmanship
Maintainable	Customer satisfaction
Reliable	Excellence
Timely	Perfection
On budget	Thoroughness
Dependable	Usefulness
Serviceable	Value
Adheres to standards	Competitive
Consistent	Utility
Repeatable	Meets expectations
Durable	Continuous improvement
Delivers benefits	Optimal
Testable	Satisfies the purpose
Reusable	Integrity
Correct	Organized
Efficient	Exceeds expectations

Definition of quality

During the early days of the quality movement, many attempts to define quality were made—definitions that focus on commitment to excellence, on freedom from defects, on marketplace success and consumer acceptance, on conformance to product requirements, and on value. They are all vaguely dissatisfying, perhaps because they each seem to focus on a specific aspect of quality and inevitably exclude many of the characteristics in Table 8.1. Another fact is that two aspects of quality emerge—the quality of the product and the quality of the project itself.

> Project quality is the quality of the project experience. Product quality is the quality of the result.

The value of this observation is to split the quality debate into two parts, enabling more focused and accurate analysis. In the meantime, most can be gained by adopting the definition used in PMBOK® (itself adapted from ISO9000), which is credible and allows a rationalization of the results in Table 8.1. The definition is:

> Quality is the degree to which a set of inherent characteristics fulfills requirements.

This definition is clearly aimed at product quality, and seems to link the subjective and objective views. The inherent characteristics are objective, and the requirements can be inclusive of the subjective.

So, this is a reasonable starting point for a quality conversation with the sponsor. If both parties accept this definition, then the vendor PM can lay down a logical progression that leads the client from her imprecise subjective views, to measurable objectives, to observable quality factors that can be built into the product.

Goal of quality

Before following that logical path, it is a good idea to step back a little and recap some background on the thought given over the past decades to the goal of quality—why do we do it, what is the purpose?

If the vendor PM and sponsor are not aligned on the purpose of the quality program for their project, this disconnect creates a risk. The following provides an outline of the primary categories of thought on this subject.

Fit for use or purpose

Two of the earliest thinkers on this matter were J. Edwards Deming and Joseph M. Juran. Deming developed the fundamentals of statistical process control in the 1930s, and Juran wrote his *Quality Control Handbook* in the late 1940s. They famously took their ideas to Japan after the war and thus paved the way for the Japanese-led quality revolution. Juran's starting point was that a product with quality must be generally fit for use and, more specifically, fit for purpose. Deming agreed, but went on to emphasize the role of the customer as a central actor in the analysis of quality.

Fit for use appeals as a simple and basic goal. A product begins, it is argued, as a means of fulfilling a need, and the congruity between that need and the usage characteristics of the product is a measure of quality. This is fine up to a point, but how do we assess a product with multiple uses, some of which are more relevant than others? For example, a water bottle is very useful to transport water, and can also be used to drink out of, but many of us would prefer a glass! Setting the quality goal as fit for purpose allows for these nuances to be introduced into the equation.

The concept of fit for purpose also raises the possibility of a range of products all essentially with the same function, but differentiated by their precise purpose. This factor, called grade in quality theory, is used to separate products included in the same use category but ranging in purpose. For example, carpeting is sold with a key durability factor being tufts per square inch. If the need for carpet is in the low traffic bedroom and not the high traffic hotel lobby, then the concept of grade allows for unneeded durability to be eliminated while still delivering a high-quality product, because it is exactly fit for purpose. This can be applied to a conversation with a customer concerning a system to be delivered with a very short production life—say a few months. Rather than suggesting a lower quality system (not a good idea), the vendor PM could make legitimate cost-saving proposals to reduce the grade of certain less relevant features—for example, documentation and maintainability.

The danger of contracting on the goal of fit for purpose is that the contractor is saddled with an open-ended commitment. The client must fully disclose his requirements so the vendor PM is left in no doubt as to the exact purpose to be met. If a client insists on including a fit for purpose clause in the contract, thus rendering the requirements open-ended, the firm has a difficult business decision. Accepting the clause is probably dependent on the perceived unknowns and the character of the client.

'Fit for Purpose' is a starting point for quality requirements, not an end point.

Elimination of defects

Delivering a defect-free product is an intuitive purpose behind any quality initiative. This goal has considerable appeal and requires little explanation. Following Juran and Deming, the second-generation quality guru Philip

Crosby pioneered an approach during his time with Martin Marietta as director of the Pershing missile program. It became known by the buzzword 'Zero Defects'. This program for engineering excellence was adopted by NASA, perhaps the most well-known implementation. NASA's margin for error is very close to zero, as we are all aware since the tragic Challenger event. Seeking such a lofty goal for quality is unfortunately an expensive undertaking, and, despite the arguments in Crosby's seminal work *Quality Is Free,* has not been totally adopted by mainstream industry. The vendor PM must understand that Crosby is contemplating full lifecycle costs and benefits, of which the project is only a part.

> Quality is not free; it's an investment.

Focus on the customer

This customer-centered goal came into prominence in the 1990s. The focus is on gaining a customer and then on retaining him. Concepts such as customer satisfaction, exceeding customer expectations, and creating a 'wow' factor are commonly quoted in this context.

Customer focus also came to mean that everyone had a role to play in finding and retaining customers—not just the sales staff. An offhand response in Accounting to a casual customer inquiry can do as much damage as a faulty product.

It has been proven time and time again that the most cost effective way to make sales is to retain an existing customer and seek repeat business, rather than searching for a new customer. Yet this lesson is often ignored. Deming made the point that though an unhappy customer may switch, a merely satisfied customer may do the same on the grounds that they could not lose much and might gain. A truly happy customer will boast about your product or service, and bring their friends or associates with them. This is true customer loyalty.

As a summary of the customer focus, consider these steps: go to extreme lengths to understand the customer's true needs; meet those needs and exceed their expectations, as merely meeting needs does not create loyalty; and be consistent and dependable because a loyal customer must feel secure with a supplier.

Compliance with standards and process

Compliance goals are centered on standards for either specifications or procedures. Compliance goals are technical matters and have a tendency to appear remote and carry less emotional appeal. There is also an unfortunate tendency for a company's motivation to be suspect, particularly when compliance can be demonstrated by certification, and certification is demanded as a mandatory criterion for selection as a supplier. Is a company seeking certification because they have a belief and commitment to quality, or to gain a place on the suppliers list?

Standards can be applied to more than process and can include materials, construction, assembly, finishing, qualifications, documentation, technical specifications, and general product attributes. They also exist at international, national, local, and corporate level. Their significance is very dependent upon the nature of the project application and the client's business environment. Based on those same dependencies, the vendor PM must be sufficiently knowledgeable to dialogue with the client and establish the degree to which standards represent a quality goal.

Conformance to requirements

In addition to his pioneering work on the demanding goal of zero defects, Crosby is also known for his idea that the goal of quality is to describe, validate, and verify the characteristics of the product or service that will satisfy the customer's requirements. To me, this muddies the waters by conflating the purpose with the definition of quality, but nonetheless, it is far and away the most commonly accepted goal within the project context and has become the foundation of the waterfall methodologies common in almost all application areas.

Conformance to requirements is a useful goal, but does create a labor intensive and expensive sequence of project activities. To be successful, it relies on both a low rate of change, and a project free of ambiguous requirements.

Dominant quality methods

Based on these goals, a variety of methodologies were developed during the 1980s and 1990s. Some have continued to expand, but most rode the wave of quality enthusiasm before falling into niche interest only. They are primarily intended for corporate implementation, and apart from RTM, it would be unrealistic for the PM to implement independently into the project environment. Nonetheless, the vendor PM should have some knowledge of the more significant, such as Six Sigma, TQM, QFD, ISO9000, and requirements-centered techniques such as RTM.

Six sigma

Six Sigma is a statistically based program with a very similar goal to zero defects. Pioneered by Motorola in the 1980s, the theory is to create processes so accurate and consistent that the chance of a flawed process is no more than 3.4 occurrences per million opportunities. This is a remarkably low defect rate, and in most companies, the difference between 3.4 per million and zero is pretty hard to detect. Part of the appeal of Six Sigma, however, is that it is statistical and can be measured, offering the possibility of incremental progress. Several large corporations have implemented Six Sigma, particularly those in the mass consumer market where the consequences of even traditionally low failure rates are very serious (like the mobile phone market). Six Sigma has also been enhanced and commercialized by consultancies, offering a much broader approach to quality than statistical process control.

Non-statisticians might be interested in a brief explanation of the original meaning of Six Sigma. Sigma is the Greek letter traditionally assigned to the statistical concept of a 'standard deviation' or a measure of data variability. Sigma can be calculated from a formula if the assumption can be made that the sample data is normally distributed, or forms a bell curve. Much data in nature do indeed form a bell curve, including the degree of error made when trying to hit a target. The incredibly interesting and useful thing about bell curves is that having calculated a value of sigma for the data distribution, consulting standard statistical tables reveals that the data within +/– one sigma of the mean represents 67% of all the data, within two sigma represents 95%, and within three sigma represents 99.7%. Yes, if you follow that progression, six sigma represents 99.99966% of the data. Counting occurrences outside of six sigma as errors, that equates to 3.4 per million.

Total quality management

TQM was widely promoted as an organizational standard for quality and when fully implemented is pervasive throughout the company. The basic tenets of TQM may be summarized as:

- Understand your customer's requirements.
- 'Everyone' has a customer.
- Perform to meet requirements.
- Implement defect prevention.
- Measure performance based on cost of quality.
- Zero defect target.
- Everyone is accountable to meet requirements.

TQM required expensive training initiatives at all levels of the organization. The big innovation was the emphasis on the universality of the customer and the payback was unarguable. This was really a new way of looking at things, requiring significant culture-change, because most employees thought of a customer as some remote entity that had little to do with them.

The innovation was to think of customers as anyone on the other end of a transaction. From that perspective, a supplier is a customer, contradictory as it sounds. A supplier could be a customer for the company's RFP, or purchase order, or invoice, and so on. Thus, designs should attempt to meet the customer's legitimate requirements for those transactions. In the end, everyone's a winner, as the company should get a better outcome from the improved transaction.

An extension of this idea is the real game changer—even people internal to the organization are customers when involved in transactions. In the project team context, there are myriad examples of possible, and actual, gains in productivity, not to mention more positive relationships and morale. Here is a case history of an accounting department's insistence on submission of weekly time cards before the end of Friday. This was deeply unpopular with the project team who, at the end of a busy week, just wanted to go home. In the TQM spirit, the vendor PM met with the accounting supervisor, and they both laid out their issues and real requirements. It turned out that the real deadline was to get time cards approved by the end of Monday, and they often just sat on the project accountant's desk till 10:00 am anyway. It was agreed that in future time cards could be submitted by 9:00 am Monday. This made no difference to accounting, and was a win for the project team as they could forget about their administration duties on Friday night, so long as they donated the twenty minutes or so over the weekend to get the chore done. Nobody minded that.

Quality function deployment

QFD is the most methodical and technical approach to hearing the 'voice of the customer'. The method centers on constructing a set of matrices, referred to as the House of Quality because of the matrix layout. These matrices purport to represent the relationship between customer requirements, the actual product, and the various departments that contribute—design, engineering, cost accounting, marketing, and so forth. The model is able to highlight areas of strong, weak, and even negative correlation. Showing these connections to the voice of the customer strengthens decision-making and trade-off analysis when circumstances require.

Requirements-focused methodology

The goal of conformance to requirements is really the purpose underlying almost all formalized development methodologies. A development methodology brings numerous benefits: both parties have defined roles and responsibilities; there is a roadmap for project progress; and importantly, a project can be estimated, because the methodology pre-defines the activities that ensure conformance to requirements. These activities include:

- A phase devoted to requirements definition and analysis;
- Review and approval activities to achieve meaningful sponsor sign-off and validation of requirements;
- A requirements traceability matrix (RTM) to prove the propagation of requirements into design and construction;
- A test and inspection process to verify that the product was built as designed and free of defects; and
- An acceptance test process to validate that the product meets the requirements.

Despite the popularity of this approach, there is a significant drawback best illustrated by a case story. Years ago, a major appliance-maker wanted to launch a new brand of ovens. In accordance with the ideas of the time they emphasized the consumers' requirements by setting up focus groups across the country made up of chefs, domestic cooks, and homemakers. Facilitated by the company, the results were fed back to the design group, analyzed, and many included in the product specifications. The year the new models were announced, the company was swept away by the competition. Why? Because that same year the competition introduced the self-cleaning oven. Irate and confused, the design team turned on their focus groups, demanding to know why they hadn't listed that feature in their requirements. The answer—"we didn't know you could do that!"

ISO9000

During the peak of the International Standards Organization (ISO) registration movement in the early 1990s, quality goals became very process oriented. The logic inherent in this approach is that adherence to a quality process ensures a quality product. The ISO9000 series was founded on this principle with many companies developing and documenting detailed business processes accordingly.

The ISO9000 standard describes quality management principles and the ISO9001 standard puts out specific requirements. Figure 8.1 gives an overview of the general environment required for ISO9001 to be applied effectively.

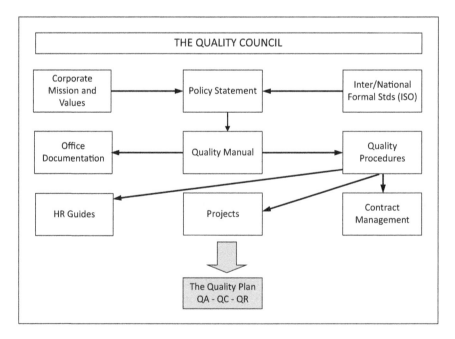

Figure 8.1 A quality management system (QMS) environment

After the environment is implemented and the location certified (technically this is called registration), the company can claim operational compliance with the implication of superior product quality. Registration must be renewed on an annual basis and only applies at the location level. Any organization involved in the production chain must also be ISO registered, or the parent cannot claim compliance. These registration maintenance costs can be quite onerous and the implemented processes themselves are sometimes criticized as expensive to run and do not really guarantee quality. In the phrase management guru Tom Peters made famous, a factory obsessed only with process could manufacture concrete life jackets and still get its ISO quality registration.

Designing a commercial response

I have theorized on the subjective and objective views of quality, reviewed the broad range of goals that could be selected for project quality, and overviewed the most important quality methodologies. How can the firm assimilate this variety and choose an approach that will make sense to every client and win profitable business? Awareness and selective training helps the firm respond, but the bedrock of a safe and affordable approach to quality is to adopt three principles.

Principles for the commercial firm

Three principles that support a successful approach to project quality:

Principle 1 The Client Pays. The client pays for the firm's services and those services naturally include standard quality activities, plus those that must be added to meet specific goals or non-standard requirements. This is why it is so important to have a conversation to understand the client's expectations before signing a fixed price contract. In some scenarios, contracts may have to be designed with some pricing flexibility.

Principle 2 If Quality Isn't an Issue, Don't Make It One. There is nothing to be gained by arguing quality approaches with a client if there is little understanding or interest. The need for education and research is if the client is wedded to a particular point of view that might jeopardize the project's success. When quality is not an issue in the customer's vocabulary, let sleeping dogs lie. Perform the project following the firm's normal standards, and a level of professionalism commensurate with the business context. Anything else is naturally out of scope.

Principle 3 The Firm Must Have a Basic Quality Method. It is apparent from the first two principles that the firm cannot be an empty shell on the subject of quality. There must be a position, not only to ensure that projects meet a standard of quality deemed important to the firm (never mind the customer) but also to explain to prospects and customers when they ask. Employees must also be aware of the firm's approach to quality and be able to explain it. The firm could adopt a position to implement and certify under ISO9000, but in the absence of a clear requirement for this costly step, the recommendation is to design and implement a more basic QMS that shows a return for the firm regardless of client needs.

Components of a basic quality management system

As a reminder of the framework demanded by implementation of a comprehensive QMS, Figure 8.1 shows the extensive and expensive scope. On the other hand, a basic QMS is designed around the few components that are relatively cheap to implement and demonstrate positive, valuable improvements. Quality must show a good cost/benefit just like anything else in business. The proposed basic QMS comprises four components:

Component 1 Policy. Executive management must write and endorse a quality policy. This policy must address the firm's expectations for quality in terms of people, processes, and technology.

Component 2 Responsibilities. Responsibility definitions for quality must be assigned. The firm's job descriptions must include specific aspects of the incumbent's responsibilities where quality outcomes or measurements are important.

Component 3 Quality Planning. Quality plans must be developed for projects. Vendor PMs must be familiar with the preparation and usage of a quality plan, often integrated with the project plan. They should be written for projects meeting certain criteria. These plans need not be elaborate but should commit to quality assurance and quality control methods consistent with the project requirements.

Component 4 Support. The firm must provide visible affordable support for quality, naturally constrained by the nature of the firm's business and revenue. Support at the high end may include a quality manager, quality assurance specialists, and quality auditors, ranging down to provision of quality training, pre-written project procedures and templates, quality tools, tailored quality guidelines, quality awards, and other appropriate recognition. At the basic QMS level, support for the project quality plan is probably the first priority.

Readers with QMS training will note that these four elements are not comprehensive. The intent is only to satisfy the need for a basic position. The balance of the chapter provides models, techniques, checklists, and templates to help put the QMS into action.

Modeling quality

The shifting nature of quality and the inadequacy of the quality vocabulary suggest that models can play a valuable role in communicating quality essentials. Communication and possibly culture-change are the main impediments to a quality program once commitment has been made at the top. There are five models that illustrate key concepts of quality and can be used either internally in the firm or in the project context. They are the Point of Quality, the Supplier/Acceptor, the Quality Triangle, the Quality Quadrant, and the Cost of Quality. Interestingly, only the first of these, the Point of Quality, directly addresses the requirements for product quality. The remainder are all focused on building quality into the project (an important distinction). The vendor PM must believe that the emphasis on project quality does indeed lead to the desired product quality. Otherwise, stop right now!

The point of quality

Adopting the definition of quality earlier in this chapter led to the recommendation to move the client from a subjective view of quality to an objective view. To promote the optimum mutual understanding of the quality targets for the project, this decomposition process should be carried to one more level—to identify quality factors.

> The quality conversation progresses from subjective goals to measurable objectives to observable quality factors.

This progression can be developed with the client using the technique of structured Q&A. The framework for such a dialogue is as follows:

Question 1. Ask directly for the client's quality needs for the product. Accept answers that are objective. A subjective answer, e.g., "Satisfied customers," triggers Question 2.

Question 2. Ask 'how' questions, e.g., "How will you know if your customers are satisfied?" Accept answers that are objective, e.g., "Fewer complaints."

Question 3. Ask 'what' questions, e.g., "What product feature will reduce the number of complaints?" Accept answers that describe observable product attributes (quality factors), e.g., "A handle would be useful."

Another example of this technique is included in Figure 8.2.

This is not an easy process. To be successful, the vendor PM requires good background in quality theory and practice, and should be able to lead the client by offering solutions to his needs by having a range of factors, features, metrics and target measurements at his fingertips. When the dialogue turns to quality factors, the PM should include a technical expert in the conversation.

Supplier/acceptor duality

This is a good framework for quality as it models the quality control implicit in any transaction when a deliverable is offered and a customer accepts.

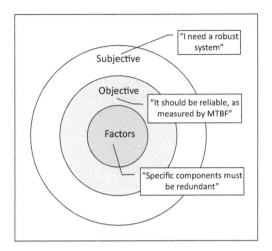

Figure 8.2 The point of quality with an example

Figure 8.3 illustrates the transaction as a balance, suggesting an equality of obligation and responsibility on both parties.

This model is familiar as the basis for concluding a project and for securing payment. The project outcomes are declared complete by the vendor PM and submitted to the customer for acceptance. There is a formal process of inspection, testing, or evaluation during which the customer validates the product. Deficiencies are rectified or negotiated and the project finally signed off. A good contract defines the details of this process, including the obligations of both parties, time limits, and conditions that create de facto acceptance. This model only works if it is in balance, ensuring that the customer wants to accept the product as much as the supplier wants to provide it.

The model has much wider applicability than just final acceptance; it can apply to any transaction between two parties included in the TQM definition

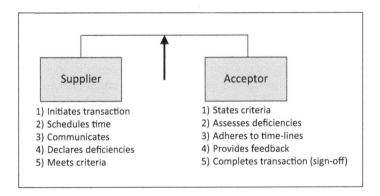

Figure 8.3 The supplier/acceptor model with protocols

of customer. A good application methodology with built-in quality will apply the model to interim project deliverables, such as specifications, designs, technical plans, components, subassemblies, etc. For example, consider a requirements specification supplied by the firm that is offered to the customer for sign-off, but, by TQM logic, also offered internally to the build team whose acceptance is required. The methodology specifies exactly what comprises a requirements specification, and if any of it is missing, it is rejected by the build team. The specs need sign-off by customer *and* builder.

All project teams are familiar with delivery urgency coming into conflict with the need for quality. Deliverables are pushed ahead in the project lifecycle with defects undiscovered in order to meet a deadline. The supplier/acceptor model embedded into the methodology offers a rational and hopefully uncontroversial solution. This will force acceptance criteria to be defined and met to the satisfaction of the acceptor. This in turn creates the right priority for the supplier, who must focus on meeting the criteria, or the deliverable will never be moved through the lifecycle regardless of deadline issues.

The quality triangle

The Quality Triangle is a model of the three fundamentals that determine quality: people, process, and technology (sometimes abbreviated to PPT). Figure 8.4 illustrates the model.

The quality movement has concentrated so much on process that the other two sides of the triangle are in danger of being forgotten. This model is a reminder and a powerful summation of the theoretical foundation for quality.

I recall making a case to a boss, arguing for the establishment of some version of a QMS program, and budget to be allocated to our projects for quality planning. He cut me off after a short while with the comment that he was supplying me with the best people in the business for my project teams, and he couldn't understand what more I wanted. Of course, I didn't know enough to make an intelligent riposte, plus my inner-self thought that perhaps he was right. Well, he was one third right, and fortunately that third was strong enough to disguise the weakness on the other two sides (but not always!). The PPT model does have three sides.

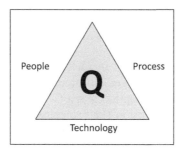

Figure 8.4 The quality triangle

> Quality is achieved by skilled people doing the right thing using effective technology.

The PPT model is so well adapted to the majority of services firms it can be used as a model for the executive quality policy statement. This is the first component of the basic QMS and the anchor for any QMS program. Many policy statements are seriously flawed because they lack specifics and thus commitment can never be seriously tested. An employee should be able to read the policy statement and know how it affects her. Details are not needed, as that is not the role of policy, but specifics are. The PPT model could also be utilized on very large projects that need a written policy on quality, as well. Following is an example of a policy template based on PPT:

1   People–Policy might address how much training is expected per year, the hiring criteria for experienced staff, the conditions under which inexperienced staff might be placed on teams, the expectation of senior staff for coaching or mentoring, the use of a commendation or awards program, etc. Motivation of employees is a consideration when framing policy.

2   Process–Policy does not deliver process, but provides a statement that may require process to be designed, or existing process followed. For example, if a vendor lifecycle is to be implemented, policy would quote the reference and state that it applies to the firm's operations.

3   Technology–Policy regarding technology is dependent upon the positioning of the firm and their business. A firm of architects famously outlawed pencils when they migrated to computer-assisted design, a cold turkey strategy that actually worked. More commonly, policy statements might state priorities for projects to leverage existing investments, or state the cost/benefit analysis rules for projects acquiring their own technology. In today's world, a statement on the quality criteria validating workplace use of Facebook or Twitter might also be very helpful.

This review of policy is a reminder that quality always flows top-down. A vendor PM is ill advised to implement independent quality initiatives if there is no drive from the firm's senior levels. There will be no support from management and the team may be conflicted; success is unlikely.

The quality quadrant

This model evolved following the incident with the client described in the introduction to this chapter. There appeared to be a need for a model to acknowledge that customer perception was a factor, that trade-offs were a fact of project life, and that quality in the project world had two dimensions— quality of the project experience and the quality of the product. Those are the rather grandiose objectives for the simple model shown in Figure 8.5. It could

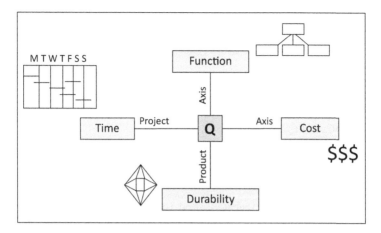

Figure 8.5 The quality quadrant tradeoff model

be made more complicated by listing factors, but it serves its purpose as a foil for a useful conversation with the client before the project starts.

In this model, quality is defined as an intersection of project requirements on one axis, and product requirements on the second axis. These high-level requirements, or objectives, act as the quality drivers for the project as a whole. Product quality is broadly defined as functionality and durability, and project quality is represented by the accomplishment of cost and schedule targets. Thus, quality is experienced when trade-offs between functionality, durability, time, and cost are adjusted for optimum customer satisfaction.

The model can be animated to show how perceptions of the significance of each point on the quadrant can be at variance. It can also be used to facilitate discussion on the trade-off of factors that might be required in order to accomplish the prime objective. If an adjustment is made, e.g., to durability, and the client dislikes the impact of the adjustment on cost, then a checklist of factors can be referenced to decide what should be added or deleted.

The cost of quality

Philip Crosby in his book *Quality Is Free* conceptualized the total cost of quality, meaning the costs of both defect prevention and defect occurrence. Crosby asserts that quality over the long haul is free because the savings from reducing rework, warranty, and maintenance costs (costs of non-conformance) outweigh the costs of defect prevention such as procedures, training staff, developing standards, and subjecting deliverables to inspections and reviews (cost of conformance). Perhaps Crosby should have called his book *Quality Is an Investment,* because the vendor PM needs a project budget for the indisputable costs of quality but the customer reaps the benefits of reduced maintenance and increased sales (for example) long after the project is over.

The value of the Cost of Quality (COQ) model is that it can be used to evaluate the questions: How much quality is enough, and how much quality is too much? These are valid questions, and challenge the assumption that the more quality, the better. The model states:

Cost of Quality = Cost of Conformance + Cost of Non-conformance.

Crosby's model is intriguing and opens up some lines of thought, but his terminology is unusual and needs to be related to the standard project terminology of QC and QA.

Quality Control (QC)–Established to find and correct defects and detect design drift. Close approximation to cost of non-conformance (CONC), though, omits post-project costs.

Quality Assurance (QA)–Established to prevent defects, such as procedures, standards, training, and methods. Close approximation to cost of conformance (COC).

Following Crosby's model, it is therefore reasonable to assume:

Project Quality Costs = Cost of QA + Cost of QC.

Figure 8.6 can be interpreted as showing the QA and QC cost curves for a hypothetical project. The curves are reciprocal—spending more on one reduces the costs of the other. This is a classic problem in cost optimization, solved in operations research mathematics by summing the curves and demonstrating that the optimum cost is where the two curves intersect.

This model also demonstrates the law of diminishing returns—spending progressively more on QA produces vanishingly small gains. The optimum or minimum cost point is when QA costs equal QC costs. In practice, few firms measure project costs for QA and QC accurately, though most experienced vendor PMs can roughly evaluate these costs. The ROT suggested by Crosby's model is that the optimum value for quality is to keep them broadly balanced.

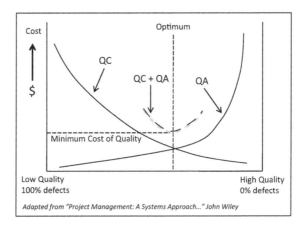

Figure 8.6 Optimizing project quality costs

The quality plan

The Quality Plan is where the vendor PM records the findings and decisions elicited by the modeling of quality for the project and any extant quality standards in the customer's environment. The Quality Plan represents the vendor PM's commitment to quality. It defines what QC and QA techniques will be applied, and the quality records to be maintained. The plan must be pragmatic and achievable, or it will fail before it starts. Often, the Quality Plan is an integral part of the overall SOW. It may be as short as a few paragraphs, or may be a comprehensive stand-alone report.

Quality in projects does not happen by accident. It happens as a result of planning decisions made by the client, the vendor PM and practitioners, who may have differing perspectives on the relative value of quality methods. Variables include the size of project, the technical issues, the relationship of the project to other work, and the client's quality objectives and priorities. As decisions are made and trade-offs are negotiated the vendor PM should recall that professionalism requires a basic standard to be met. Ultimately, the Quality Plan defines the level of quality management judged appropriate for the project.

There are two suggested formats for capturing the Quality Plan. The first is a traditional report format using a customized template adapted to the type of project. The second is a checklist, very efficient to use and easy to review. The firm, as part of their quality support role, should prepare templates for both these formats and issue guidelines for their use. The examples that follow are drawn from experience but are not necessarily applicable to all projects.

Quality plan report format

This template represents a comprehensive format suitable for a stand-alone report for a project with extensive quality requirements:

Quality Goal and Supporting Strategy. The client's overarching goal of quality, and key elements of the strategy. Strategy might highlight items such as methodology, requirement for cost/benefit, critical alternatives and decision points such as checkpoints, unusual roles or use of subcontractors, any special emphasis on document reviews and approvals.

Quality Objectives. Quality objectives should be specific and measurable. Reference to critical and agreed quality factors in the product is appropriate, but the details are migrated to the product specifications report.

Organizational Roles and Responsibilities. This starts with a clear statement that the vendor PM is responsible for quality, in line with the agreements and funding supplied by the sponsor. Specific aspects of responsibility for quality are usually delegated to senior practitioners and client personnel.

Training Requirements. Practitioners in certain project roles will be expected to have training or certification to a required level. Plans that rectify training deficiencies are identified. Project-specific training, such as new team member induction, is identified.

Documentation and Records. Identification of project documents that are critical for quality (typical examples—design specifications, technical specifications) and important characteristics of those documents required to ensure quality. Quality records include briefer documents with significance for quality such as approvals or review minutes.

Procedures. Definition of procedures to be adopted by the project to ensure quality. Typical examples include handling issues, changes, decisions, reviews, testing, inspection, audits, status reporting, approvals, and sign-offs.

Quality Tools, Techniques, and Checklists. Identification of specific QA/QC techniques that will be used on the project and an identification of the types of problems to be solved and when they would be applied.

Metrics. Identification of quality metrics and associated record-keeping that are indicative of progress towards objectives, or are representative of quality performance on the project as a whole. Typical examples might include measurements of errors, defects, complaints, rework, breakages, rejects, unresolved issues, pending change requests, and counts of any events deemed relevant.

Budget. As with all plans, the quality plan enables estimation of schedule, effort, and resource requirements associated with quality activities. The plan includes estimates of QA/QC efforts and the responsible resources.

This comprehensive format suggests a scenario where the client has expressed specific quality requirements. The vendor PM could well be counting on support from the firm to prepare this report and assist with its implementation. If a basic approach to quality planning is more appropriate, the checklist is the way to go.

Quality plan checklist format

The utility of a checklist is to present all methods that the firm's experts have concluded add to the quality of a family of projects executed by the firm. They can then be reviewed and selected as appropriate. It is tailored to an application area and needs effort for its development. Table 8.2 is based on methods from the software development world and lists guidance on what might be included in the checklist.

The checklist could be expanded to include a sign-off for the vendor PM, and anyone in the firm carrying QMS responsibility.

Quality techniques

A technical discourse on quality techniques is not entirely within the scope of this guide, but to support the important work of the vendor PM in preparation of the quality plan, especially if using the checklist approach, I am including overview information in Table 8.3. The specifics of QA/QC are linked to the nature of the application, so for this section I have drawn on a background in software development.

Table 8.2 Guide to development of a quality plan checklist

Guide to a quality plan checklist	
Quality method	Guidance
1 Deliverable review plan	Create a checklist of all deliverables for the firm's typical projects, e.g., Reqts Specs, Design Specs, Test Plan, etc. Those checked for the project must state deliverable title, draft date, due date, reviewer.
2 QA reviews	QA reviews are appropriate on larger projects, every 3 months. If checked, state planned dates, reviewer.
3 QA audit	QA audits use third party reviewers and raise formal CAR reports. Might be unusual in a basic QMS. If checked, state planned date, auditor.
4 Methodology	Selection of methodology can influence quality. If checked, list lifecycle phases.
5 Standards	List any corporate, local, national or international standards that must be followed.
6 Planned re-use	Re-use of existing proven material is a reliable method to reduce embedded defects. If checked, list software, utilities, documents.
7 Quality tools	Examples would include automated test tools, test case generators, configuration management, requirements management, etc. If checked, list existing or acquired hardware or software products.
8 Major checkpoints	Anticipate and record formal points in the plan for client assessments. If checked, list, dates, participants, decision.
9 Quality techniques	Create a checklist of QA/QC techniques supported by the firm. Table 8.3 shows techniques that could be considered.
10 Quality records	Create a checklist of quality records used by the firm. Table 8.4 shows QR that could be considered.
11 Metrics	Create a checklist of typical project metrics.
12 Date of next Q plan update	List date. The checklist should be reviewed and revised at appropriate intervals during the project.

The checklist is structured as QC, QA, and Generic. In practice, these distinctions are often fuzzy, and in any case, much of industry does not abide by these formal definitions. The important point is understanding the applicability of the technique, and not debating whether it is QA or QC.

One point of theory that can contribute to appreciating the objectives of QA/QC and help in correct selection is the distinction between the terms 'error' and 'defect'. In casual discussion, the distinction is seldom drawn, but these are the best definitions in the context of quality management and their usage in this guide:

Defect—A failure, or deviation of the product from the technical specification, that requires rectification and rework. Usually applies to the result or the product, but can also apply to subassemblies and components specifically if they are subcontracted.

Table 8.3 Quality assurance and quality control checklist

	QA/QC techniques checklist		
No.	QC technique	QA technique	Generic technique
1	Acceptance criteria	Checklists	Brainstorming
2	Acceptance testing	Checkpoints	Cause and effect diagram
3	Component (unit) testing	Commonality	Cost/benefit analysis
4	Deliverable review	Deliverable definition	Decision matrix
5	Inspection	Design	Deployment flowchart
6	Integration testing	Grade of material	Metrics
7	Interface testing	Instruction manual	Nominal group technique
8	Performance testing	Methodology	Pareto chart (80/20)
9	Regression testing	Performance standards	Scatter (correlation) diagram
10	Statistical sampling	Procedures	
11	Stress (destructive) testing	Product handover	
12	System (product) testing	Quality audit	
13	Trend analysis	Requirements specifications	
14	Walkthrough	Reusability	
15		Roles and responsibilities	
16		Standards	
17		Teamwork culture	
18		Training	

Error–A mistake, a correctable misunderstanding, a detectable deviation from requirements specifications, standards, procedures, that can be corrected before the product is built. Usually applies to interim deliverables.

An objective of QC is to find and then fix defects and errors. The QC techniques Table 8.3, though drawn from experience in software, is not particularly specialized and, with one or two exceptions, might be transferrable to other application areas. It is open for debate whether techniques more oriented to finding errors are QC or QA. I included them in the QC list. They are listed in alphabetical sequence.

An objective of QA is to prevent defects and errors. Casting the net widely in such a cause seems reasonable, and so the QA list in Table 8.3 contains elements that might be considered project attributes rather than techniques, but are influential on quality. They are listed in alphabetical sequence.

The techniques in the generic list in Table 8.3 are used for project problem-solving and decision-making and have a bearing on quality. They may serve either QC or QA purposes. There is a long list out there—these are the most likely to be useful in typical projects. They are listed in alphabetical sequence.

Table 8.4 Quality records checklist

Quality records checklist			
1	Change log	9	Issues log
2	Completed checklists	10	Measurement logs
3	Corrective action request (CAR)	11	Project sign-off
4	Customer satisfaction survey	12	Requirements traceability matrix
5	Deliverable approval	13	Review comments, or review report
6	Discrepancy report	14	Test results
7	Evaluation form	15	Tracking forms
8	Handover report	16	Walkthrough minutes

An additional checklist for quality records kept during the project is shown in Table 8.4. Quality records are declared in the quality plan. These records are mainly used for QA/QC analysis, to support continuous improvement, and to help maintain project control. Some are also important to retain as proof of certain events, of approvals, and for reference during an audit.

Commitment and motivation

In this concluding section, the people side of the quality triangle is examined in more detail. This covers the nature of the management commitment and organization required, and how to obtain the very best performance from employees.

The nature of commitment

Quality implementation must come top-down. There are many reasons for this, but a few stand out. First, without clear direction from the top, quality anarchy will prevail. Each project will deal with the issue in haphazard fashion.

Secondly, even though the 'customer pays' principle protects the firm from unfunded project quality commitments, there is an investment needed for infrastructure, and that is management's responsibility. For a smaller firm, this need not be a major cost item. There is some necessary development work to be done on the basic QMS so that the vendor PM is not starting from scratch, but most of the ongoing cost is the support for quality, and that is definitely an item that can evolve as the firm grows.

Third, however it's sliced, extra work is needed when quality is addressed, even though there may be a payback later. Employees are smart enough to realize that extra work not mandated by senior management is looking awfully optional.

The commitment of management to the quality path must be evident, both in their willingness to fund the initiative and in their own behavior. The vendor PM wants his firm's management at his side when he realizes that implementation of a true quality environment on the project may require some level of culture change. Even the most charismatic of PMs may find that a tall order.

What do I mean by culture change? Examples of observed team behavior will illustrate the nature of the change that might be needed:

Example 1. The response to a new request to review a document before release to the client is indicative. If the reactions were defensive, accusative, alarmed, or paranoid, that would suggest a warning. Positive and welcoming would be the good news.

Example 2. Introduction of a quality standard in an area of weakness, perhaps a requirement for documented, formatted trouble reports, may be welcomed or criticized. Keep your ears open around the water cooler the next day.

There's more to a quality culture than that, but it's a start.

Management roles influenced by quality

One of the elements of the basic QMS is definition of quality responsibilities. These extend further than office management and the vendor PM, but these roles have the most impact on a serious quality implementation.

Role of office management

- Endorses the quality policy statement
- Authorizes and funds the required quality infrastructure, such as procedures, methodology, training, templates, and checklists
- Empowers vendor PMs to prepare and implement quality plans
- Models and exemplifies the values of the firm
- Chairs a periodic meeting of vendor PMs (quarterly) to specifically review quality issues and results being achieved, as well as to hear recommendations

Role of vendor PM

- Responsible for project quality
- Prepares and implements the quality plan
- Plans, resources, and authorizes reviews
- Takes action on review recommendations
- Takes issues and recommendations to the quarterly office quality meeting

Advanced quality management

A next stage in QMS evolution is to assign a specialist quality manager. Up to this point, the day-to-day burden of quality management has resided 100% with the vendor PM and the resources she can delegate within the scope of her project team. The assignment of a quality manager changes this and moves the firm beyond the level of a basic QMS. The firm is now creating management accountability that relieves the over-worked vendor PM and, as shown in Figure 8.7, is organizing for quality within the firm, beyond project boundaries. This includes the creation of a Quality Management Council (QMC) that provides a formal forum for review of escalated quality matters. Both the quality manager and delivery manager sit on the QMC.

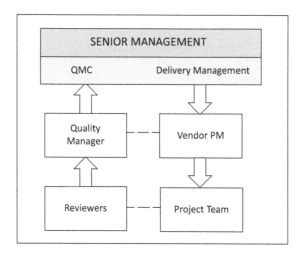

Figure 8.7 Organizing for quality within the firm

The quality manager organizes and chairs the QMC and takes overall responsibility for development and implementation of the quality standards within the firm. There is also a major project support element in the role.

Role of quality manager

Specific responsibilities might include any of the following:

- Active support for the quality infrastructure;
- Active QA/QC support for vendor PMs;
- Review (sign off) all projects' quality plans;
- Maintain a roster of internal reviewers, their availability, and specialization;
- Monitor and support progress of the quality plans;
- Check on the effectiveness of reviews;
- Periodically review quality records, or carry out internal audits as per quality plans;
- Provide support, mandate, and review templates for reviewers;
- Ensure reviewers understand review objectives;
- Discuss significant findings with vendor PMs;
- Provide consolidated feedback and assessments to the QMC, a representative management body that meets quarterly to oversee the quality agenda.

The emergence of a quality manager and a QMC modifies the roles of office management and the vendor PM. Office management can be removed from the immediate issues and the infrastructure maintenance chores. The PM can find assistance in executing the quality plan, and a specialized resource with whom she can raise quality issues. She also has ready access to a manager who accepts responsibility for quality matters that are broader than a single project.

Design for motivation

Psychological states that motivate

There is an abundance of literature available that theorizes on the motivation of employees—two classic authors are Maslow and Herzberg. The problem for the vendor PM is that the factors described in these theories, and others, are largely beyond the power of the PM to influence.

The attractions of Hackman and Oldham's model of work motivation, *Critical Psychological States*, are that the job dimensions in the model are largely under the PM's control, and the outcome includes the high quality of work performance that is sought. The model hinges on establishing work conditions so that the employee experiences three critical psychological states. This sounds forbidding, but these states are simple to describe and match our common-sense experiences. Figure 8.8 illustrates the model.

If employees experience an increased degree of these three states, they will feel better about themselves and improve their performance. The three psychological states are defined as:

1   Experienced Meaningfulness of the Work—The degree to which the individual experiences the job as one that is generally meaningful, valuable, and worthwhile.
2   Experienced Responsibility for Work Outcomes—The degree to which the individual feels personally accountable and responsible for the results of the work.
3   Knowledge of Results—The degree to which the individuals know and understand, on a continuous basis, how effectively they are performing.

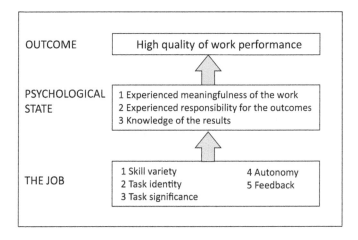

Figure 8.8 Critical psychological states for high–quality work

Most project managers would agree that these are states they wish their team members to experience, and through their planning, organizing, controlling, and leading of the project would seek to bring that about. In other words, these states match very well the natural objectives of project management.

Job dimensions that motivate

Researchers have also discovered five core dimensions of work that have a key role in establishing these states and they will outweigh any other influences in the workplace and effectively determine the quality of work. Every vendor PM, with some thought, creativity, and diligence, can design a project in which some, though perhaps not all, of these five dimensions are satisfied:

1   Skill Variety–The degree to which a job requires a variety of different activities, skills, and talents.
2   Task Identity–The degree to which the job requires completion of a whole and identifiable piece of work.
3   Task Significance–The degree to which the job has a substantial impact on the lives or work of others.
4   Autonomy–The degree to which the job provides substantial freedom, independence, and discretion.
5   Feedback–The degree to which carrying out the work activities results in individuals obtaining clear information about their effectiveness of performance.

At this point, the reader is probably thinking, surely bonus plans and other financial incentives have some role to play here? Yes, they do, but research findings on this issue are virtually unanimous, and it is not quite what you might expect. Rewards have an influence, but it is positive only on tasks that are well defined, and primarily require focus and a 'drive to the line' attitude. Tasks that require knowledge work and creativity actually suffer the reverse effect. That is, offer an incentive and people do lower-quality work, and most often finish last.

Motivation theory usually emphasizes that a manager cannot motivate an employee—that individuals can only motivate themselves. That is probably true, but we are extraordinarily fortunate that, as project managers, the nature of our mandate and of project work itself provides us with every opportunity to use our creativity to establish motivating conditions.

9 Managing the resource pool

Projects that operate in any setting—government or private sector, in-house or contracted—appear to suffer from one common complaint; an actual or expected shortfall in the required resources. This may be either in skill set, or quantity. If frequency of risk factors selected for the risk rank assessment were analyzed worldwide my guess is resource shortage would be near the top!

The usually tiresome cliché about employees being a company's greatest asset comes to mind again, because in the professional services, business people truly *are* the greatest (maybe only) asset—and they are the product. What is being sold is a service, and without someone to perform it there is no product. Everyone has a price. It is therefore unsettling to note that not only does the firm face apparently unceasing resource challenges, but resources are at the center of the business model. It is reasonable to conclude that analysis of resource requirements, current capability and productivity, and active planning and modeling would be essential techniques for every professional services firm. If a resource management practice is defined as the means by which the firm supplies their product, then it is surely a number one priority.

The chapter opens by describing a robust hiring practice and then covers the definition of operational metrics, a solid resource planning process for management, and supporting reports, techniques, and strategies. Topics not covered here are the softer people management skills such as communications, conflict management, motivation theory, negotiation, delegation, exercising power and influence, stress management, and so on. The interested reader could refer to Verma's *Human Resource Skills for the Project Manager* for exactly those topics. I am dealing with nuts and bolts issues and specifically those that affect the operational capability of the firm.

Hiring practice

Managing the firm's resource assets starts with hiring, and it's undoubtedly the most important thing the firm does. Even firms with a low-process culture have written rules for hiring. Firms that consider themselves agile take their time over hiring.

In every hiring scenario there are two perspectives vying for ascendance—does the candidate have the potential to do the job, or does the candidate have the experience to do the job? Then the key attributes of technical skill, personal skill, leadership skills, credentials, qualifications and pedigree are added. Finally—always important but paramount in professional services—will the candidate 'fit'? Never hire if there is a suspicion it's the wrong decision. It's too expensive.

The statement of role

Every job position in the firm needs a defined and written statement of the role (SOR). These are prepared once and reviewed and updated periodically, perhaps every year. The specifics are totally dependent on the firm's application area and how broadly their positions are defined. In software development, an SOR might be generated for the roles of Developer, Analyst, Technical Specialist, Consultant, Project Manager, and Sales Executive. Perhaps each has two or three seniority levels.

If the firm follows a supply-side model, it may be hiring to build bench strength for potential opportunities, but it is more likely that there is an actual project to be staffed. If this is the case, the SOR should be supplemented with a more specific statement of the planned project assignment.

Researchers into the origins of human resource productivity and high performance find a correlation with a complex range of indicators: past experience and achievements, professional or peer standing, competencies, occupational knowledge, technical skills, personal skills (including managerial and professional), behavioral traits, and personality. For most hiring, it is reasonable to treat this as a high-level checklist and to select out the detail requirements known to be important for the role. Technical skills and knowledge map directly to the work to be performed, and experience requirements are usually related to the seniority and leverage inherent in the role.

Personality and behavior

Regarding the perplexing indicators of personality and behavior, consider each of the following recommendations when building the SOR:

- Ignoring personality is a bad mistake, whether hiring a sales executive or developer. What is the best way to state these needs without a degree in psychology? One useful approach is to simplify the matter into organizational and cultural 'fit' or chemistry. The SOR should then identify the critical groups and individuals with whom positive chemistry is required.
- Behavioral traits are the observable manifestations of personality and can be neutral, positive, or negative in relation to the role. Referring to a checklist will trigger some requirements. For example, one role might

suit a natural skeptic; another role, someone who is painstaking; or yet another role, someone who does not interrupt or is patient and unhurried.

- If a family of behavioral traits is an essential role requirement, consider adopting a behavioral model based on the Myers–Briggs type indicators. For example, the Thomas System identifies four fundamentals—dominance, influence, steadiness, and compliance. Each of these brings certain benefits and values to the firm—how do these match the role requirements? The Personal Style model endorsed in Chapter 3 gives a different view of similar data and measures individual preferences on four axes: driver, analytical, amiable, and expressive. The model can be given a business orientation: strategic/creative, entrepreneurial/builder, organizer/improver, and technical/sustainer. How much does the role demand of each of these behavioral traits? The role fit with the model's measurements can be plotted on a diagram, similar to the example in Figure 9.1. This uses a spider diagram to show the role preferences, in this case primarily organizer/improver, with a strong component of strategic/creative.
- Although it is improbable that traits can be learned (or unlearned), personal skills can definitely be learned, though learning may come more naturally to those with certain behavioral traits. Skill checklists can help here, and examples for the SOR might be: must respond well to leadership, accept direction and suggestions, and logically plan the work to be done. Discussion on this is deferred to Chapter 11 under the topic of training.

Evaluation criteria

A well-stated SOR will lead naturally to the evaluation criteria. As guidance, keep the criteria focused on the important attributes already identified in the SOR, perhaps supported by checklists and sorted by must, want, and desirable. An example of a straightforward evaluation matrix is shown in Table 9.1.

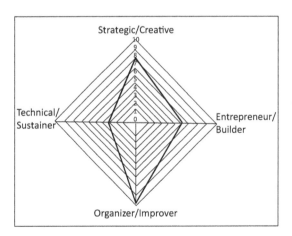

Figure 9.1 Criteria for preferred role behavior

Table 9.1 Example of a candidate evaluation matrix

Candidate evaluation matrix			
Criteria	Weight Out of 10	Rating 1 to 5	Score
Business knowledge	5	4	20
Application knowledge	9	3	27
Delivery of results	10	2	20
Communication skills	7	5	35
Relevant experience	8	2	16
Analysis techniques	4	5	20
Traits fit	6	4	24
Chemistry fit	5	3	15
Total points			177
Hourly rate			$195.00
VALUE = PRICE per point			$1.10
Best possible value			$0.72

The draft criteria should be analyzed to ensure they map to requirements, are objective or at least observable, and that it is clear how each criterion is to be measured. Questions should be drafted that provoke a response indicative of the criterion.

Be careful not to make optional or gradable criteria mandatory. A gradable item such as 'Experience' should not be mandatory, but highly weighted and then graded—better than stating 'Must have 5 years of experience' (what if a very good candidate has 4 years?). Stating that a PM candidate 'Must have PMP Certification' may exclude candidates with equivalent or better credentials. On the other hand, stating 'Must have RCMP clearance' would be an evident mandatory in the context of the project assignment.

Two criteria that may stray from being objective are chemistry, which can only be assessed as acceptable by co-workers, and behavior. If a behavioral model has been adopted, then a numerical scale that measures 'weak' to 'strong' should be plotted on each axis, as illustrated in Figure 9.1. When considering candidate assessments, these business-oriented descriptors should not be misunderstood as signifying the presence of skill or achievements. They are only measures of *behavior* that represent the individual's preferences; they magnify, or diminish, any relevant skills that are present.

Selection process

Once candidate submissions are in hand, a consistent selection process should be used, though different techniques can be selected based on the role being hired:

Apply a low cost screening process to establish a short list.
* Submit the candidate short list to techniques that will enable all of the selection criteria to be scored. Techniques to be considered include: interviews,

presentations, work product inspections, take-home case studies, aptitude tests, problem-solving scenarios, and references.

- Pre-plan for the interviews using a question list that probes the past, explores future potential, and is tailored for the role. Develop standard question sets for each SOR being recruited by the firm, though the interviewing manager can customize them.
- Conduct interviews following guidelines on who should interview, and whether to use an interview panel format. Panel interviews add a touch of reality, allow the hiring manager to listen more, and minimize emotions of all participants.
- Evaluate the criteria scores as a team. Note that the example in Table 9.1 takes a strong business view by calculating a value metric ($ price per point) based on the proposed billing rate for the candidate.

A carpentry rule applied to hiring—measure twice (or thrice) and hire once!

Guidelines for interviewing

Good preparation is the key to a good interview. Conduct interviews following these proven guidelines:

- Create demand at the start by summarizing the SOR and emphasizing the position's importance, and then keep 100% control by preparing and tabling an agenda, including the questions.
- Don't measure the candidate purely on a match with the SOR, but discuss performance objectives and how they could improve the role.
- The first question asks how the applicant's background fits with the SOR. The second question should ask candidates what they have achieved over and above the needs of their previous jobs. This immediately signals the primary expectations of the firm.
- Ask open questions and do not lead. "What are the most significant recent technical advances in your field?" is better than, "how do you keep up to date?" which is better than, "I expect you have to read a lot to keep up-to-date, don't you?"
- Measure performance, character, and personality traits in this order: first, measure performance traits (initiative, competence) objectively. Then, determine if character (integrity, responsibility) and personality (appearance, affability, poise) enhance or detract from performance indicators.
- Listen more than talk. The suggested ratio of interviewer to candidate talk is 1:4.
- A good candidate will possess self-knowledge, so for some of the more subjective attributes, simply ask the candidate. For example, ask the

candidate to draw a spider diagram showing preferences for strategic, entrepreneurial, organizer, and technical (if that was the model selected for behavioral criteria).

- Never make an offer until it's certain it will be accepted. Use the offer to maintain open communications. Uncover objections by asking candidates how they feel about an offer. Get a start date from the candidate before giving it and probe if they hesitate.

Perhaps this is more of a personal preference than a guideline, but I am a firm believer in not wasting my time or the candidate's, and, as most interviews go for an hour, if it's obvious the candidate is not a fit after 15 minutes of discussion, best to terminate the session right away.

Sample question sets

Behavioral traits and questions

Research findings suggest that a candidate's past behavior is the prime indicator of future performance success. Five open-ended questions have been shown to bring out key points of a candidate's behavior:

1 Aggressiveness, Confidence, Judgment, Discernment–Ask about a time the candidate had to weigh options to make a critical work decision.
2 Assertiveness, Self-Worth, Personal Values–Ask about a time the candidate had to take a stand on something and would not compromise.
3 Stress, Commitment, Intensity–Ask about the most stressful deadline they have met in the past six months.
4 Competitiveness–Ask about a time the candidate gave 110% to obtain a goal.
5 Mission of Service, Loyalty, Teamwork–Ask about a time when they went the extra mile for a client, co-worker or project.

These questions are adapted from a body of hiring knowledge known as patterned interviewing. This theory suggests there are dominant patterns in our working behavior and in the future these patterns will be repeated.

Project manager question set

This summarized set of questions for the role of project manager has proven reliable over the years:

Question 1. You have read our SOR for the PM assignment. Tell me how your background fits?
Question 2. How do you view the responsibilities of this position? Would you suggest changes?

Question 3. How was your last project organized? What would your suggestions be for our project?

Question 4. What do you think the minimum control processes are for our project?

Question 5. In the client environment, would you prefer to report to a more technical manager or a business manager? What are the pros and cons?

Question 6. Why were you selected for your last assignment?

Question 7. What are your successes and challenges with managing the client's staff and their contractors?

Question 8. Some design decisions have a long-term impact not understood by the decision maker. How do you deal with that?

Question 9. How do you keep the product construction aligned with the specification? How do you keep the specification from being incorrect?

Question 10. How do you control quality?

Question 11. What is your recent experience of working with a steering committee? What was the composition? How did it work? How could it have been improved?

Question 12. How have you worked with stakeholders in your last project? What methods did you use to minimize communications failures?

Question 13. Why do you like project management?

Essential resource metrics

Another pithy expression that I frequently quote is, "if you can't measure it, you can't manage it." It's a good guide to the limits of management, as well as an encouragement to get out the measuring stick. Some metrics can be cheaply measured, but others can cost substantial effort and should be subject to a cost/benefit analysis. The cumulative cost of the four resource metrics being put forward here is non-trivial, but they contribute to just about every technique of resource management invented. For people-intensive professional services, these metrics are the core of the business.

The metrics cover the work being done by the firm and the effort and resources required to do it. They are inextricably linked and are essential if the firm is serious about resource management. These metrics are the estimate, the actuals, utilization, and availability.

Measuring the work

The unit of work is taken as the project, or if more discrimination is required, the deliverable. Work loads the resource—too much and the firm is under-capacity, too little and it's over-capacity. Effort supplied by the resource is applied to the work and is measured in units of hours.

There are two aspects to the measurement—the measure of past effort, or the 'actuals', and measurement of future effort, or 'estimate to complete' (ETC) or simply 'estimate'.

The first essential discipline is a standard practice for capturing the hours expended on project deliverables. This is a function of the firm's time capture system described in Chapter 10. The second discipline is to capture the estimate of effort still to be spent on project deliverables. This is captured in the PM's project management tool, and also summarized in the PSR.

Knowledge of the actual effort spent, and the estimated effort to be spent aggregated over the work of the firm is the foundation needed for the key resource metrics and is also a fundamental of project management.

> If the project manager does not know the actuals and estimates, he might be managing something, but it's not a project.

Knowing actuals and estimates is valuable but does not go far enough. The added dimension is time. Knowing the timeframe for the effort spent and the effort planned in the future is essential to determine the historic productivity of the firm, and the resources needed to meet the future workload.

This can be illustrated by an example using a hypothetical project with an estimate of 10,000 h or $2.5M. Measurements from last month indicate that actuals were 400 h, against an estimate of 600 h. Thus 33% less effort was delivered in the month than was planned. This might mean trouble.

Another important time-related metric is burn rate. In the example, the project burn rate is 400 h/month. If the project is in the mid-range of the S-curve this might be a typical rate for several months. Translating the burn rate to priced dollars, at a rate of $250/h, gives a burn rate of $100,000/month. Do the simple-minded mathematics pointing to a 25-month project match expectations? The vendor PM keeps on top of her project not only by detailed planning and tracking, but by learning to crosscheck conclusions and reality check commitments using quick ROT and high-level project mathematics.

> Develop personal ROTs and use them to assess day-to-day conclusions and decisions.

Measuring the resources

There are two metrics associated with resource loading and they are the inverse of each other. The first is utilization, usually expressed as a percentage; the numerator is the project hours, and the denominator is the available hours. The second is availability, also expressed as a percentage.

Utilization is the time spent on project work. It is historical and can be measured for the practitioner, the project, and the business unit. Utilization is also looked at from a future perspective, in which case it is the estimated effort that will be spent on future project work, sometimes referred to as 'expected utilization'.

Availability is the inverse of expected utilization. If utilization for the next month is expected to be 80%, then availability is 20%.

Practitioner utilization is the prime metric, but aggregation to project utilization is also useful. Assuming that a sample project with a burn rate of 400 h/month has a resource allocation of four, there is now data for the utilization calculation assuming the denominator is given as 150 h/month per resource.

Project utilization = Project hours/Available hours = 400/600 = 67%.

This immediately tells the PM that she could increase utilization if the source of the 33% lost utilization can be identified and reclaimed. Note that if the loading was three resources, then project utilization is 90% and a different conclusion might be reached.

Similar aggregation sums can be done for each business unit and for the firm as a whole.

Resource utilization for the firm

Utilization tells the PM a lot about the condition of the project, but the main interest for the firm is at the business unit and company levels. A reasonable approximation for the firm is:

Revenue = Average utilization × Average rate × No. of practitioners.

This implies a few simplifying assumptions, but surely indicates the importance of utilization as a metric. This leads to important variations giving rise to the following family of metrics and associated definitions, which should be standardized in the firm.

Definition of utilization metrics

In most firms the chosen unit of timeframe is the month. These are the common monthly metrics:

Standard Hours–Hours available for work from the standard calendar.

Available Hours–Standard hours less statutory holidays, vacation time, other time off.

Working Hours–All hours allocated to designated time codes.

Billable Hours–All hours allocated to time codes signifying billable project work.

Total Utilization–Working hours/available hours.

Billable Utilization–Billable hours/available hours.

Other Utilizations–Of interest are sales, training, and admin utilization.

There are alternative preferences for these definitions. For example, some prefer the utilization percentages with the denominator as working hours, rather than available hours, to constrain all percentages to 100% or less. I prefer to see the possibility of greater than 100%, as this is indicative of overtime.

These metrics can now be tuned to planning numbers that reflect the firm's business model. For example, the sales force may be either self-sufficient or may rely on billable practitioners for occasional sales assistance. The latter scenario might reduce average billable targets by, say, 15%. If the firm's quality policy is to provide 15 days of training per year, then billable targets must be reduced again by an average of 7%. These metrics can be reported for the business unit and monitored by management for exceptions to the normal range.

> Never forget that billable utilization is correlated to revenue.

Resource planning

Resource management and planning are the most important parts of a professional services manager's (PSM's) job. PSMs could be regarded as resource managers, responsible for the efficient utilization of their practitioners. The annual planning effort sets the stage for balanced utilization during the year, but is highly dependent on the forecast of the sales executives and any constraints or requirements from the firm's business plan. Resource plans are inherently variable and require monthly review and reforecast.

Annual plan

The PSM creates a resource plan in conjunction with the annual business plan that provides sales forecasts and budgets. The resource plan is based on assumptions about the work remaining on existing projects and the timing and resources required for new projects. The plan usually identifies:

Headcount–The planned headcount for the PSM's unit, planned changes during the year (new hires, layoffs), and the triggering events for the changes to occur.

Contractors–The planned use of sub-contractors.

Billing Rates–Adjustment of the firm's billing rates by level according to market analysis and internal cost review.

Rate Table–The rate table, updated to include all practitioners, each allocated into billing levels and standard costs provided by Finance for each billing level.

Billable Target–A billable utilization target calculated for each practitioner, for each business unit, and for the firm overall.

This resource plan and planned annual utilization should broadly reconcile with the annual business plan including services revenue and the margin plan. The most useful format for going forward with the resource plan is a list of practitioners by business unit as shown in Table 9.2 that can be easily updated during the monthly forecast.

Monthly forecast

The resource plan is updated with a revised utilization forecast on a periodic basis. Usually, this is done as part of a monthly analysis. The forecast is a rule-of-thumb assessment based on the PSM's knowledge of upcoming contracts and sales activity.

Forecasting factors

When preparing a forecast, the following factors are taken into account:

• Confirmed contracts
• Business outlook and possible contracts
• Practitioner's utilization target
• Recent year-to-date utilization history
• Special situations and risks
• Practitioner's available time in the period.

Forecasting template

Table 9.2 shows the generalized template for the resource forecast. The ideal is to list all practitioners in the unit, but some conventions are required to ensure consistent measurements when subcontractors or part-timers are employed.

Table 9.2 Simple resource utilization forecast template

Resource utilization forecast						
Business unit		xxx	For period		xxx	
Date of report		dd/mm/yy	Available hours		xxx hours	
Employee	Level	Utilization target	Committed billable hours	Vacation hours	Utilization forecast	Comment
xxx	x	0%			0%	
xxx	x	0%			0%	
xxx	x	0%			0%	
xxx	x	0%			0%	
Business Unit	xxx	0%	xx	xx	0%	

The template in Table 9.2 can be enhanced with additional information such as a three-month forecast, alert flags, and client/contract references.

Monthly resource review

A management procedure that complements the monthly forecast is for all business unit PSMs to meet in conference with the senior business manager. The broad intent of this meeting is to optimize resource utilization over the firm as a whole. The forecast from each PSM is consolidated and tabled for the review. The objectives of this review are to:

* Analyze variances in utilization.
* Identify possible actions to reduce negative variances, including resource loans to other business units.
* Identify ways and means to improve the firm's overall performance.
* Other resource-related issues of concern to all PSMs.

Trend analysis is used to determine if assumptions or conditions have changed and are significant enough to necessitate revisions to the annual business plan. Agreement is sought on proposed actions that might impact more than one PSM, and strategy developed to mitigate client issues that might arise. Reports that provide recent period and year-to-date utilization information are also useful for reference at the review, though the focus is on the near future.

Project resource plan

At the project level, resource planning is a part of conventional project management though not always done to the standard required for professional services firms. All projects, except the most trivial, should have a resource plan and be discussed with the PSM.

These days, it is essential that the project data be maintained in a project management tool, though, surprisingly, exceptions still can be found. A good PM tool can generate a perfectly functional resource plan from its standard reports set. The output should show the hours of effort (expected utilization) required per month over the time horizon of the project from each generic resource level (e.g., Developer, Analyst, PM). Naturally the near term (within 3–6 months) data are expected to be the most reliable.

Reliability of the resource plan is the biggest impediment to creating a practical consolidated forecast of utilization and the PSM must strive to get the best possible plans from her PMs. As the project proceeds, generic resources are updated with the assigned practitioner, better estimates for future activities become available, and inevitable stops and starts in the schedule are accommodated. The most consistent way to deal with these problems is to agree with PMs to submit a reforecast resource plan to the PSM for their project at the end of every month.

Resource management

Effective resource management relies on accurate information to enable good monitoring and decision-making. Some of the issues with reliable planning information have been acknowledged, and although automation of planning reports is feasible, GIGO will still be a factor. This should not be the case when it comes to historic utilization (actuals) reporting, and the PSM can expect a reliable utilization report. In addition, there are a number of supporting techniques and strategies that can be drawn on to assist with short and long-term resource management.

The utilization report

The source of utilization data is the backend of the time reporting system shown in Figure 10.4. As these systems also feed financial needs, accuracy of data is a prime requirement and procedures will be in place to manage and correct time cards. This provides assurance that utilization information is reliable, though missing time is always a risk. It is up to the PSM to ensure that all monthly time has been reported, approved, and is included in the report. As a broad check on this, all reported time per employee must equal or exceed available time in the period.

Utilization categories

Time is reported according to detailed time codes specified by the firm, and as part of the reporting logic, these codes are aggregated into each of the utilization categories of interest to management. These categories are—billable, sales support, administration, training, vacation, and perhaps others. A typical report format is shown in Table 9.3.

Table 9.3 Resource utilization report format

Resource utilization report											
Business unit			*xxx*		*For period*				*xxx*		
Date of report			*dd/mm/yy*		*Available hours*			*xxx hours*			
	Billable		*Sales support*		*Training*		*Admin*		*Vacation*		*Total*
Employee	*h*	*%*	*h*	*%*	*h*	*%*	*h*	*%*	*h*	*%*	*h*	*%*
xxx												
xxx												
xxx												
xxx												
Business unit	xx	0%	xx	0%	xx	0%	xx	0%	xx	0%	xx	0%

The data displayed for each employee is simple—hours per period and utilization percentage for each of the categories.

Employee anomalies

There are some potential employment-class anomalies to be resolved, best handled as follows:

Part-Time Employees—utilization is calculated based on available hours, but available hours are reduced to match their part-time contract.

Contractors—by definition, sub-contractors hired for project work are only compensated for billable work and their billable utilization is thus 100%. They can be listed on the report, but a decision is needed to determine if they are included in utilization metrics. (My preference is to exclude as they cause distortion.)

Joiners/Leavers—Resources who leave continue to have their utilization recognized in year-to-date reports. Adjustment must be made to available hours for resources who join/leave mid-month.

Using the report

Resource planning and management is probably where the average PSM spends most of his time. A reliable resource utilization report is essential as a window into the work of the unit. This permits utilization tracking at the individual and unit level to determine whether billable targets are being met, and whether any exceptional time has been booked to other categories that deserve to be investigated. The report also helps the PSM (retrospectively) manage approvals to ensure that authority table rules are being followed regarding time booked to projects, extracurricular work, training, conferences, vacation, and others.

The utilization forecast and actuals report are obviously of similar format and comparison of the data is clearly a requirement. Both documents can easily be expanded to show forecast and actuals by month and quarter, and year-to-date information. Automation should offer an opportunity to build more comprehensive versions of the report and possibly to merge with the forecasting template. Merging utilization with a periodic manual forecast to create an integrated actuals/forecast utilization report is recommended, though it might require custom development.

Techniques and strategies

Resource management items of particular note in the professional services world include planning for contingencies, performance, and career management.

Resourcing contingencies

It's a rare occurrence for the resourcing plan to unfold through the year without diverging from the expected plan or encountering unanticipated events.

In the case of more work materializing than planned, and the firm's resource review failing to identify an internal candidate from another unit, initiating the hiring process is the first option. Probably, and with good reason, the firm has a process that requires approval of the headcount increase. There must be some basis for considering the expansion in headcount to be sustainable. If it is not, or the market is too tight for hiring to provide a competitive or timely solution, then the PSM needs access to some contingency options:

Friendly Third Party. It's a good idea to keep an association with competitors in the local market, and perhaps even a closer relationship with firms in the same services business that are not directly competitive. I worked for a firm that specialized in contracts that supplied full project teams to the client and took considerable responsibility. In this case, I kept in touch with a different kind of firm who specialized in résumé selling and placed individual subcontractors with clients for a fee. Even though their costs were higher than an employee, having reliable resource availability in a contingency situation was reassuring.

Trap-line. Nowadays I suspect a trap-line should be called a network, but I still like the old term. These are people who are known already, who have traits that would fit with the firm, and whose skills match opportunities that occasionally arise. They are people to keep in touch with, who can always be trusted in semi-confidential situations, who might consider openings as an employee or contractor, and whose referrals are always valid.

On the Bench. The other thing that can happen to a plan is that work goes away. The firm's resource review helps locate work in other units, though if travel is involved this is potentially unsatisfactory with the employee. Even less satisfactory is absence of billable work and time spent 'on the bench'. This is the worst management scenario faced by any PSM. If real work cannot be found there are always standby internal jobs that keep people busy. (Maybe these days a standby Uber license is a good idea!) Placing idle staff on existing projects to provide extra 'free' help or to gain some training is another consideration, but never a popular one. Morale inevitably begins to erode and if the situation persists for 2 or 3 months, continuing employment has to be called into question. Often the employee takes matters into their own hands, finds another job and resigns. The alternative is termination by the firm, which involves a serious assessment of the employee's performance and value to the firm before proceeding down that disagreeable route.

Always have a management alternative and maintain your options.

Performance management

Performance Appraisal. This is the apex of performance management, supported by periodic formatted feedback, coaching, and career management.

Assessing an employee's performance is another tough part of the PSM's job. I have never found a manager or an employee who actually looks forward to the occasion. Perhaps that's why it's often poorly done. (Assessing skill levels and identifying a training program is a related topic, but is discussed in Chapter 11.) The firm has many decisions to make regarding the appraisal. Structured or unstructured, rated or qualitative, use of the bell curve model or not, 360-degree input, self-evaluation or manager only, formal or informal—I think I have seen all variants, and enjoyed none of them! But these are my recommendations:

Appraisals must be done.

- The process is formal and there should be a discernable link with compensation.
- Focus on results achieved on billable projects, linked to the performance chains described in Chapter 6 and the SOR for the position.
- 360-degree input is flawed so don't do that, but PSMs should seek input from PMs. Practitioners should be aware of this.
- It should not be an annual 'big deal' but more a consolidation of feedback offered to the employee throughout the year. Feedback adheres to some format specified by the firm to ensure consistency. It's a responsibility of the PM to provide this feedback, with the PSM generally kept informed.
- The employee's input should be solicited and voluntarily submitted prior to the appraisal, but self-evaluations for performance topics (as opposed to skills) are not a good idea.

Reviews. The PSM must make it her business to attend as many review meetings as she can. These may range from periodic project reviews organized by the delivery manager and attended by the project manager, to issue-related meetings with the client, or steering committee progress meetings. The role is to be there and to respond to resource-related issues and take away the requested action plans. These are also valuable opportunities to observe staff in a client setting and to ask gentle, informal "how are we doing?" questions.

Lifeboat List. Another very instructive appraisal technique is the lifeboat list and requires no participation from the staff at all. It is entirely subjective, informal, and opinionated. Beforehand, each PSM must prepare a forced priority list. Hence the rather morbid lifeboat analogy—if the ship is sinking, who is saved first, and last. Obviously, this forces hard thinking about who has the most value to the business, and who the least. The managers must then meet, present and defend their list to their peers. This can offer many productive insights, cause some positive changes of mind, and lead to some action plans beneficial to the firm that might not otherwise have happened.

Improvement Programs. Management's responsibility is ultimately the quality of the product and value for the client's money. Based on the feedback program, on the lifeboat list, on observation, client satisfaction surveys, and documentation of the performance appraisal, an occasional, necessary responsibility of the PSM is to administer a performance improvement program (PIP). This is almost always attributable to a failure of the hiring process, hence another saying from the HR business, "we failed, you're fired!" To be completely fair and to comply with government labor law, the PIP is an attempt at recovery, in which the employee is told clearly and in writing the improvements expected and the minimum results required over a defined period, usually three months. If these are not achieved, then the employee is terminated.

Career management

Management experts have said, "employees don't leave the company, they leave a manager." Although not always true, it's a strong factor in probably 70% of cases, and reminds the firm, again, to hire or promote managers with care, and to provide training. That leaves the 30% who simply leave because they don't see a future or don't fit the culture. The mature firm who has moved beyond boutique beginnings definitely needs to consider retention policies and should offer a clear explanation on how to build a career progression within the firm.

It's not an easily discussed topic, but inevitably the best career option for many employees is to leave the firm. Market-driven firms exist in a dynamic environment, and even technically secure practitioners decide to move to more stable companies with defined hierarchies and consistent work patterns. A background in a services firm and a string of good client references can offer very good credentials for an employee looking to leave.

How then can the firm build a vision of progression for those who they wish to retain? The most common and logical solution is to define skill streams (Developer, Analysts, PM, Sales, etc.), and then designate progressive promotion levels within each stream. Migration between streams should be on offer, linked to competence assessments and training schemes. The more challenging element is to assess and promote wisely into the management ranks; this becomes highly dependent on the nature of the firm, its size, and the involvement of owners, the executive, or the board. From my experience, managers emerge from either the ranks of project managers or sales executives. Exceptions to this occur more often in the larger complex firms who have moved into outsourcing, technical specializations, internal development of reusable product, methodologies, and maintenance or technical practices. These firms offer more obvious migration opportunities into management for practitioners with a technical background.

To promote career progression, the more typical tools of career management include mentoring, coaching, and the appointment of career managers:

Mentoring. Currently enjoying a trend, there seems on the surface to be a strong demand for mentors, except they are either self-appointed, or appointed by management or worthy professional associations to help the newbie. There is a misunderstanding about mentorship, because what is usually being offered is coaching. The employee chooses a mentor; she is not thrust upon him. There is no appointment or job description, and often the mentor is unaware he has been selected. The mentor is senior, established, respected in his profession, demonstrates traits that the employee admires, and is in a position to help. I can think of only four mentors in my career, and two were my direct bosses. This advice came from my first boss who always held my gaze such that his conversation seemed direct and convincing. He noticed my eyes looking away too frequently and weakly, so he suggested I look at his nose. It works. He rose to be VP of the very large firm for which he worked.

Coaching. The term comes from sports but now applies to everything, including life. Unlike mentoring, coaching may not be voluntary, and definitely addresses one simple ambition—performance improvement. This may be the ambition of either the boss or the employee, though hopefully both. It may also be the ambition of the team. In O'Brien's delightful pocketbook *Who's Got the Ball?*, the opening point is that every team has to know the game they're playing—thus the substantial coaching differences. Using the sports analogy overlaid on business teams, she explores the differences in coaching football, basketball, and baseball. The book is filled with coaching tips and techniques that apply to just about every kind of project team.

There is a structure to good coaching of individuals, as well as choosing both a good time and a private place for it. If both parties agree, then coaching can be provided by anyone who possesses superior knowledge or experience. Coaching happens on innumerable occasions in a firm with a good culture, and during a career, many people may act as coaches. Vendor PMs are ideally placed to provide coaching, and I believe it is such an important aspect of their job it should be written into their SOR.

My own experiences as coach have seen most success in dealing with problem scenarios related to the job in hand. My role has been to coach using a problem-solving method and assist with solution formulation, or to teach a specific technique and assist with its application. There were cases when the employee directly leveraged my own experience and knowledge to the benefit of her work and ultimately the client. This is why I believe the project manager is a natural coach for the firm and why it's unnecessary to build more career management structure. Project managers should be recognized more widely for this role. Admittedly, this is from the perspective of a large project-based firm and different conclusions might be reached if there are few PMs and an overloaded PSM.

Career Managers. In a worthy attempt to embed coaching into the firm's culture, one line of thought has been to appoint subordinates to the PSM with the title of career manager and assign to each a group of practitioners based on certain criteria. These career managers are not managers at all (that would be unaffordable), but senior practitioners who fulfill their career management relationships with other practitioners in between project work. There is more involved than just coaching, as it can include training plans, assignment plans, and performance appraisal, all of which must be approved by the PSM. The problems are that the career manager may not be interested, or good at coaching or, indeed, any form of management. The practitioner may not be interested, either. I remember being told by a practitioner very clearly during one inept session when I had this role that he was "perfectly capable of managing his own career." I tend to agree.

10 Finance matters

For many readers, I suspect the Finance Department (a generic term I will use for all matters financial and accounting) is a mystery. Numbers that were simple enough and made sense when they left the project come back in accounting reports that seem unrecognizable. This chapter is not a primer on accounting—that is not my profession—but it is an explanation suitable for vendor PMs of the relevant issues and the interpretation that accounting principles place on project data. This purpose will be served by examining a model of the services business, then describing the key interactions between the PM and Finance through the vendor lifecycle, providing explanations, typical problems, and examples along the way.

The role of Finance is generally in the background and not fully appreciated by practitioners, except for procedures they engage in such as time recording and expense reimbursement. However, the range of responsibilities important to the health of the firm is large, and at least includes the list in Table 10.1. Of course, only issues that directly impact the vendor PM's responsibilities are discussed here.

The department must also ensure compliance with GAAP (Generally Accepted Accounting Principles), its replacement based on IFRS (International Financial Reporting Standards, now generally implemented in Canada, United Kingdom, and Europe), and in the case of public companies

Table 10.1 List of common finance department responsibilities

List of finance department responsibilities	
Cash flow	Payroll
Contract processing	Project accounting
Financial analyses	Purchasing
Foreign exchange management	Receivables
General ledger	Records retention
Invoicing	Sales accounting
Management reporting	Standard costs
Operational plans	Standard rates
Payables	Tax accounting

in US jurisdictions, US GAAP and Sarbanes–Oxley (SOX). Enacted in 2002 following a series of corporate scandals that left shareholders and other stakeholders with considerable losses, SOX created a need for stricter financial governance and made corporate directors individually accountable for the accuracy of financial reports.

What companies need to comply with SOX? All publicly traded companies in the United States, including all wholly owned subsidiaries, and all publicly traded non-US companies doing business in the United States are effected. In addition, any private companies that are preparing for their initial public offering (IPO) may also need to comply with certain provisions of SOX.

There is a fine line between financial success and failure in everyday life, and this is also a red line for the vendor PM. Crossing it places the project into the dreaded category of bleeding project, which can rapidly consume profits from healthy projects.

> A bleeding project means costs can only exceed revenue.

In extreme cases, where other remedies cannot be found, bleeding projects can lead to bankruptcy. Unfortunately, just keeping on the right side of the red line won't ensure financial success either. The turning of a slender profit might keep the firm from bankruptcy, but it is not going to finance expansion, research, training, and fairly compensate the shareholders.

Modeling the services business

Figure 10.1 shows the high-level relationships between the common entities of a services business and illustrates the fundamental financial drivers of a typical firm. This may be a little more complicated than instructions I received years ago as a new manager that "this is a simple business, you must juggle the customer, the staff, and profit, and don't drop any of them," but unfortunately, the real complexity is in the execution and not the modeling.

This model prompts many questions concerning the health of the business today and the forecast for tomorrow. These questions might be:

- What is the aggregate margin-to-date and forecast margin for all projects?
- What are the revenue and forecast revenue for all projects?
- What are the costs and cost forecasts for all projects?
- Which customers generate repeat business?
- Who provides most of the firm's margin?
- What is the relationship between revenue and 'Services to Customer'?
- What is average practitioner utilization?
- What services are most in demand?
- and so on.

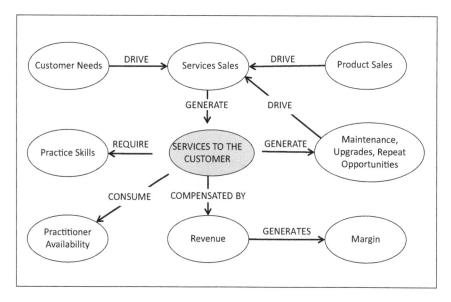

Figure 10.1 Entity relationships in the services business

It is the job of Finance to develop codes, structures, and procedures that allow these questions to be answered, and to sponsor or provide the information systems that give the answers. Many questions raised by the model can suggest performance metrics, or key performance indicators (KPI) for the business.

Key performance indicators

Examples of KPI for professional services:

Sales EMV–All sales opportunities expressed as Value × Probability (Expected Monetary Value).

Backlog ($)–Value of booked work, but not yet recognized as revenue.

Backlog (Months Work)–The number of months work represented by the backlog value. A commonly accepted healthy number is six months.

Monthly Revenue ($)–Value of revenue recognized per month.

Billable Utilization %–The percentage of time spent by practitioners on billable work.

G & A %–The percentage of costs allocated to General and Administration. These are thought to be more controllable than sales and practitioner costs, and although the target number is dependent on business factors specific to the firm, ratios of 10–12% are likely targets.

Gross Margin %–Value of revenue less direct costs, expressed as a percentage of revenue. Hugely dependent on the competitive environment and the firm's business model, but, on average, services have to run on margins of 50% or more to sustain an acceptable bottom line of 10–15%.

Comparison to Plan–Almost all of these can be turned into variance KPIs by comparison with the annual/quarterly plan.

The firm selects from these KPIs for reporting by Finance, which then form the basis for management's essential monthly business review.

During the bid phase

When the sales executive and vendor PM possess a good knowledge of commercial contracts and the firm's policy on what is acceptable, they form a stronger team and are more influential in client situations. A sound understanding of essentials such as common types of contract, rate setting, and standard costs of the firm, mixed with informed creativity, pays dividends when strategizing a business solution for the client.

Types of contract

There are three types of contract generally found in the services business. For each type, variations have been devised to satisfy the needs of the parties in particular situations.

> The three types of contract are fixed price, time and material, and cost plus.

Fixed price (FP)

Fixed Price, also known as Firm Fixed Price, or Lump Sum, is the simplest to describe, but potentially the most difficult to administer. An FP contract requires the firm to deliver specified deliverable(s) or services in return for a defined payment. Because the amount is defined, this type of contract is generally seen as shifting risk from the customer to the firm, though this benefit can sometimes be overstated. I have seen several situations where the firm has failed to deliver (bankruptcy, lack of resource or capability, *force majeur*) and the liability and the risk for the deliverable then return to the customer.

FP contracts require the firm to be diligent in gaining strong understanding of the deliverable specifications and hence the work to be performed. This is referred to as the project scope and is documented in a SOW. The firm must then protect itself from scope change—two sources are to be considered.

First, the client may change the specifications after the pricing has been agreed. A method must be defined in the contract that gives the firm the right to quote a new price that includes the required changes, or offer other reasonable alternatives. The right of the client is defined to accept or reject this contract change. An obligation to deal with such changes expeditiously is expected. Managing change requests is often challenging, as the original specifications can be ambiguous and the client's attitude is sometimes resentful of apparent demands for additional funds. He has paid his price and considers he now has a ticket for the 'all-you-can-eat' buffet.

The second source comes from under-estimation by the firm and a failure to allow for risks and complications that invalidate the estimate. There is a possibility that this source can be funded by a change order if the client was instrumental in setting the parameters for the estimates, especially parameters that characterize complexity. This possibility explains why skill and diligence are required in setting the basis for an estimate and carefully reviewing it with the client.

Time and material (T&M)

Time and Material is the most commonly encountered contract type, especially for smaller jobs or where deliverables can't be totally described. T&M means that the firm is reimbursed at an agreed rate for every hour of work provided. Thus, payment is based upon hours worked and not deliverables. Any expenses or materials consumption incurred as part of the work effort are billed directly to the client, usually with a small uplift to compensate for administration costs. (This practice seems to depend upon local custom—some companies, especially in US jurisdictions, will accept a 10% uplift as reasonable, others will refuse to consider it.) The risk for these contracts generally remains with the client, though attention should be paid to performance clauses and the possibility of withholding invoice payment. Another hazard for the firm is the implication of providing an estimate in the contract, or even verbally. This can create a moral commitment, if not a legal one. Care must be taken, as virtually all T&M contracts will be capped, or subject to an upper limit. The contract must be explicit that the only obligation of the firm is to deliver the hours to the value quoted. If the deliverable or services described in the contract are incomplete when the hours have been consumed, then the options are to either approve a contract extension so work can continue, or to stop work with the deliverable unfinished. I have seen situations where ill-considered statements have created such a weight of moral commitment that the firm continues work and finishes the job, but leaves the extra hours unbilled though still chargeable to the contract.

Cost plus

Cost Plus type represents the least risk to the firm, as it guarantees all costs will be covered, plus a negotiated profit. These contracts are more common for very large and complex endeavors, often with government as the client. Examples might be Research and Development, Defense Procurement, or Advanced Weapons Development. Costs are carefully defined and must then be tracked. Categories of covered services costs might include employee wages, employee overhead, expenses, administration, management, office costs, maintenance costs, and so forth. These costs must be fairly allocated between multiple projects. Record keeping is critical, as contracts will stipulate the right of the client to audit the firm (all books opened) and can specify adjustments and even penalties if inaccuracies are uncovered.

The profit component is usually negotiated using one of two methods. The first method is a simple lump sum added to the bill. This does at least provide some incentive for the firm to complete within estimate because overruns will start to dilute the percentage profitability, as the profit remains fixed while costs increase. The second method is to add a percentage of cost to the bill. This is most advantageous to the firm as there is no penalty paid if overruns occur, but, on the other side of the coin, no monetary incentive to keep costs in line.

Common contract variations

Within the generally accepted standard contract types just described, many variations can be designed to address specific issues. The following describes the most commonly encountered and their purpose.

Fixed upper limit (FUL)

This common variant of the FP contract, also known as a Fixed Ceiling Price, is often found in government business. The deliverable(s) must be provided for the price quoted but, unlike FP, invoices are for hours worked up to the price limit. Should the work be completed under the upper limit, only that amount may be charged, leaving "money on the table", as the firm's management sometimes complains. This is the root of the complaint about FUL; the firm must take all the risk and exercise all the care, as for FP, but enjoys none of the rewards of extra margin if costs are lower than estimated. Nonetheless, if rates are set with the necessary margin embedded (as they should be) and the FUL price includes a fair contingency, then there is little reason for complaint. I have run many FUL contracts with good results for both client and firm. In many cases, an FUL contract can be a sound solution in risk scenarios where the client wants price protection and will not countenance T&M, but is loath to automatically pay the large fixed price needed to cover the contingency deemed adequate by the firm. The promise of a lower billing if risks are less severe pleases the client, and should be acceptable to the firm.

Shared risk/reward

There are many variants of FP that seek to balance financial risk and incentives. The basic intent is to modify the FP agreement so that the firm enjoys less uplift to margin if the work is completed under budget, because a portion of it is returned to the client. This keeps a 'win/win' atmosphere in place if estimates originally accepted by the client turn out to be over-estimates. The common negotiation is a 50/50 split, which means if the project completes under budget, the firm retains half of the cost reduction, and the other half is returned to the client as a reduced billing.

There is another version of this to deal with overruns. Under this agreement, if the project overruns the FP the firm can then bill for 50% of the overrun costs (usually up to a new limit). The intent of this might be to encourage the firm to take on higher-risk work, knowing that the overrun billings will at least keep the lights on!

Variable rate T&M

In cases where T&M is obviously the right approach, but the client wants to impose some incentive for the firm to meet an estimate, work may continue after the estimate is breached but at a reduced rate. This continues until a new upper limit is reached or the work is completed.

Incentives and penalties

Contracts of any type can have incentives (bonuses) and/or penalties applied. The usual purpose is to reward early or punish late delivery. These are often set at a cumulating amount per day, which, if not capped, represents an added risk. They are common in application areas such as construction and sometimes sought by zealous clients in other areas not quite so suited. Application areas where they don't work include activities where there is a high degree of co-dependency. For example, in software development with mixed teams of developers and users, responsibility for delays may be ambiguous. A procedure for delay management is appropriate if penalties are in the contract.

My experience with these kinds of contract has been decidedly negative, and so I always try to eliminate such clauses from the agreement. They strongly militate against client/firm teamwork and sidetrack management effort into proving or disproving claims.

Payment based on usage

In specialized cases, the firm may agree to take payment in the form of fees or royalties based on usage of the product being built. This is only for well-capitalized firms, as there is a cash flow issue to be addressed, not to mention increased risk of non-payment. It could be an attractive proposition for the firm if coupled with a long-term follow-on operating and maintenance contract, or if the product application represents a strategic direction for the firm.

Joint venture

An even more collaborative form of contract is the creation of a joint venture partnership. This is encountered in cases where both parties wish to onward sell the product to other customers, each party contributing relevant expertise to achieving this objective in return for negotiated joint venture revenue. It can also be used to resolve situations in which intellectual property is a commercial issue. These contracts are complex and the financial benefit envisaged by the client is often over-estimated. They are inherently very high-risk, and the firm will be reluctant to discount or to defer significant product development revenue, which the client might request.

Inflation adjusted

This variation can also be applied to many different types of contract and compensates the vendor for inflation over multiyear contracts. The basic agreement is to allow rates to increase based on an agreed index such as the government-published CPI (Consumer Price Index). This is another reason to ensure that even FP contracts include a current rate schedule so change orders in current and future years can be calculated without argument.

Rate setting

Almost every bid—an exception is value pricing—requires clear understanding of selling rates (price), internal cost rates (cost), margin, mark-up (or uplift), and discounting rules. These parameters of the bid are embedded in the bid estimate template used for bid preparation and management review.

Hourly rates for price and cost are held in a rate table; an example is shown in Table 10.2. If the company is small then rates are assigned for each individual, but for larger numbers of practitioners, the more practical approach is to grade practitioners into levels matching the skills and experience that the firm provides and then assess a rate for each level according to demand and perceived value in the marketplace. This framework will provide five to ten different levels of resource that form the basis for a rate table. These levels, once designed, are rarely modified. List prices are set for each level and reviewed annually to reflect inflation, cost pressures, changes in the marketplace, and management's planned margin for each level.

Costs for each level are set using a standard costing techniques. Every practitioner has been evaluated and assigned to one of the defined levels. Finance then calculates a standard cost for each level based on salary and overhead of all practitioners at that level. The annual update also accounts for level

Table 10.2 Example of a rate table

Rate table—price and cost based on level					
Level	Title	List price/h ($)	Cost/h ($)	Margin (%)	Mark-up (%)
3	Project Manager, Business Analyst	180	100	44	80
2	Senior Developer, Tech Analyst	150	75	50	100
1	Developer, Tech Programmer	120	50	58	140

changes as the practitioner evaluation may change as she acquires new skills or moves from one role to another.

Sales executives must understand that the planned cost of the work is based on the standard cost for the level required, or for the nominated practitioner. The only way to reduce planned costs is to choose a lower level or reduce the work. During execution, actual costs are an entirely different matter. If the only way to staff a project is to deploy a practitioner with a higher standard cost than planned, then that's too bad. If the same amount of effort is required as planned, then costs will be higher and margins lower—that's the accountability of the professional services manager.

Although the rates are fictitious, Table 10.2 demonstrates a common principle of rate setting. Margin is generally higher than the average for lower level resources who can be leveraged by their more experienced colleagues. Billing multiples, a key factor in many firms' business models, are discussed in Chapter 11.

I have shown both margin and mark-up in the table to make the point that the percentages are different—significantly so. Margin is based on dividing price minus cost by price, and mark-up on dividing price minus cost by cost.

Thus, a 50% margin is a 100% mark-up. Make it your business to understand the difference, unlike one salesman of my recollection who was instructed to place a margin of 20% on a one million dollar subcontract. He interpreted this as mark-up, underbid the contract, and lost the firm significant dollars.

Standard selling rates are just the beginning of the pricing game, but they provide a benchmark for profitable business. T&M rates can be reduced and an FP bid may be discounted by a lump sum, but rules are set using an authority table to ensure management control of these decisions. Occasionally there is an opportunity to price above the standard list. There is no legal or moral reason why not, so long as the firm can argue (as it always has to) that value will be delivered. The most common vehicle for high margin bids is 'value pricing' that dispenses with the rate table entirely. Value pricing may have several interpretations, but is usually seen as an opportunity to include a re-usable deliverable in the overall bid, priced at fair value but estimated at very low or zero cost because the effort has already been expended and paid for.

Firms with multiple locations must establish interoffice rates for practitioners temporarily assigned to another business unit. Rather than negotiate each occurrence, a better practice is to establish a corporate policy based on a reasonable business rule. For example, the borrowing office reimburses the lending office for the practitioner's costs, but retains the revenue earned.

Cash flow

Finance likes to see every project generate a positive or at least neutral cash flow. This means that sufficient funds are flowing into the project from ongoing payments to cover the ongoing costs (primarily staff salaries) of executing the project. If not, loans from the bank are needed to cover the gap, and financing charges must be added to project costs. This is normal practice for large firms, but can be difficult for smaller firms or those at the beginning of their growth. I have known firms who have made it their policy since inception to avoid operating loans, and have successfully managed their business without them.

Figure 10.2 illustrates a typical cash flow projection for an FP project showing positive results. Cash flow is primarily a concern of FP projects. The monthly or more frequent invoicing method for T&M work generally keeps revenues in step with costs.

The main factors that determine cash flow are the frequency and amount of progress payments, and the nature of the cost curve. Progress payments on FP projects are usually tied to deliverables or to the achievement of critical milestones. Clients for larger projects understand the need for ongoing payments to be made and will collaborate in the development of a fair payment schedule which will either appear in the client's RFP or in the firm's proposal. It eventually forms part of the contract.

Contentious points include the upfront payment point and the amount paid on final acceptance. The firm might consider awarding of contract to

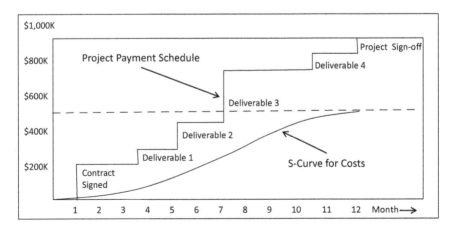

Figure 10.2 Cash flow chart showing payments and cost S–curve for FP project

represent a valid payment point for, say, 25%. An alternative milestone is the approval of the detailed plan for the project. Upfront payments are important for the firm if unusually high costs are incurred early, or if revenue from deliverables isn't generated until much later in the project. In such cases, the cost curve deviates from the classic S-curve and includes a front-end load, and there might be a long gap in the step for payment.

For final acceptance (not to be confused with holdbacks), an amount of 10% usually seems reasonable to the firm; customers think more in terms of 25%.

For small projects, with duration in the order of three months, these considerations tend to apply less, and there is one payment of the full amount on completion.

For budgetary reasons, a customer may wish to pay for deliverables in advance of delivery. This is less favorable than it seems, as although this practice helps cash flow, the amounts can't be entered as revenue until the work is done, according to rules of revenue recognition.

A last point on cash flow—in reality there are delays in cash requirements compared to the S-curve. It is simpler to estimate the curve based on the concept of accruals, the date a cash commitment is incurred, rather than the date the cash is actually required. For example, labor costs are accrued to the project throughout the month, but payroll must only be met at the end of the month. Subcontractor goods or services are costed as incurred, though invoices from suppliers are usually on payment terms of 30 days. Since the same logic applies to customer payments, also paid in arrears, both payments and costs should 'even out' so the S-curve approximation still gives a usable result.

Other financial pitfalls

Other financial issues can arise from requirements in the RFP and must be reviewed with Finance to ensure they are acceptable. These include incentives, types of bonds, and accounting technicalities surrounding the delivery of product bundled with services, all of which can cause headaches.

Incentives to perform

There are two common areas of client concern—apprehension that the firm will not bid or negotiate in good faith, and fear that, having been awarded the contract, the firm will fail to deliver. The first is dealt with through a device called a bid bond arranged by a specialized third party. The firm commits a sum (usually not very large) that could be forfeited to the client if, having agreed to bid, the firm does not adhere to the terms of the invitation including failure to bid. The bond may also include terms to secure damages for the client if the firm withdraws from contract negotiations.

There are several ways to incent delivery performance to the client's standard. A third party can arrange a performance bond similar in concept to a bid bond. Performance bonds may have considerable value, in some cases comparable with the contract value itself. Another mechanism is the Irrevocable Letter of Credit arranged through the firm's bank. Unlike the performance bond, this does not require the handover of cash to a third party, but does obligate the bank to honor payment should the aggrieved client present the Letter. Obviously, conditions that will permit this (performance/delivery failure) must be carefully defined. Finally, the most common method used by clients is the payment holdback. This does not involve a third party or arrangement costs, but is built into the contract. The client retains the amount, perhaps 10–20% of contract value after acceptance, so it must not be confused with the acceptance payment. The contract will stipulate how long after acceptance before holdback can be released, and the conditions for its release.

Apart from the bid bond dealt with before the bid, these issues are usually vigorously negotiated during contracting. Finance must be given a heads–up when they are unearthed during the bid phase because they add considerable financial risk.

Accounting rules on revenue

Non–standard, more complex projects can be subject to accounting rules that affect revenue recognition during execution and need to be approved by Finance during the bid phase, or the firm will be in for a very nasty surprise later on. I recall one case in which these rules were misunderstood, resulting in the possibility of absolutely no revenue being recognized until the entire project was delivered 24 months in the future. These rules are applied under US GAAP, or IFRS in Canada and Europe, and apply specifically to firms that are publicly accountable. A vendor PM working for a smaller private firm would still be wise to have some awareness of these rules as the firm may choose to comply as a matter of internal policy.

Unfortunately, revenue recognition is a complex and specialized topic. For example, US GAAP lists over 200 different sources of revenue recognition! IFRS, on the other hand, contains only very general (IAS 18 Revenue) rules that require more judgment from the firm to apply correctly. As a result, it is not uncommon for companies reporting under IFRS to apply US GAAP rules as representing best practice. Companies that report under both US GAAP and IFRS generally have similar revenue recognition policies.

Citing examples of revenue issues, such as bundled and other complex bids, involves a little more accounting alphabet soup. A common accounting reference will be SOP 97-2. This refers to the AICPA (American Institute of Certified Public Accountants) Statement of Position number 97-2, covering VSOE and multiple element accounting. These rules, which are only cursorily summarized here, affect internal allocation of revenue between elements and when it can be recognized. They target the following: bundled bids (mix of services, software product, maintenance, etc.); separate deals not explicitly bundled but which must all be completed for the client to benefit from the functionality; deals which employ a selective discounting method; and deals which include a future product for which fair value cannot be demonstrated (no independent sales have been registered, or does not appear in the sales price book).

> Complex revenue recognition is not something to try at home alone—talk to your project accountant.

There are sometimes ways of restructuring the deal to avoid the issue, or at least reduce the impact. Worst case, if the only way to secure the deal is to incur these rules, then at least the bid decision is made transparently, with no future surprises.

During the initiation phase

The assigned vendor PM is on-board by the initiation phase, and must make it a priority to assimilate all of the bid and contract documents. She must have a seat at the negotiation table, even if she is not a signatory. The PM will also be interested in the structure of the booking when the project value is recorded into the accounting system. This structure will shape the operational reports essential for project managers as well as accounting. Whether both needs can be satisfied depends upon the accounting systems capability—at a minimum the booking should record costs for each of the project deliverables as this will enable deliverable cost tracking.

Contract negotiation

Most work is performed under a written contract. In law, a contract need not be in writing for a contract to exist, but it's the sensible thing. Firms prefer to use their own specialized standard contracts because then there is no doubt about the terms and conditions being agreed to, but often the client proposes their own standard. This is often less than perfect, as the client's standard may be general purpose and not tailored to the work (construction, engineering, software, consulting) being tendered. Additional time must be spent agreeing the inclusion or exclusion of terms, and in some cases laboriously word-smithing the client's text to meet the firm's requirements.

Contracts usually follow a self-contained all-in-one structure assembled from a number of elements generated during the tendering, bid, and initiation processes. Figure 10.3 illustrates the structure of a typical contract. These elements may be combined in many ways, but are usually assembled

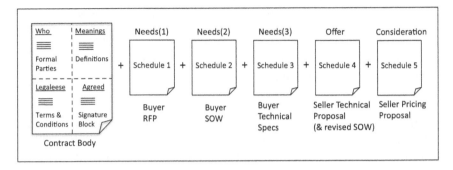

Figure 10.3 Formal structure of a contract plus schedules

as a naming of the Parties, Definitions, Terms and Conditions, and Sign-off block to form the body, plus numbered or lettered schedules.

When a series of contracts with the vendor are envisioned, contracting can be streamlined by structuring the agreement in two parts. The first part is a general legal section often called the Master Services Agreement (MSA) and is separately negotiated and signed. Then, as project work is identified and committed, a new section, or schedule in contract lingo, is added for each defined piece of work or SOW.

Overview of contract elements

The key elements of a contract can be grouped as follows:

The Parties. The first page of the contract declares who are engaging in the contract using proper legal names and any abbreviations used subsequently. A contract with more than two parties could conceivably be written, but is not usual. Subcontractors are separately contracted, and if the prime wants to ensure 100% flow-through of all terms, the usual tactic is to include the customer contract as a schedule to the subcontract.

Definitions and Preamble. Technical or specialized terms that might be misunderstood are usually gathered into a Definitions Paragraph. (The internals of a contract are always numbered and referenced as paragraphs.) A key paragraph to look for in the Preamble is a declaration of the Order of Precedence. This defines the hierarchy or sequence in which the contract documents shall be read to resolve a possible ambiguity, or even contradiction. Clients frequently insist on positioning their RFP at the top of the heap, so if there are two ways of interpreting a commitment, the RFP statements will receive precedence in a court of law.

Terms and Conditions (T&C). A contract may include 20–30 paragraphs defining the terms of the deal, and the discussion so far has touched on several of them. Most are mundane, but those that can cause difficulties for the firm have already been discussed in Chapter 3.

Schedules 1, 2, and 3 (RFP). An RFP (Schedule 1) describes the problem situation and type of solution required, designed to solicit the best possible proposals from vendors. Content includes an introduction, purpose and objectives, proposal requirements including standards to be adhered to by vendors, functional requirements, policies and procedures for award, and contract terms and conditions. The client may choose to supplement the functional requirements by appending a draft SOW (Schedule 2 for services) and/or Technical Specifications (Schedule 3 for product).

Schedules 4 and 5 (Proposal). Every firm has their own preference on the layout and content of a services proposal. The first rule, however, is to give the client exactly what they asked for in the RFP. Sometimes, for internal reasons, the client requests all pricing to be presented separately, leading to a Technical Proposal (Schedule 4) and a Pricing Proposal (Schedule 5). The SOW included in Schedule 4 is either the version originated by the vendor, or a revised version of the client's SOW distributed with the RFP.

Signature Block. Contracts can be bound with one authorized signature, though most firms have internal rules requiring additional, specific signatures based on contract value. Being a signatory means that authority is granted to bind the firm. These are usually senior managers and executives, but the actual names are identified in a formal resolution of the board of directors, periodically updated.

Setting up a new project

The financial booking of the project triggers project setup and is a collaboration between Finance and the vendor PM. Usually, three associated systems are involved: the first concerns time collection and approval requirements, the second, project reporting, and the third, client invoicing. They are influenced by the technical systems operated by the firm; namely, the time reporting, the project management, the accounting, and invoicing systems. A typical architecture is shown in Figure 10.4. The more integrated these systems are, the less periodic reconciliation is required, and the easier life should be for everyone.

Project booking

Finance has rules concerning documents that must be present before the contract value can be booked and counted as part of the firm's backlog. The determinant is usually value. A signed contract is usually preferred for any value because delivering services is always subject to contractual conditions that both parties want documented, but for smaller amounts a client purchase order may be adequate, or even a copy of the firm's offer for sale or quotation, countersigned by the client.

Time reporting

The time system is the bane of the services firm and sadly unloved by practitioners. The data entry requirements should be kept minimalist while

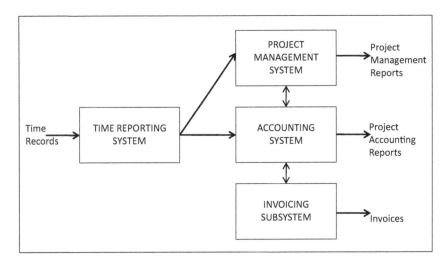

Figure 10.4 Basic architecture for project accounting

meeting the needs of Finance and the PM who generally requires more detail to maintain his project plan. Finance may not require the same detail, though the client's needs are also a factor (primarily on T&M work). Most accounting systems apply a pre-defined set of codes that must be selected by the practitioner when reporting time for project work.

The PM informs Finance about the practitioners who will be billing time to the project so the proper permissions can be set. The PM also double checks that the resource is booked at the selling rate as per contract (for T&M work). Any additions or changes as the project proceeds must also be authorized by the PM.

At the end of each period the PM reconciles values that are not processed though the integrated systems. An example might be subcontractor time and invoices.

Project management

Good estimating practice is to estimate at the highest level at which accuracy is possible, therefore that is the level at which time must be tracked. Smaller, familiar projects can be confidently estimated at the deliverable level and the vendor PM can still sleep soundly at night. In other, more complex, 'never-done-anything-like-it' projects, the estimate is at the activity level so the vendor PM must track time at the same level. Attention to this during setup pays off during execution when the project accounting report properly reflects the details needed by the PM to keep control of project time and costs.

Generally, more expensive integrated systems allow the most flexibility to set up projects based on PM requirements. Standalone systems are not so accommodating, being driven primarily by Finance needs.

One cause of confusion is setting up for contingency. Contingency work-hours or cost must be entered as planned costs during the booking, but must *not* be accessible to time charges—there can be no 'activity' called contingency. If an activity goes into overrun, time continues to be charged there until complete, consuming costs the estimator was farsighted enough to allocate to the plan as contingency.

Invoicing

Finance generally invoices on a monthly cycle for operational convenience. For T&M projects, time charges authorized by the vendor PM (or services manager) and factored by the contracted rate for the practitioner are included on the invoice. Some customers require time allocation at the activity level, or explanatory comments to be shown on the invoice; most are satisfied with the totals by resource against the contract. During booking, these requirements are established and set up in the system. For FP projects, invoicing is quite different. The payment schedule is defined in the contract and requires the close attention of the PM.

A wise practice for complex projects is for the vendor PM to double-check the setup before the project is opened for time and cost recording by running a preview version of the project accounting report with no actuals. The purpose of the check is to ensure that the revenue, costs, and planned margin match those agreed on the bid estimate, and that any adjustments from contract negotiation have been properly incorporated. In cases where technical accounting needs (e.g., SOP 97-2) have modified the revenue numbers, the PM must understand the impact and reconcile back to the bid estimate.

During the execution phase

A good setup during project booking should ensure the operational procedures during execution work smoothly and with good communication between the vendor PM and Finance. However, when project troubles and exceptions arise, disconnects are possible. Understanding these accounting issues helps the PM provide the right information and maintains good internal communication.

Revenue recognition

The pragmatic world of project management and the conservative world of accounting can collide over the issues of revenue recognition (more simply called 'revenue'), so this is a good place to start. Figure 10.5 shows the flow of the firm's lifeblood from booking, to revenue, to receivable, to cash. Revenue

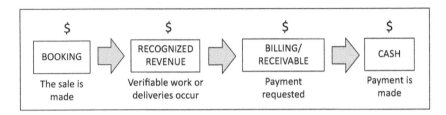

Figure 10.5 Flow of assets in the services firm

connects the booking to cash, and earning it is in the hands of the vendor PM. Sales executives get the booking and Finance gets the cash, but the PM earns the revenue (though the recognition method is applied by Finance).

Revenue earned by the project, hence the firm, is governed by accounting rules compliant with the requirements of IFRS. Some of these were touched on in the bid phase discussion.

Revenue, from an accounting perspective, is a very different transaction from billing, when the customer is asked to pay, or from cash, which comes later and is something you can put in the bank. Revenue is important, covered by rules, rather less tangible, and the vendor PM is in the middle of it. For revenue to be recognized there must be a reasonable expectation of collection. Finance can be expected to ask for evidence of this from the PM.

> If revenue exceeds cost, the project has a gross profit. Summed for all projects this gives a gross profit for the firm.

Revenue has the attention of managers, executives, and shareholders, and so it's important to get it right.

Revenue for T&M

When T&M work is billed, the revenue can be safely recognized if the contract is sound and makes clear the agreement is purely for the supply of hours worked. The situation may be less clear-cut if contractual conditions have been attached, such as assurances of quality or delivery, or acceptance conditions. In such cases, Finance may look for additional evidence before recognizing all revenue. In the general case, the presumption is that T&M work is billed and recognized on a periodic, usually monthly, basis.

Although T&M revenue is legitimately assumed to be low-risk, the vendor PM must remain alert to customer satisfaction and the firm's obligation under contract. There is always a duty to work in a professional manner consistent with the standards of the firm. If issues are arising, it would be cautious to suspend recognition as the customer may halt payment. Mitigations for such risks include securing a clear reporting line to the client project manager who is authorizing all work, having a reasonable scope of work (even though it is not FP) that can be tracked and managed, and devising frequent informal checkpoints for assurances of acceptable work along the way.

Revenue for FP

Revenue recognition for FP work is conventionally assessed using one of two methods. The first method requires the calculation of a percentage of completion (POC), which is then applied to planned revenue to determine revenue that can be recognized. The second method requires revenue values to be assigned to milestones, deliverables, or work packets and the revenue is recognized when the milestone etc. is completed. The method chosen is the prerogative of Finance, but it remains the responsibility of the PM to provide data for revenue recognition whatever method is chosen, usually as part of a monthly, auditable project status report (PSR).

The first method is known as the POC, or 'Percentage of Completion' method. The PM periodically, usually monthly, assesses the percentage of the total work of the project that has been completed. There are techniques for doing this, based on principles of earned value, and can be calculated in the PSR. Although this appears scientific, there is always a strong element of judgment involved, which is another reason to keep contingency in play. Contingency has the effect of lowering POC to a more cautious level as it is added to the EAC (denominator) in the formula POC = $(AC/EAC) \times 100\%$.

The simplest units to use for AC and EAC are hours and are widely used. However, some financial analysts believe that a POC based on project costs for AC and EAC is preferable because it keeps recognized revenue more closely aligned with costs. Differences between using hours and cost as a unit are only really significant if, for example, very high-value resources are used at the start of the project and then discontinued. The cost POC would then be higher than the hours POC.

The second method—Milestone (or Deliverable) recognition—is inherently cautious, and relies on placing a value upon project milestones. A milestone is a planned project event of significance, and is often taken to be approval of a work packet, deliverable, or group of deliverables. When the milestone is reached, the revenue is recognized. Referring to IFRS and the contract, Finance may conclude that if the client requires acceptance, then revenue can only be recognized when milestones are accepted. This would rule out the POC method. Using the Milestone method, revenue increases in a series of steps and usually lags behind project costs. To reduce the impact of this phenomenon, best practice is to make the recognition milestones small and discrete—such as work packet completions. Some of these milestones may also be billing points, but many are not, which is a reminder of the difference between revenue and billing.

A cautious approach to revenue is probably good, as the last thing anyone wants is a reversal of revenue. This is a risk in the POC method if not properly managed. Careless estimation of ETCs (sometimes lazily and incorrectly taken as the BAC minus AC) may cause POC to advance excessively. When the chickens come home to roost, the vendor PM finds that EAC has risen so precipitously that the POC takes a step back and, to continue the metaphors, this really puts the cat among the pigeons!

The opposite can be a problem too. The reality of business is that at certain periods of the year there is pressure to meet targets, and the search for revenue may land on the PM's doorstep. There is really no kudos to anyone in increasing POC without a rationale, so this must be resisted. Nonetheless, protecting the integrity of the project while at the same time staying sympathetic to business reality is probably the best posture to adopt. One reasonable negotiation might be to reduce or entirely release remaining contingency if the project is nearing completion and operating in the 'green' zone. This will boost POC by several points and for a small number of large projects might conjure up a fair chunk of revenue.

The method to use—POC or Milestone—comes down to a trade-off on the strengths and weaknesses of either approach. The POC method is generally most favored because it is easily applied to projects of all sizes, and yields a more realistic assessment of revenue, with the big assumption that the POC is accurate. The Milestone method is inherently more reliable because a milestone can be assessed as either complete or incomplete. If it is complete, 100% of revenue is applied; if incomplete, then 0%. On the other hand, the lag in revenue compared to costs may be unacceptable. The solution to the lag problem is to apply revenue to many small, discrete work packets, but this requires intensive planning and is cumbersome for accounting systems. A compromise might be to supply a milestone completion to Finance chosen not just from 0% and 100%, but also 50%.

Revenue for bundled product

If the firm manufactures or procures product for onward delivery to the client and the client requires professional services before business value is delivered, then the product revenue cannot be recognized until those services are delivered. The usual method is to recognize product revenue in step with the services, using the project POC to recognize both. Of course, purchase and delivery of product not requiring services can usually be fully recognized on delivery.

Financial procedures interfaced with projects

The bulk of Finance's activity during execution lies hidden from the vendor PM and is of no concern. The procedures operated by Finance that do touch on the project were discussed in the initiation phase, though during execution significant related issues can arise.

Time reporting

The vendor PM must treat time reports with utmost seriousness and with little forgiveness for delinquency. Time reporting operates on a fixed cycle—weekly is the best compromise—and everyone must be trained on the system. All time entered must be coded according to the established conventions and must be approved by an accountable manager, usually the PM. All staff must be clear on their duty to report all hours worked, especially those on client projects. It is the prerogative of management to determine whether all hours logged to the client are billed or not. This is not a decision made by the employee at point of data entry.

Billable vs. chargeable hours

Billable Hours–Most firms interpret these as approved hours worked on a customer project, or a maintenance agreement (which may be prepaid), within agreed scope and legitimate under the contract. They are therefore revenue generating, can be allocated to the project, and justify a billing. Billable hours can be sliced and diced in many ways for utilization analysis. A useful subset of billable hours is project hours—utilization that earns new revenue. This removes pre-paid and similar contract work where contract revenue is recognized using different methods.

Non-billable Hours–These are hours neither billed nor charged to a project, e.g. internal work, sales, absence, and administration.

Chargeable Hours–There is a distinction between chargeable and billable hours, which many firms find useful. If, in the judgment of management, time charged to the project should not be billed, they are classified as chargeable hours but not billable. Chargeable hours contribute to cost, billable hours to revenue. As an example, if the client has a sustainable objection to an amount of billable hours, the firm may agree to remove the amount from billable, though they remain chargeable.

It is the role of management to confirm chargeable hours are billable.

Billable utilization is a common measure of the revenue-generating capacity of employees and it is usual for an annual target to be allocated. In aggregate, they become a target for the business unit and a useful KPI to monitor during the year. The best definition, recorded over a monthly period is:

Billable utilization = Billable hours/Available hours.

This formula can give an answer >100%, which I consider a useful feature to highlight overtime. Some managers prefer to eliminate this by using 'Worked hours' as the denominator.

Expenses

Project profitability calculation means it's vital to identify and bill project expenses. There is another dimension, however—all practitioners want to be reimbursed promptly for their company and project expenses! Most firms are canny enough to link expense and time systems, so if you do one, you must do the other. This can be an incentive to timeliness. It is also convenient and common to use the same system for both company and project expenses. A 'billable/non-billable' code can be used to differentiate, or a separate section of the form designated.

Vendor PMs must be aware of the contract agreement concerning expenses. For example, expenses may have been included in the total fixed price for the project, in which case the amounts are chargeable, but not billed to the client. Alternatively, in T&M contracts and in FP contracts with a variable expenses allowance, expenses can be billed separately to the client.

Invoicing

To forestall potential problems, the smart firm ensures vendor PMs are engaged in the invoicing process. This usually means the PM reviews and approves a pre-invoice document. For simpler projects, such as T&M, this takes the form of a pre-bill list sent to the PM. For most FP projects, a facsimile of the invoice is reviewed before it is sent. The purpose of this review is to acknowledge that the client is expecting the bill, the amount matches the payment schedule, and the work represented by the billing has been performed.

Reserve analysis and loss provision

For higher-risk projects, or for any large project that experiences a significant risk event, Finance may exercise its prerogative for loss provision. Reserves may have been set aside for this eventuality at the start of the project, independent of contingency, but if that was not done or proves inadequate, Finance may opt to review and take provisions for loss on a quarterly basis. Although no one likes to do this, the result is a smoother absorption of unplanned costs rather than a procrastination until the last quarter when the vendor PM finally wakes up to the fact that she ain't gonna make it!

During the completion phase

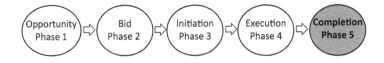

Financial anxieties during the run-up to project sign-off mirror what is at stake during completion. Concerns are particularly high if the customer negotiated significant holdback or a performance bond. The vendor PM must be prepared to supply accurate assessments of what issues might arise and what are the possible solutions. In most circumstances, the PM simply focuses on the accomplishment of project sign-off and presenting the sign-off report to Finance so the final invoice can be sent.

After sign-off, there are some important administration items to be completed. All deliverable and project sign-offs should be confirmed as filed. If there are invoice collection issues, little is normally expected from the vendor PM other than to ensure key records are auditable. The PM should prepare all relevant project records, such as copies of deliverables, change orders, decision requests, customer status reports, etc., for archive. This will assist the firm in the event of continuing collection issues, post-project audit requirements, or any form of contract dispute that might arise.

Upon completion of project activities, time reporting ceases and the vendor PM authorizes the closing of time records. Any subcontractors must also go through agreed completion or acceptance processes and their final invoices presented for payment.

Although the project is now complete and the PM certainly sees it that way, it always takes some time for final invoices, final payments, and closing expenses to flush through the system. At that point, the project is financially closed and the conscientious PM can prepare the financial analysis section of her completion report for presentation to the firm's management. At a minimum, the analysis includes revenue, costs, planned, and actual margin.

11 Building a successful services firm

Introduction to core business concepts

There is a danger that in my enthusiasm, I leave the reader with the erroneous impression that the implementation of a vendor lifecycle and assorted practices is a recipe for success in its entirety. Success is, unfortunately, not so easy. The methods described are, after all, only an extension of project management theory and practice—an elementary vendor methodology. I believe it is the right approach to the work of the professional services firm and puts the vendor PM and the firm on the right road, but it won't do all the running for you.

It is not in the scope of this guide to cover all topics that contribute to the successful services firm, as pleasing as that would be. Nonetheless, in acknowledgment that methodology is only part of the success puzzle, this chapter is a summary of the complementary areas of knowledge needed to prepare a services firm for business.

Supply vs. demand management

The firm faces a fundamental decision on how to attack the marketplace—whether to manage the business on the basis of supply management, or demand management. The answer is complex and is based on the type of service being supplied, the competition, the business cycle, the availability of hirable talent, and so on. Both strategies carry risks; supply management can incur short-term financing needs, while demand management can miss a sudden upsurge in opportunities and has some reputational concerns. A supply-based strategy is generally more positive for employees and for profits, and maps well into a growth environment. A demand-based approach means managing to the backlog, which implies a willingness to hire and lay off staff, or use part-timers and freelancers in the firm's workforce.

Balancing the organization

For the firm to operate at its optimum economic potential, it is essential to understand the staffing ratios that drive a properly balanced services business. Most firms define just three levels for this analysis: senior, intermediate, and junior.

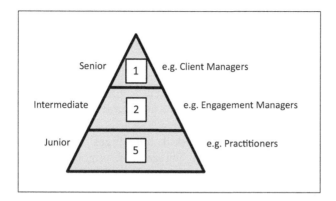

Figure 11.1 Sample ratios to balance a professional services firm

These are not job titles, but job titles will map to them. In the colloquial, these levels are sometimes referred to as the 'finders, minders, and grinders'.

Balance between these three levels requires a rule of thumb ratio based on the type of business, as illustrated in Figure 11.1. These ratios might be typical of a public accounting firm, but are different in other applications such as software development. In this example, for every client manager (a senior) the firm should employ two engagement or project managers (intermediates) and five practitioners (juniors). These ratios should stay constant as the firm expands.

Each level is characterized by an expected utilization and a billing multiple allowing the population of each level to be planned. As the firm grows, it is essential that these ratios be maintained, or the firm will start to encounter significant operational difficulties. Based on growth expectations and turnover assumptions, career paths through the levels can be planned. This provides clear incentives to employees, who can see a route to their career position. Frequent promotion from the lower levels also provides management with another screening possibility (screening at hire is the first). Employees who fail to be promoted a level after the implicit time period—maybe 4–6 years—often decide to leave the firm. This turnover is not always a negative, and may be essential at the junior level to maintain the balance.

> Too much staff turnover is a bad thing, but so is too little.

Client management

Services firms can easily lose their way if the hyperbole of sales and marketing starts to obscure the real secret of the services firm's sales success—skilled client management. It's more than just the ability to form a relationship, and people with client management skills justifiably occupy the senior level of the firm. Depending upon the details of the business model, people at this level may retain a personal billing target, but their value is in their skill at finding and maintaining clients while leveraging the firm's lower levels. Many factors contribute to this, but in terms of describable process there are three elements in play:

1   Diagnosis–The ability, as an outsider, to listen, to understand, and to analyze the client's problem and his needs and then to propose and persuade the client of the solution.
2   Interaction–This is a complex skill, but hinges on an almost universal need of the client for genuine engagement, ongoing attention, and responsiveness to feedback. The services business is rarely built on a sales approach that only consists of specifying, pricing, and delivering a product.
3   Trust–There must be a degree of trust between the parties, making integrity a vital personal attribute for meaningful diagnosis and interaction.

These characteristics mark a client manager from a salesman. A client manager also draws skillfully on the firm's practitioners and those associated with ongoing work for the client to create the concept of an account team. This leads to a practice known as team selling and, if led by a skilled client manager, is a very effective approach.

Billing multiples and the marketplace

This is the art and science of optimizing the firm's economics in a given marketplace, and with a balanced workforce. Regardless of the application area, services projects fall into one of three types, with sometimes a degree of mix:

Type 1 Intellectual. A problem is to be solved that demands brainpower, highly specialized or technical knowledge ('smart people').

Type 2 Experience. The problem requires the capability that comes with practice, with the knowledge of what works and what doesn't, and with insights into the many different circumstances that can frame a problem ('the grey hairs').

Type 3 Procedural. Interpreting and following a methodology that addresses the problem. Systems thinking and strong analytic skills will get the job done.

As a generalization, Type 3 Procedural projects have the need for less senior resources. Conversely, Type 1 Intellectual and Type 2 Experience projects tend to require more seniority. This model leads to the most powerful economic tool at the disposal of the firm—leverage.

Leverage allows the services firm to bill out their less senior resources at increasing billing multiples. The billing multiple is the ratio of the

Table 11.1 Sample billing multiples

Sample billing multiples	
Level	Multiple
Junior	2.5–3
Intermediate	2–2.5
Senior	1.5–2

market-billing rate for an individual, divided by their cost rate (including overhead). As an example, a junior whose costs are $100/h might be billed out at $250/h for a billing multiple of 2.5. The billing multiple for juniors will be significantly more than for seniors. Across businesses and application areas there is no standard, but Table 11.1 illustrates the principle.

Leverage is illustrated in the sample by the fact that juniors can be placed at 50% more than the billing multiple of a senior. This explains why seniors may account for, say, 40% of the compensation, but only 20% of the revenue. It is their ability to leverage a talented junior who is prepared to accept compensation for their level, but can be billed at a higher multiple because of the involvement of the senior. The client sees this as providing assurance for the work and giving him access to the firm's depth through the supported junior. The junior sees this as opportunity for growth during a period of apprenticeship, and the firm earns what is termed as surplus value. Examples of leverage at work are seen in Type 1 Intellectual projects where juniors are employed in research, in development of material from a senior's specifications, or inclusion in brainstorming sessions. Regardless of the project type, juniors must always work under the supervision of an intermediate or senior; this coaching and supervising relationship also justifies the surplus value.

> Skilled leveraging is the key to higher profitability.

Standard operating procedures

Proceduralization is not the theme of this guide, which instead emphasizes the flexibility of practices, techniques and checklists. The natural starting point for any desired procedure development would be the processes from the vendor methodology postulated in Table 4.4. To these would be added the financial procedures implied in Chapter 10 and the relevant responsibilities identified in Table 10.1, plus the remaining 'head-office' functions from the organization chart in Figure 5.6. Such a top-down development of procedures is an extreme, and would result in a very bulky manual.

The degree of proceduralization in a services firm, indeed any firm, is always a point of controversy. From experience, I can be positive on two

Table 11.2 Standard operating procedures

Standard operating procedures for the firm	
Contingency estimating	Leadership and management training
Continuous client satisfaction monitoring	Practice development
Contract administration	Project management and support processes
Contract review and approval	Project status and progress review
Employee feedback and appraisal	Proposal development and sign-off
Employee retention	Quality review
Employee skill development and training	Resource planning
Employee utilization and availability	Risk review
Estimates development and sign-off	Subcontractor management
Hiring	Time and expense reporting
Invoice approval	

points: you can have too much, and you can have too little! Certainly, the development of a full procedures manual is unrealistic. The solution is to find a balance point for the firm, and adopt a basic set of Standard Operating Procedures (SOP). One way to identify SOP candidates is to assess from the perspective of risk management. These are not project-specific mitigations or transference strategies, but are standards built into the way the firm does business that act to reduce risk. SOP can be regarded as a prioritized selection of procedures, implemented individually as point solutions rather than as an integrated methodology derived from a top-down process analysis. The list of SOP in Table 11.2 pulls together one view of the scope of these procedures. Financial SOP have not been included.

If these procedures are poorly implemented, or are suspended, collective project risk inevitably increases. Without rectification, the firm should not expect to sustain the project success rate for the long-term.

Delegation of authority

Most companies experience difficulties with regularizing a delegation policy as they grow from their entrepreneurial roots into an inevitable bureaucracy. Early on, the founder and owner makes the decisions and delegates informally, and perhaps on a situational basis. Over time, as the firm grows and a management hierarchy comes into being, levels of authority must be designed. The discussion on the RAA model in Chapter 5 gave the efficiency arguments for this.

A useful technique for designing and documenting delegation rules is the Authority Table, also called a Delegation Matrix. The table can be made as simple or as complex as required—it can grow with the firm. It is also unambiguous and an excellent tool for communication and management control.

Table 11.3 Examples of use for the authority table

Authority table examples	
Authority granted	*Position*
Approve discounts over 25%	Senior Business Manager
Approve CRs up to $50K	Project Manager
Approve project budget increase	Professional Services Manager
Approve bid with Risk Rank 4	Vice President
...	
Bid/Project situation	*Business requirement*
FP project is >$500K to bid	Bid review is mandatory
FP project is >$100K to report	Written report using standard PSR
FP project is >$100K and Risk Rank 4 or 5 to report	Written report for executive dashboard
...	

The first example in Table 11.3 shows the type of authority being granted in the first column, and the position in the firm that holds the authority in the second column. The first line clearly shows that a Senior Business Manager is required to approve a discount of 25% or more.

The second example in Table 11.3 shows a less common use for the table, but one that fits well with a theme of the guide—that a 'one size fits all' philosophy in dealing with bid or project situations is usually asking for failure. The solution is to design simplified tools or process requirements for simpler projects and to use an Authority Table to document the policy. The first line clearly shows that a bid review is mandatory only for an FP project over $500K.

Taking care of the employees

Despite its cliché status, and despite being endlessly dished up in corporate vision statements, the assertion that people are the firm's greatest asset comes to mind again. In the services business it really does deserve thoughtful consideration and action. On reflection, there is not much else on the asset register, and what does come to mind, such as the contract backlog and perhaps the firm's reputation (goodwill), rests largely on the employees.

The caring process starts with the hiring practice described in Chapter 9. The hiring procedure must be rigorous and capable of selecting smart, ambitious, and motivated recruits with demonstrable skills and a fit to the firm's culture. Although not always possible, it is best to hire primarily at the junior level and focus on recognizing potential, developing the staff, and promoting internally. This policy will contribute to maintaining balance, and the prospect of promotion is a strong motivational incentive for ambitious juniors when staffing into the intermediate levels. Compensation must be set somewhat above the average for professionals in all branches of the discipline, and carefully designed performance-based incentives should be available to everyone.

The middle tier—the intermediates—must receive special attention. The first reason is that they have now probably been through two hurdles; hiring, and the first significant promotion. The firm has an investment in their development, experience, and future potential. The second reason is that they occupy a unique position in the firm that submits them to significant pressure. Most people in the services business actually thrive under pressure, but that is usually the pressure that comes from contributing to the project—to find the solution, to create the deliverable, to get the sign-off—when there never seems to be enough time. The intermediates are unusually pressured because they must cope with time and performance demands from both sides of the firm's structure. As is expected, they are demonstrating their fitness for seniority by acting partially in that role, such as picking up some client management responsibilities. At the same time, they have not left their practitioner role behind and are still called upon for some grinding. All this, as well as minding the day job!

Augmenting the firm's capability

There are a handful of concerns that deserve attention, as addressing them is a prerequisite to integration of the practices and methods in this guide into the conduct of the firm's business. This is especially true of a firm that has reached a certain size and is encountering setbacks or resistance to moving forward. These concerns are: culture change, skills assessment and training, document storage, adapting the delivery management role, and leadership.

Culture change

Resistance to change is a cultural phenomenon and afflicts all efforts to modify how people work and how they look at problems and priorities. It seems to be a facet of human nature. It has been recognized for at least 20 years, and a body of practice known as change management has since grown up to address it. The project marketplace as a whole is still a long way from universally recognizing this as an issue to be dealt with professionally. I am sure many readers have witnessed large corporate projects struggle because the culture change required was lagging the project implementation.

The same trap can await the implementation of new practices in the services firm. Failure to change the culture predictably retards or even eliminates benefits. Furthermore, even when recognized and planned, changing the culture always seems to take longer than expected.

Examples of resistance to change

- Project managers resist the notion of a shared delivery accountability and the intervention of a delivery manager.

- Sales executives may complain about the lack of total authority, the intervention of a delivery manager, and the occasional conditional or delayed responses to the client.
- Sales executives resist additional 'paperwork'.
- Many, in particular more mature practitioners and PMs who rely on their intuitive approach, resist formalized methods such as consistent risk assessment and estimating standards.
- Reviews are sometimes regarded as unsupportive and vehicles for criticism, rather than tools of quality.
- PMs used to unstructured environments fail to support more structured tools such as the internal status report, and do not act as mentors to more junior staff.
- Some staff exhibit a degree of cynicism about the effectiveness and value of risk alert assignments (red, yellow, green).
- Senior management don't 'walk the talk' and only pay lip service to the new working methods.
- And so on.

I hope that those who have read to here will have little trouble framing rebuttals to these attitudes and beliefs—so I can move on to methods that can effectively manage the culture change needed in the organization.

> A change in methodology requires a change in culture.

Levers of change

Andrea Shapiro, in her book *Creating Contagious Commitment*, named her methods 'levers of change' and developed an approach that seems particularly suitable:

Lever 1 Contacts. Establish a program that encourages the advocates of change to schedule regular and periodic contact with an assigned group of those known to be apathetic.

Lever 2 Mass Exposure. Plan for communication events (primarily one-way) such as 'concert hall' training (rather than seminars), motivational speakers, mass emails, and additional corporate PR giveaways such as coffee mugs, T-shirts, web apps, and fancy screen savers.

Lever 3 Hire Advocates. Evaluate the pros and cons of hiring consultants from the outside to supplement existing internal advocates.

Lever 4 Shift the Resisters: Determine the criteria for removing or transferring people who are resisting the change.

Lever 5 Infrastructure. Establish guidelines for investing in infrastructure to support the change.

Lever 6 Walk the Talk. Establish a plan, and non-judgmental feedback methods, to help senior management lead the implementation by example. This would detail specific opportunities to demonstrate decision-making and actions that are consistent with the change.

Lever 7 Reward and Recognition. Create, budget, and advertise a rewards and recognition program such as small gifts with some status value, custom awards, dinners-for-two, and bonuses. Parallel to the program, encourage senior advocates to use thank-you notes, even words of praise and encouragement for good performance related to the change.

Before launching any major change initiative, understanding and selecting from these levers could remove the risk of proceeding based on the assumption of staff acceptance. It will also provide useful feedback on implementation progress by monitoring the migration of staff through stages of resistance and apathy to internal acceptance and explicit advocacy.

Management skills assessment

A large part of the services manager's job and a concern of the firm's PMs are centered on the skills and experience of the practitioners. What, though, about management skills? Because professional services is such a people-centered business, weak management is very damaging and difficult to fix. It is expensive to make poor hiring decisions at the management level.

Whether assessing a services manager or project manager, there are two aspects of management skills to consider. The first are personal skills, the second are leadership skills. There is actually a third class of technical skills, but that is dependent upon the firm's application area and the pervasiveness of technology. Technical project management skills are reviewed in the next section on Training.

Personal skills

Most assessments of personal skills deal with generalities like communication skills, empathy, listening, ability to solve problems, willingness to delegate, and perhaps even charisma! I have found great utility in a detailed checklist of 25 attributes presented in Table 11.4.

The attributes in the checklist are phrased in a style designed for self-assessment. The implementation method involves each manager completing the checklist and then discussing the results with their immediate superior. An alternative approach is to rephrase the questions and have the assessment done by the superior and then discussed. Perhaps a yes or no response is too stringent, in which case a five point rating for each attribute could be designed—1 for weak, 3 for good, 5 for strong.

The discussion will naturally examine any differences of opinion on the rating, but should also center on more future-focused questions and develop actions. For

Table 11.4 Personal skills assessment checklist

Personal skills assessment checklist

---

1 I accept accountability, do not pass the buck.
2 I am aware of operating costs.
3 I am responsive to the firm's leadership and act on suggestions.
4 I am thorough, but don't overwork the problem in terms of its value to the project.
5 I arrive at supportable, practical conclusions and decisions.
6 I communicate well with all levels.
7 I consider cultural and other non-financial implications in making decisions.
8 I demand high standards of myself and others.
9 I ensure that the team know their objectives and those of the project.
10 I exercise good judgment in directing the team and delegating responsibility.
11 I get to the heart of the problem quickly—follow a problem-solving method.
12 I give effective feedback, positive and negative, to the team.
13 I handle a large and varied amount of work.
14 I have strong convictions, but am flexible when new information is provided.
15 I know when to make the decision and when to clear it with others.
16 I logically plan the work.
17 I maintain optimum control over the team.
18 I make effective use of people and resources.
19 I measure my own and others' performance against objectives.
20 I plan and implement development programs for the team.
21 I require minimum supervision by management, follow through on my own initiative.
22 I seek and accept added responsibility.
23 I take calculated risks if warranted by the situation.
24 I value teamwork and collaboration, but understand when an alternative leadership style is needed.

---

example, one question might be, "which areas of weakness are holding you back, and what do you intend to do about it?" Another related question is, "which areas of relative strength are of most benefit, and how will you build on them?"

Leadership skills

In the class of leadership skills there is some unavoidable overlap with the personal skills class, but Table 11.5 lists the 28 attributes collected from various sources over the years that have proven most valuable.

I have never seen this list used in a formal assessment process and I don't believe it is suitable, but as an informal checklist to peruse occasionally during the rigors of a project, it can serve to vitalize and motivate a PM in a direction he might have been ignoring.

Performance management

It's impossible to present material on skills assessment without seeming to spill over into performance management, which is fully reviewed in Chapter 9.

Table 11.5 Leadership skills assessment checklist

Leadership skills assessment checklist	
1 Accept criticism	15 Influencer
2 Adaptable	16 Issue resolution
3 Awareness of environment	17 Negotiator
4 Coaching	18 Open and approachable
5 Commitment	19 Persists
6 Communication	20 Positivity—failure not an option
7 Conflict resolution	21 Professional
8 Credible	22 Recognizes potential
9 Decision maker	24 Results focus
10 Delegation and empowerment	24 Sensitivity to people
11 Experience	25 Trigger motivation
12 Follows up	26 Trusted
13 Fosters team skill development	27 Visible
14 Gives credit	28 Vision

There is naturally a connection, but performance management is a formal process and is largely concerned with the achievement of project objectives over the review period. It usually ends up with a performance rating and must become a part of the firm's SOP.

Topics for performance reviews can be adapted from the performance chains in Chapter 6. For example, meet delivery requirements, meet planned margins, manage team effectively, and maintain positive client relationship. Topics can always be added for evaluation, like stakeholder communications, use of PM techniques, and efficient project administration. On the other hand, I had a remarkable boss at one time who, when I asked for the performance review form, reached for the pad on his desk, tore off a sheet and— gave me a blank sheet of paper!

Project management training

This section looks at project management training based on the POCL model, and at short training events covering the essentials of the firm's standard project lifecycle and their elementary vendor methodology.

A key benefit of the POCL model, introduced in Chapter 2, is that it immediately provides the firm with a universal foundation for the training of vendor PMs, regardless of specific project methodologies. Training is important for every project manager, but is a core competency for the services firm.

POCL skills

Training topics fit naturally into each of the four POCL categories:

1   Planning Skills–Many courses and workshops can be found. Things to look for in the curricula include scope and activity planning, estimating,

budgeting, scheduling, quality planning, risk planning, resource planning, communications planning, contracting, and procurement.

2   Organizational Skills–Checklists and techniques exist, though there are few public courses. There are some who believe that organizational ability is an innate characteristic, thus making it harder to learn for those who do not possess it. Organization skills cover areas such as team structure, roles and responsibilities, procedures, documentation, project files, project logs, checklists used in planning and control, and general 'start up' skills.

3   Controlling Skills (including Monitoring/Tracking)–Many courses and workshops can be found. Curricula should include issue and change management, meeting management, supervision skills, time management and prioritization, personnel performance management and feedback, technical methods including earned value and critical path analysis, and specialized methods such as quality control and risk analysis.

4   Leadership Skills (including Communication)–Many courses and workshops can be found, though in this area many also believe that leadership is an innate characteristic, thus making this ability much harder to learn for those who do not possess it. Topics that fall into this category include delegation skills, negotiating skills, conflict resolution, 'dealing with difficult people', delivering feedback, motivation theory, social style profiling, influencing people, situational awareness, intervention strategies, presentation techniques, decision methods, teamwork development, and more.

Operational project skills

The vendor PM also requires training in two additional areas, both of which are specific to the firm and their operational procedures. The first is the standard project lifecycle and associated development methodology that the firm will use to perform work on the majority of projects. Chapter 3 explains how this is the backbone of client project integration. The second is the vendor lifecycle and methodology components proposed in this book. Chapter 4 describes the core components.

Vendor PMs are also expected to be familiar with the client organization for which their project is being conducted, and with the methods and technologies of the application area they are implementing. It is likely that this knowledge comes more from experience and personal study rather than training.

Example training program

Training is now widely acknowledged as an essential adjunct to change. I sometimes feel that, necessary as it is, the benefits of training can be elusive unless an effort is made to match the training to the real need and what is practical in a busy corporate environment. This is especially relevant in a services firm. One of the success factors for training has to be a reasonably motivated attendee. Another is to keep the sessions brief and maximally engaging for the attendee. It is hard to get good training results with a resister or someone who is just too busy to be there!

Presuming that the attendees do not require basic project management training, a program of training in the elementary vendor methodology is laid out in Table 11.6. A selection of these modules is also applicable for managers, sales executives, and senior practitioners in the firm.

None of these modules require more than 3 h attention, and the tutorials are generally 1 h or less.

> Training only succeeds when both parties appreciate there is a need and understand the value of the chosen training method.

Training options

The training program in Table 11.6 could be applied to, for example, a new PM joining the firm who needs to get up to speed on 'how things are done'. Faced with an immediate need to prepare standard reports, he could register for a 'how-to' tutorial. To get a more in-depth review and discussion on the practices, he could schedule the relevant seminars as per his requirements.

Based on the standard program, modules can be assembled to efficiently meet individual needs. The modular approach makes this possible. For example, new sales executives may not wish to take all modules, but a mandatory program could be assembled based on: Benefits of the Methodology, Sales Executive Briefing, Business and Finance Basics, Revenue Accounting, How to Complete a Bid Estimate, and How to Complete a Risk Rank Assessment.

Table 11.6 is based on only two training methods—seminar and tutorial. In practice, there are many training options available and a good program will select the most efficient based on the material, the audience, and the time available, as well as the desired outcome. These methods include:

> Half-day Seminars–Formatted with combinations of lecturettes, group work, demonstrations, individual exercises, and discussion. A half-day seems optimum, though 1 day and possibly 2-day sessions can work.

> Tutorials–Formatted for very small groups or teams with a common interest and customized from the standard training modules to meet very specific 'how-to' training needs, often identified by the teams themselves after a period of implementation experience. Usually designed as 1–2 h sessions. Non-interactive tutorials can be delivered by video.

> Workshops–Formatted to give a group an opportunity to develop and practice a new techniques skill, sometimes using real project situations for the case work. Usually 2–4 h.

Table 11.6 Modules of an elementary vendor methodology training program

Firm's sample training program	
Seminar	Tutorial
Accountabilities definition practice	How to complete a bid estimate
Business and finance basics	How to complete a project status report
Estimating practice	How to complete a risk alert assessment
Executive dashboard	How to complete a risk rank assessment
Lifecycle mapping practice	How to complete a work estimate
Performance evaluation	How to develop a lesson learned
Quality management practice	How to develop a RAA and RAM
Revenue accounting	How to develop the risk register
Risk management practice	How to get project sign-off
Roles and responsibilities in the firm	How to interview
Sales executive briefing	
Vendor methodology—architecture and benefits	

Lunch 'n' Learn–A less formal means of responding to training and information needs, usually formatted as a 20-minute lecturette or video topic as attendees eat a lunch. This is followed by a question and answer period, and/or group discussion.

Online Interactive–Using conferencing technology such as Webex or GoToMeeting is an increasingly popular means of training a geographically dispersed population, specifically in a detailed skill that benefits from demonstration and can be accomplished in an hour or less.

Video–A non-interactive medium that can be scheduled to meet the needs of the learner, formatted to transfer highly detailed skills using technologies such as recorded Webex, PowerPoint, Captivate, or Camtasia. The optimum is to create segments that can accomplish an objective in 20 minutes to a maximum of 1 h.

The modules of the sample program address knowledge transfer, technique skills, or other very detailed skills such as template use. Building a training program for the firm means selecting the best delivery method for the topic, assembling the topics into modules, and then offering the optimum mix of modules to the trainee or trainee group.

Document storage

A discourse on document storage may seem prosaic, but deserves coverage—if you can't find it, you may as well not have it. Fortunately, today's technologies give us no excuse for not finding documents, especially those that are naturally structured. Most bid or project documents are created from templates or forms, adhere to a naming standard, are associated with a particular

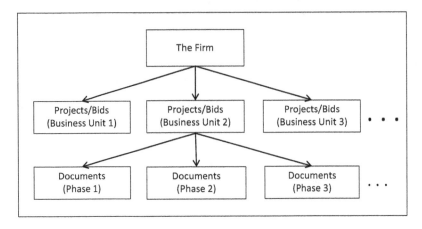

Figure 11.2 Recommended document storage hierarchy

phase of the lifecycle and with a business unit, and need to be analyzed based on readily identifiable data such as name, date, value, risk rank, etc.

A basic storage hierarchy that meets most practical storage needs is shown in Figure 11.2. Documents are either attributed or physically located based on three primary keys—the business unit, the project or bid code, and the phase of the vendor lifecycle. Even if documents themselves are not coded (which is easy and recommended, e.g., PSR for the project status report, etc.), with knowledge of the vendor methodology, anything can be found quickly.

Implementation principles

Experience with establishing and using this type of document storage system suggests adhering to a set of principles as follows:

- Use a technology accessible to everyone in the firm.
- Avoid excessive use of hierarchies: documents should be retrieved using minimal clicks.
- Maintain a unified purpose: the system is for vendor methodology filing, not general-purpose project filing.
- The storage is for bids and projects, which can be differentiated but are not segregated.
- Keep only current documents, not earlier drafts or versions.
- Maintain open access.
- Manage filing and updates so that multiple authors are permitted, but in a controlled environment.

Example set of requirements

In this example of document storage requirements, SharePoint is the reference technology, although any similar collaborative document management product can undoubtedly meet these needs:

- One example of implementation uses the firm as the folder for projects/bids, and uses project/bid as the folder for documents. To minimize clicks through folders, business unit is coded as a project attribute and lifecycle phase as a document attribute.
- All projects/bids are allocated a unique code following a standard.
- The code differentiates bids from projects and is updatable from bid to project if the bid is won.
- A bid may be tagged with an approval designation.
- Projects/bids may be filtered by value, risk rank, type of contract, and more complex logic such as all unapproved bids over $250,000.
- Projects/bids should be scrollable within business unit, and within the firm (in code sequence).
- All documents shall be accessible, and listed, through the project/bid code.
- A document can be downloaded for read-only.
- A document can be checked-out for update by a permitted user, and the updated document re-filed with an annotation of who made the change.
- Documents can be removed for archive.

Prior to implementation, there may be some more detailed design points worth thinking out. For example, there are good and bad coding systems—a good project code is a standard client abbreviation and a sequence number. An example of ease of use suggests all screens must be viewable without horizontal scrolling.

Organization of delivery management

The evolution of a delivery management role as the firm migrates from a decentralized to a centralized structure, or as the requirement for delivery processes becomes evident, is not always cut and dried. As the firm grows, the role becomes increasingly necessary, but for various reasons, the firm is sometimes unable to make the commitment to a full delivery management (DM) structure. This section offers some alternatives, presented as three scenarios. Before continuing, the reader might like to review Table 5.1, which distinguishes the role of DM and professional services management (PSM). The three scenarios examined are: Strong DM, Matrixed DM, and Weak DM:

Scenario 1 Strong DM. This scenario is the baseline and would be the usual operational model for a large firm with mainly large projects. The DM is directly responsible for the project management function, and building and maintaining this capability. In this scenario, the DM/vendor PM team manage all the firm's FP projects and any T&M projects where the firm has taken on a project management responsibility through tendering their own project manager. The PSM is responsible for all other work, managing the practitioners, and supporting the sales force.

Scenario 2 Matrixed DM. This scenario retains the project oversight role with DM, but moves the personnel management responsibility for vendor PMs back to the PSM. Thus the PSM controls all project management and practitioner resources. This structure typically operates with less DM resource, and the threshold for triggering DM engagement might be established in the authority table. For example, "all FP projects valued at $100K or more are overseen by DM."

The strength of the vendor PM function is also a factor when designing how projects are managed in this scenario. It is less likely that dedicated project managers will flourish in this scenario. It is possible that staff inexperienced in project management will be assigned to a vendor PM role and will also retain significant practitioner responsibilities. A 'Lead Practitioner' whose main job is project work, but who is also assigned typical vendor PM responsibilities, may manage smaller projects. Alternatively, a fully qualified PM within the business unit might manage multiple small projects.

The authority table and a RAM matrix are useful tools to maintain clarity in this environment with multiple responsibility options.

Scenario 3 Weak DM. This scenario fits the limitations of the small firm with one or two locations. In this case, the job of delivery manager does not yet exist, and all elements of the role are allocated to the PSM. This additional burden constrains the amount of management attention that can be given to methodology implementation. The vendor PM function may not flourish in this scenario.

Management costs are a factor when the firm migrates through these scenarios, and this tends to favor the flexibility of the matrixed DM model. The nature of the PSM network is also a significant factor. A firm that operates in a variety of business environments (e.g., government, retail, manufacturing, etc.) or with different suites of complex products, may choose to optimize the practitioner organization by establishing PSM units in each of these specializations. This implies the likelihood of more than one PSM per location. Full DM coverage under scenario 1 may then both be unaffordable and potentially under-utilize the PSMs. The solution then points towards the matrixed DM approach.

Leadership

Adopting the practices and organizational methods espoused by this guide is a matter for the senior level of the firm's management. The methodology must fit with management's long-term vision for the firm—the type of projects to be undertaken, the growth targets, the character of the clients they want to work with, the business approach to be encouraged, the nature of the work environment, and the internal organizational relationships. The notion of a vendor methodology being a piece of the firm's vision is a worthwhile connection. Business guru Joel Barker's video *The Power of Vision* presents guidelines for vision implementation, and it seems like a plausible general approach to adopting any methodology.

Vision implementation model

Barker's implementation may be summarized in four steps:

1   The vision must be leader initiated. It must come from leadership's appreciation of the value the vision confers on the firm in terms of business success, competing in the marketplace, and relationships with their clients, their employees, and potential hires.
2   The vision must be shared with employees and receive their support. Every employee must understand the benefits that can flow and see their role in its functioning.
3   The vision must be comprehensive and detailed. Generalities will not be adequate. The vision must describe how things are to be done and where each member of the firm fits.
4   Finally, the vision must be positive and inspiring. The greatest contribution of leadership is to maintain a visible, persistent confidence that the results are within grasp and that the benefits can be achieved. They must, by their own commitment and focus, inspire the community to reach for those same results.

A corporate vision must be leader-initiated, shared and supported, comprehensive and detailed, positive and inspiring.

To achieve these noble actions, leadership may wish to appoint a day-to-day implementation manager with a focus on results while they assume the role of sponsor. This manager will need to demonstrate many of the skills of a project manager, most notably communication skills, identification of CSFs, objective setting, documentation management, organizing skills, experience with role and responsibility definitions, process change management, and process design. It seems apparent that this would be an excellent assignment for a newly appointed delivery manager.

Transforming a firm from an informal ad hoc working style to a formalized, more structured approach is not a trivial undertaking. Perhaps it is worth taking a leaf from the project management book and first defining what is meant by success. Implementation can then proceed in a controlled and steady fashion with objectives monitored and visibly achieved. I hope this guide helps along the way.

12 Toward collaborative procurement of services

The ideas in this chapter were originally submitted in a white paper to the PMI Global Congress 2015 and presented by the author to the conference on October 13, 2015.

Fully collaborative procurement is the vision—a rational, collaborative procurement and delivery process, in which buyer and seller work together to optimize the results for both parties. The premise is that a new foundation must be laid: a collaborative methodology. The requirements and architecture for such a methodology are described, and an overview provided of the five integrated phases that serve both vendor and buyer. Longer term, a consortium of committed buyers and sellers is needed to bring about a true joint, integrated, subscription-based methodology.

The material presented in this guide so far could be developed into a full vendor methodology, but it's possible that larger gains are to be found in a different direction. The six core practices (introduced in Chapter 2) will gain more in utility by added integration with the customer instead of specialization into the vendor's world. The vendor lifecycle, merged with the buyer's procurement phase, seems an obvious starting point for a new commercially focused methodology that brings the vendor and client together at the business level in the same way as the shared project lifecycle brings project management together at the PM level.

The ideas outlined here will expand the commercial project environment (Figure 2.1) to address critical joint management requirements and will integrate these methods into a joint methodology where it is practical to do so (Figure 12.1). This will result in benefits to all parties.

The idea of collaboration is not new. The concept of 'just-in-time' supply management and inventory reduction could not have been achieved and become standard in many industries without customer and supplier collaboration. The CPFR (Collaborative Planning Forecasting and Replenishment) model is an ambitious extension into a multi-vendor environment that is meeting with some success. These initiatives are intended primarily for the manufacturing world, and the unique issues of professional services procurement have not so far been satisfactorily addressed. The main challenge is to offer collaboration at the front-end where scope, estimates, risk, and quality might be uncertain or ambiguous, whilst at the same time maintaining a fair and competitive environment.

Problems in the marketplace

Currently, buyers and sellers tend to operate as silos, creating communication tangles, misunderstandings, and unnecessary complexity, as well as sometimes causing project failures. Procurement, as generally understood by clients, is almost entirely focused on the selection and contracting of the vendor firm. The actual delivery of the project, which is surely the real goal of procurement, is left to oversight by a steering committee and maybe occasional audits by the procurement department. Paradoxically, although skeptical buyers might feel otherwise, my case histories suggest that more savings will accrue to buyers than vendors if a collaborative approach is adopted. One area overlooked in such assessments is the frequent over-dependence on the vendor. Buyers tend not to properly examine methods used by their vendors, often fail to ask for meaningful status, fail to train their own staff, delegate the vendor to deal with risk and quality, and often, by default, let the vendor PM entirely drive the project.

A common framework that supports a collaborative approach would eliminate direct and indirect costs for both parties, create a more effective project environment, and vastly improve communications by jointly establishing a set of ground rules and practices to guide the parties through procurement, project execution, and completion. Collaboration does not simply mean work is performed by one party and signed off by the other. The parties agree to a jointly defined allocation of work and management, and both sign off on the results.

Avoidable loss

Experience points to some general categories where current procurement methods suffer from a number of failings:

- The RFP lacks clarity, is cancelled, or withdrawn and reissued.
- Vendor selection does not filter unqualified candidates, is subject to misrepresentations, allows incorrect estimates, and may be prejudged.
- The contract may be the incorrect type, contain inefficient terms, and excessively delay start-up.
- Project execution introduces brand new causes of failure, and traditional causes are intensified (refer to Table 3.1).

Illustrating with some selected case histories can better exemplify inefficiencies created by current practices.

Very ambiguous scope

The firm was given insufficient time to respond to an RFP, so the business manager needed an estimate quickly. I was asked to prepare one over the weekend, with an independent estimate prepared by my colleague. We met on Monday morning to work together prior to meeting the boss with our conclusions. The problem was—my estimate was $100,000, my colleague's was $1M, and neither of us could read the scope any other way. The boss wisely no-bid.

This case is old and was a learning experience on many levels. The interesting thing is the loss for the firm was minimal, but the client (a government department following their procurement rules) wanted the firm to do the work but didn't even get a bid to evaluate. The project went to a main competitor and was not a success.

An inadequate budget

The firm had been associated with a large client for a number of years doing small consulting projects and some T&M advisory work. A very large project was in the works, but following their process the client told the firm nothing about it, except the application area and that they were looking forward to the firm's bid following release of the RFP.

The bid was very expensive to assemble, and required the firm to team with a local specialist. The proposal was high-quality and the firm expected to be short-listed with a good chance to win the bid.

The day after the RFP closing date the business manager received a call from the client's procurement manager advising him that the firm's bid could not be accepted as it was well outside the allocated budget. The firm discovered later that all bids were over the budget. From recollection, the firm's bid was $5M and the budget was $3M. The firm's bid costs were $50,000, and three other firms bid incurring similar costs.

Best-price competition

The firm was chosen as a preferred supplier of projects along with two competitors. There was a backlog of project work. Laudably, the client wished to streamline procurement, and this was the method chosen. The problem was that, as a condition for joining the preferred vendor consortium, all firms had to respond with a proposal to all RFPs, involving a lot of proposal and sales support work by all competitors. Inevitably, communication with the competition was ritualistic and distrustful, causing projects to operate as silos even more than usual.

After a while, each firm started to gain superior expertise and experience in certain of the client's application areas, and this made them a more natural choice for the users. The procurement rules continued with the added twist that the erstwhile competitors could forecast the favorite. To justify their consortium approach, the procurement manager would not endorse the user's choice until the chosen firm was negotiated down to 10% less than the lowest competitive bid. This negotiation was not only disruptive but the knowledge of these undocumented rules led to some gaming of the system.

Despite the best of intentions this approach did not end well. The firm left the consortium.

The thin ray of hope

The client had issued a major RFP that came with a mandatory implementation date such that the after-work pub talk was mission impossible. Nonetheless, the firm could not ignore the opportunity, as it was well placed to perform the project with the proviso that they could not guarantee the schedule as presented in the RFP.

At the short-list presentation, the firm reviewed some carefully designed options that were judged to achieve the bulk of the client's demands, which were politically motivated. The client made it clear these deviations were not compliant and wanted commitment to their 'plan'. I remember, as the proposed vendor PM, struggling for the right words and saying, "there is a thin ray of hope their plan could be achieved!" My boss, to his credit, did not overrule my paltry expression of a risk analysis, but did give me a wry smile and some performance feedback over a beer later.

A firm was selected that was prepared to make the commitment, and the project was not a success. In fact, it was a disaster, eventually costing several times the planned cost.

All of these situations were avoidable. Obviously, bids can be cancelled, scope can change, pricing can be challenged, and schedule needs are important, but if all parties can be transparent about the factors in play there is a much better chance of the client getting mostly what she wants and the vendor community left with the knowledge that their efforts were valid and not wasted. Case histories testify—there must be a better way.

The case for methodology

A better way would focus on a collaborative approach and still protect the client's confidentiality and expectation of a competitive response. A methodology endorsed by all parties would seem to offer the best prospect of improving the situation.

Without formalization, just like standard project management, attempts to improve the record of project contracting will be sporadic, temporary, and based on heroic measures by rare combinations of exceptional people.

The proposition is that the major benefits of collaborative procurement can only be achieved by a new methodology. This formalization deserves a name, and as a working title I suggest *Total Collaborative Procurement* (*TCP*). Using the qualifier 'Total' is a reminder that successful procurement is much more than just getting a qualified vendor selected for the project. Success demands that the entire delivery cycle is addressed. The client must abandon the idea that all risks and problems are delegated to the vendor. Projects are always a joint endeavour.

Requirements for a TCP methodology

Based on this background and the intent of the TCP, some general requirements can be defined:

Formalized Method–The TCP must be written and must have structure.

Scope–Procurement, including both vendor selection and project delivery must be covered.

Lifecycle–There must be a definable lifecycle that makes sense to both buyer and seller without attempting to subsume activities that truly must be internal or confidential.

Business Considerations–The theme must be business efficiency and convergence of business interests by both parties.

Management Positioning–The TCP role is supervisory over the vendor and client PMs.

Integrated–The practices, techniques, checklists, and documents specified by the TCP are, by definition, integrated and open.

Compatibility–The technical specifications of the methodology should be consistent with project management standards.

Delegation–The methods must support business decision-making by the PMs.

Flexibility–The TCP must offer multiple paths though the engagement based primarily on complexity criteria.

Generality–The method should be implementable at a generalized level without the need for process specification or excessive detail within the TCP.

Documentation–There should be minimal demand for documents, consistent with management clarity and accepted best practice.

Proposal for total collaborative procurement

In response to these requirements, the commercial project environment has been reconfigured. The resulting architecture in Figure 12.1 is equally recognizable to client and vendor. This model represents a blending of methods currently used independently by vendor and buyer, with adaptations that support an integrated approach.

A joint TCP lifecycle is a challenge to the existing paradigm. It will initially engage multiple organizations, some in competition. The model must be kept simple and the description kept at the highest level of abstraction capable of providing practical guidance.

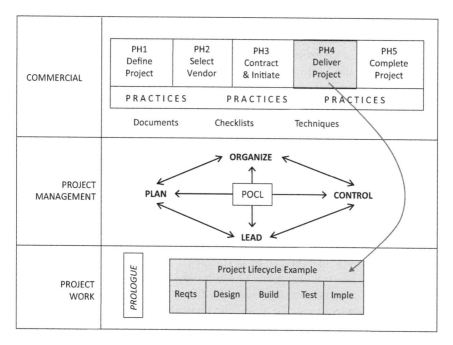

Figure 12.1 The TCP architecture

TCP architecture

The architecture is layered. Three layers are envisaged: the commercial layer, the project management layer, and the project work layer. Though the model borrows the techniques of project management, the primary context for the TCP is business; for the client, procurement is primarily a business operation, and for the vendor, delivery is the fundamental business of the firm.

Level 1: Commercial

Five phases are defined. Each phase specifies joint practices. During each phase these practices are deployed either partially or in their entirety. The six core practices presently defined are seen as essential. There could eventually be as many as 10–15 practices specified. Each practice generates joint documents, utilizes common checklists, and works with recommended techniques.

Level 2: Project management

Project management addresses the work of the project, but is also linked into the commercial level. To provide the client and vendor with maximum flexibility, project management is defined using the functional model described in

Chapter 2. These functions operate repetitively and definitely not as sequential phases. This clearly distinguishes project management from the lifecycle phases that characterize the commercial and project work levels. The TCP is not a prescription for project management, but could provide documentation lists, checklists and techniques generally applicable to each POCL function. As an example of this, and to demonstrate the links with the commercial level, the Organize function should include the core processes proposed in Chapter 2, e.g., change and issue management, acceptance, status and discrepancy reporting, sign-off, decision requests, and transition to operations.

Level 3: Project work

The concept behind Level 3 is entirely borrowed from the ideas in Chapter 3 that insist on a common project lifecycle so that the client and the vendor views of the project are identical. This is essential if the client and vendor PMs are to manage jointly without friction. It also permits the integrative practice of lifecycle mapping to be performed.

The project lifecycle in Figure 12.1 is purely for illustration purposes and the TCP does not and cannot specify the lifecycle content, but does specify that the lifecycle technique be used. The Phase 4 Deliver Project is the oversight phase (or 'wrapper') for the project phases contracted for delivery. The illustration shows all phases from Requirements to Implementation, or 'big bang'. An alternative might be to contract using the rolling wave so that the first contract is for Requirements and Design, and the second is for Build to Implementation. This is illustrated in Figure 4.2.

To recognize that early project work is commissioned before the formal existence of a project and appointment of a client PM, Level 3 identifies a Prologue phase. Activities in this phase flow from the Phase 1 Define Project and, for example, might comprise the client's Feasibility Study.

TCP design requirements

The design of each TCP phase requires a specification for each of the five phases using the following design template:

Goal–Statement of the overarching purpose of the phase.

Objectives–Specific measurable outcomes from the phase that contribute to the goal.

Exit Criteria–Conditions to be met that allow the phase to close.

Practices Used–The practices useful during the phase, some partial, some fully deployed. The six core practices currently identified are: Lifecycle Mapping, Accountabilities Definition, Joint Risk Management, Estimate Counseling, Quality Target Development, and Joint Resource Management.

Practice Documents–Joint reports or practice outputs.

Other Joint Documents–Documents generated by the phase and jointly released by project management (TCP does not cover documents prepared independently for internal use).

Outline of the TCP phases

This section provides a preliminary specification for each of the phases using the design template, and how each phase might use the relevant core practice(s). This should give the reader better insight into how the TCP promotes collaboration.

Phase 1: Define project

Collaboration is important at this early stage, but jointly approved documents are unrealistic and few are expected. A revolutionary characteristic of this phase is the early involvement of vendors and their anticipated role in shaping the project.

Goal. This is primarily the client's preparatory phase to create a blueprint of the project and for the vendor a preliminary decision on bid/no bid.

Objectives. For larger projects the objectives of this phase can be spread over a significant timeframe. A preliminary scope must be assembled and sufficient data collected to enable a cost/benefit or feasibility study. Links to the client's strategic plan must be established and budgetary forecasts approved. The marketplace is approached with an RFI or other announcements, a list of vendors drawn up, and expressions of interest established. Vendors can respond to the project definition and evaluate the opportunity according to a variety of criteria.

Exit Criteria. Preliminary project scope and a list of competitive vendors willing to bid.

Practices Used. Preliminary estimate counseling, a consultation between the client and prospective vendors with the intent of assisting the client with budgetary information and assessing opinions regarding scope, risk, and assumptions. Preliminary Joint Risk Management, an early development of a brief risk rank assessment between the client and prospective vendors with the intent of both parties assessing an early measure of risk rank and assisting the vendor with their bid/no bid decision.

Practice Documents. Preliminary risk rank assessment.

Phase 2: Select vendor

Collaboration focuses on a diminishing set of vendors as successive qualification and filtering activities yield a checkpoint with the invitation to bid (RFP) issued to a long-list of vendors. Formal evaluation results in a short-list of vendors who are then invited to finalist events.

Goal. The goal is to identify a preferred vendor and, in most cases, a runner-up.

Objectives. The client generally adapts the objectives of classic procurement to confirm a long-list of vendors, to prepare and distribute the RFP, to review and evaluate proposals, and to choose the winner and runner-up. The vendors are focused on developing an estimated, compliant solution, preparing the proposal and bid response, assessing and mitigating risk, and completing their own internal review procedures. The client will use partial or full versions of the practices as filtering activities progressively through this phase, specifically to validate the SOW and determine the long-list, short-list, and winner.

Exit Criteria. A selected vendor willing to enter contract negotiations.

Practices Used. Preliminary Accountabilities Definition, Preliminary Quality Target Development, Joint Risk Management (Rank), and Estimate Counseling.

Practice Documents. Draft List of Project Roles and Responsibilities, Quality Objectives, Risk Factor Checklist, Risk Rank, and Basis for Estimate.

Other Joint Documents. Statement of Work.

Phase 3: Contract and initiate

Collaboration shifts from the sales focus to delivery and an increasingly operational mode as both project managers are now assigned. A checkpoint occurs with contract agreement in principle, failing which contract negotiation moves to the runner-up.

Goal. The goal is to secure a contract for project delivery with a qualified vendor and kick off the project.

Objectives. Both parties must take this opportunity to clarify the specifics of joint project operations before contract agreement. This includes the core project processes and associated delegations, the key features of the project plan and QMS, and a lifecycle map. Early 'agreement in principle' with the winner is essential to avoid lost time if negotiations must move to the runner-up.

Exit Criteria. Contract signed and kick-off meeting held.

Practices Used. Lifecycle Mapping, Quality Target Development, and Accountabilities Definition.

Practice Documents. Lifecycle Map, Quality Plan, Project Organization, and RAM Chart.

Other Joint Documents. Contract, Project Procedures Manual, Communications Plan, Project Gantt Chart, and Initiation Checklist.

Phase 4: Deliver project

Collaboration during delivery should be marked by a high degree of openness, frankness, and an effective forum for problem and issue resolution.

Goal. The intent is to accomplish the work to build the product and to demonstrate that the vendor has met, or is meeting, the project objectives.

Objectives. Phase objectives are formed from a subset of accepted project progress metrics such as milestone achievement, resource assignment, deliverable approvals, payment schedule, phase schedule, issue resolutions, discrepancy solutions, etc.

Exit Criteria. The product should have been subjected to client acceptance testing and determined adequate for its intended use. The vendor and client agree to a Joint Completion Plan that documents outstanding tasks to be completed, the outcome of any negotiations, final change requests, and plan modifications.

Practices Used. Joint Resource Management and Joint Risk Management (Alerts).

Practice Documents. Project Resource Utilization, Departmental Resource Availability, Risk Indicator Checklist, and Risk Alert.

Other Joint Documents. Joint Project Status and Progress Reports, Change Request Reports, Issue Reports, Discrepancy Reports, Decision Reports, Acceptance Reports, Test Plan, and Project Completion Plan.

Phase 5: Complete project

During completion both parties are influenced by potentially conflicting goals to complete the project quickly, but completely. Collaboration is facilitated by prior agreements on process, criteria, and priorities.

Goal. The goal is to sign off the project.

Objectives. At the center of this phase are the previously endorsed completion criteria and the new Completion Plan. Both parties should focus on its management and achievement. The transition plan to migrate to client operations and support must also be executed, though the role of the vendor in this (training, maintenance, etc.) would be determined by contract and may not be a precondition for sign-off.

Exit Criteria. The project is signed off.

Practices Used. Joint Resource Management.

Practice Documents. Project Resource Utilization, and Departmental Resource Availa bility.

Other Joint Documents. Transition Plan, Project Sign-off, Lessons Learned, and Completion Checklist.

Practice descriptions

The TCP target is to provide full specification for each of the six core practices according to the following design template:

Practice Description–A reasonably structured explanation of the practice; the intent, roles who participate, inputs needed, outputs generated, and general guidance on how to deal with common issues.

Documents Created–These are outputs from the practice for which templates are available.

Checklists–Specification of generic checklists included in the practice to improve efficiency.

Techniques–Explanations of specific techniques employed by the practice.

The following draft practice descriptions and technique identifications provide preliminary guidance pending further development using the above template.

Practice 1: Lifecycle mapping

The client and the vendor must share the same view of the lifecycle, the work to be done, and the project management to be applied. The answer is to recognize the role of the project lifecycle as the backbone of project integration. The mapping process integrates project management explicitly into the work of the project, shows the management activity supplied by both client and vendor, and maps their management deliverables into the same phases of work as project deliverables. This practice, which reinvigorates the project lifecycle, is described in Chapter 3.

Practice 2: Accountabilities definition

Lack of clarity in management, stakeholder, and team accountabilities is a leading cause of project inefficiency and sometimes failure. A willingness by both parties to define accountabilities during the vendor selection phase and in more detail during contracting avoids problems later in the project. Two techniques are recommended—a project organization or structure chart, and RAM charts.

Structure Chart. The project organization chart is an essential tool for visually communicating the critical roles within a project, and the context of the project within the client organization. Most charts will fall into one of three classes: parallel management teams; technically led teams; and business led teams. Each has its own strengths and weaknesses. Roles and reporting relationships can then be drawn. From the vendor side: vendor project manager, technical manager, professional services manager(s), sales executive, sales manager, delivery manager, and business manager. From the client side: client project manager, sponsor, technical manager, operations manager, contract manager, resource manager(s), and user(s).

RAM Charts. The Responsibility Assignment Matrix provides the PMs with the extra precision and clarity needed for activity and deliverable management. Most PMs are familiar with the tool, and it is possible that both vendor and client PMs will have developed their own chart. That, of course, is the problem. The true value of the RAM is when it is jointly developed in a working session, and issued as a project document signed off by both client and vendor.

These techniques are described and examples given in Chapter 5.

Practice 3: Joint risk management

The challenge is to bridge the marked difference in risk perception between the sales executive, vendor PM, and the client. A salesperson trying to make a project sale tends to view risk as an annoyance, and presumes that the delivery side of the organization should accept it as an everyday challenge. The vendor PM will tend to assume an analytical posture and start drafting a risk register with only sketchy information available. On the client side, unfortunately, the likely attitude is that risk is something they really don't have to worry about as it is to be downloaded onto the vendor! Unfortunately, if the vendor fails to deliver, for whatever reason, the consequences eventually fall back into the client's lap. Risk can never be fully delegated, and the best approach is to work jointly, using risk factor and risk indicator tools adapted to the project.

Joint Risk Assessments. Project outcomes have generally been observed as more positive in contracted projects where the client and vendor operate joint risk assessments. Teams seem to be influenced to perform collaboratively in other areas as well, and the project atmosphere is more positive.

Risk Factor Analysis. The risk factor model shown in Figure 6.5 is a good starting point. The standard set of facets for a specific project family, e.g., the Team, Contract, Size, Solution, Technology, and Customer, can be adapted for joint use, with the expectation that the Customer facet is probably best divided into two or three more specific facets to provide better accuracy. For each facet, a checklist of risk factors is developed and designated as base, compounding, or mitigating factors. A joint management team applies the risk factor checklist to estimate a risk rank for the project, set between 1 (very low risk) and 5 (very high). Both parties can use the rank to condition their estimates and their own internal procedures, but its important function within TCP is to highlight the most effective path through the TCP methodology. In other words, the rank metric can be used to condition next steps, rather than subjecting all projects to a 'one size fits all'.

Risk Indicator Analysis. When a project starts executing, everything changes. The risk rank, valuable in the planning phase, loses relevance. The specifics in the risk register gain in value, and become the team's primary future-focused risk tool. A tool is therefore needed that is responsive to the project as it presently exists. The risk alert model shown in Figure 6.6 is the basis for assessing whether the project is in trouble, heading into trouble, or on track. The model focuses on the strength of the links that keep the project aligned with project objectives. From the vendor perspective, these performance chains are delivery, financial, team efficiency, and client relationship. Significant adaptation work must be done to expand these chains to properly represent the client's view of the project's objectives, or success criteria. A checklist of these is shown in Table 3.7. The state of each chain is then characterized by a risk indicators checklist, which yields a composite red, yellow, or green alert. The TCP will suggest protocols to be invoked based on the value of the project alert.

These techniques are described and examples given in Chapter 6.

Practice 4: Estimate counseling

With collaboration as the theme, the reader might be wondering how on earth the parties can collaborate on this topic and still operate in a fair and competitive environment? I believe some aspects can fit a collaborative approach and offer real benefits. Vendors can be invited to provide budgetary estimates, without the allocated budget necessarily being shared. Buyers can give estimating advice to vendors who do not necessarily share the specifics of the resulting estimate. Currently, the emphasis on isolating the client's budget from the vendor's estimate in the cause of competition tends to work against the interests of a viable and successful project.

A major technique to counteract this tendency is for both parties to avoid wedge issues that cause inefficiency, lead to inaccurate estimates, and benefit no one. A wedge issue drives the client and the vendor further apart for no good reason, to the detriment of getting a good proposal. This key point is illustrated in Figure 12.2, which suggests mutual understanding of the requirements and solution will generate a convergence of budget and estimate, whereas wedge issues lead to divergence.

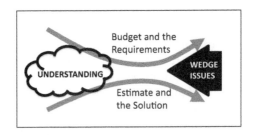

Figure 12.2 The effect of wedge issues on budget and estimate

Partial list of wedge issues

The Acceptance of Ambiguity by Both Parties—The client should strive to remove ambiguity from their requirements, and the vendor should not hesitate to question if it is encountered.

The Conflation of Estimate and Price—These are two different data. An estimate is first expressed in work hours or days, then it is priced. The parties should not argue about one, when they mean the other.

Avoidance of Decisions that will Impact the Estimate—A diligent client will endeavor to have these decisions made before releasing the RFP.

Unreasonable Choice of Contract Type—Don't try to squeeze a T&M project into a FP pot! Both parties should be knowledgeable about the variety of contracting types and options available that can protect the legitimate interests of the parties and still provide a competitive deal.

Reluctance to Discuss Assumptions—Assumptions are essential to a realistic estimate, but can also be the refuge of the lazy. Ambiguities and open decisions must be covered by assumptions if the questions are not answered.

Subterfuge to Evade Discussion on Risk and Contingency—This is one of the hardest wedge issues. Contingency can be buried in 'support' activities to avoid being stripped out—hardly a collaborative approach.

Accepting an Unreasonable Approach (e.g., 'big bang' for ill-defined projects)—This is related to contract type, but if the contract type is fixed, then both parties might collaborate on a revised approach that will better meet all objectives.

Limiting a joint estimating practice to the resolution of wedge issues is probably the current bound of feasibility. Chapter 7 discusses other possible candidates for collaboration, such as complexity baselining, but these await experience with the first TCP version.

Practice 5: Quality target development

One of the more difficult tasks of the vendor PM, and one not always achieved, is establishing a meaningful understanding between client and vendor on the subject of project quality. Why should that be?

Quality is difficult at the best of times, more so in a commercial relationship. Both parties prefer dealing in subjective terms—vendors will talk about the objective of customer satisfaction; clients will talk about the need for everything to "work the way we want." Sometimes slogans (Quality is Job 1) are mistaken for quality policy, and serious engagement ends there. Sometimes neither party has had adequate training on how quality best applies to their application area, and neither do they have a sharable quality system in place. Without a solid reference point, selecting and pricing the right quality standard is hit or miss.

TCP uses a framework that translates subjective expressions of future states to objective measures that represent project targets to be discussed and agreed. Uncomplicated models help to establish project protocols and trade-off options that will best meet these quality targets. The techniques proposed, and the quality plan component of a basic QMS that will factor the results into the project plan, are summarized below:

Quality Objectives. The vendor and client open a dialogue using the 'point of quality' model that will move the client's expression of needs from the subjective to the objective, which can be measured. The technique uses 'what and how' questions and is illustrated in Figure 8.2. The vendor PM should not sign up for objectives that cannot be achieved within the scope of work as that may result in frustration and failure. The end point of the technique emphasizes quality factors that support objectives and are tangible. They can be observed or tested to be present in the deliverable, or not.

Supplier and Acceptor Protocols. Quality theory endorses the necessity for active acceptance of goods by inspection. This concept can be broadened to suggest that the relationship between seller and buyer at the time of delivery places an onus upon the acceptor as well as the supplier, illustrated using the Supplier/Acceptor model in Figure 8.3. These protocols are effective for interim deliverables and other important project transactions, not just for final product acceptance. Optimum results arise when the duality of the relationship is in balance. Insufficient attention to the acceptor role, and quality may suffer. Too much may create diminishing returns and add unnecessarily to time and cost. The dynamics are based on the default positions of the supplier who is saying, "Get it done and get paid!" versus the acceptor who is saying, "Do it well and get it in use!"

Trade-off Analysis. Trade-offs are a fact of project life. The Quality Quadrant model in Figure 8.5 arose to acknowledge that client perception of the project as a whole was just as important as the quality factors carefully built into the product itself. In this view, quality has two dimensions: the quality of the execution (usually experienced as time and cost), and the quality of the product (experienced as functionality and durability). Sometimes clients have difficulty in truly assessing their priorities when trade-offs are needed, and this model is a good framework for such an analysis.

Quality Plan (a QMS Component). A QMS, by definition, is pre-existing and unlikely to be developed collaboratively by the parties unless there is a project backlog allocated to the same vendor. Typically, a QMS is implemented at the corporate level, and is *applied* to projects. Exceptionally, the client will have an ISO9000 environment, or similar, into which the vendor must fit, but in the event that there is no QMS to anchor the project, the best solution to meet the basic need is to jointly prepare the key component—a quality plan. Included in the plan are the results of developing quality objectives, determining acceptance protocols, and framing trade-off analysis. A quality plan checklist is shown in Table 8.2.

The collaborative approach to quality uses most of the techniques fully described in Chapter 8.

Practice 6: Joint resource management

Resource constraints seem to dog most projects, and appear in risk registers so often it is almost business as usual. In the commercial world, the problem is exacerbated by the reluctance of the parties to communicate their plans and status. In this particular practice, more frankness is required, and I also believe that clients would benefit from adopting some of the techniques employed by many vendors. Another viewpoint is that the project, no matter how it was contracted, is in reality a joint venture between the parties and the best chance of success is to accurately plan the resources invested by each party and then actively manage that plan to deliver on the commitments.

Rational project resource planning can only occur when useful resource data are collected and analyzed to provide project and client departmental information. This requires implementation of systems and procedures to collect the needed resource effort data, utilization, and forecast availability. This is used to create a Project Resource Utilization Forecast and a Departmental Resource Availability Forecast. The parties are now positioned for worthwhile collaboration on project resourcing. This would take the form of a joint resource review meeting between the project managers and relevant resource managers from both client and vendor. The discussion includes a current view of contingencies such as resourcing alternatives, training or coaching, trap-line for hiring, third parties, and any contractual issues that will have an influence. As a result, both PMs will take away a common view of their resourcing plan, the associated risks, and their alternatives.

Resourcing processes, reports, and techniques that can be adapted are described in Chapter 9.

Other practices

The six core practices belong in the initial version of TCP, but there may be arguments for establishing additional practices to encompass other jointly prepared documents. Candidate documents or activities for inclusion in a collaborative practice include: short-listing, project initiation, scheduling, project status reporting, performance management, communications, changes, issues, reviews, deficiencies, deliverable acceptance, lessons learned, and project sign-off.

Many of these reach into existing PM methods and require less innovation to operate jointly, or are less controversial. Practice definition might be overkill. Meanwhile an enthusiastic vendor and client could immediately adopt, with mutual agreement, at least some of the core practices as point solutions independent of TCP development.

Implementation prerequisites

The description of the envisaged TCP is admittedly presented from an idealistic viewpoint. Although elements of the approach can be, and have been, successfully implemented as point solutions, the TCP can only move forward if other conditions in the commercial project environment are met. These include the following: an increased awareness of the need for commercial skills in the repertoire of both vendor and client PMs, an acknowledgment that trust between the parties is essential though extraordinarily difficult to earn and retain, and that a rule book and even an umpire might be the best way to shepherd in a significant change in the procurement paradigm.

Commercial skills

The need for knowledge of standard project management processes and their supporting techniques is now widely recognized. Although unrealistic as a prerequisite, a vendor and client PM who both happen to be certified in the standard prevailing in their jurisdiction will enjoy a communications advantage. A less obvious issue is the need for business and organizational knowledge, and for business delegation to be granted to project managers. This signals the need for a training model that equips PMs with skills for the commercial environment they will be working in, as they move into professional services or their company moves to outsource project work.

The skills assessment and training advice offered in Chapter 11 is directed at vendor PMs, but with some adjustment could also provide a client PM with an appreciation of the commercial context, common issues, and their resolution. Prior to adopting TCP, both client and vendor PMs would need to be trained, and so part of the package would include training, perhaps even certification.

As commercial project management reaches into the financial and operational side of the business, there must be a matching acknowledgement that project management knowledge and discipline is needed in the business. The vendor whose business success is based on project success must build project management thinking into their business model and their practices. Project risk, quality management, and relevant project status are just three examçples. Similar logic applies to the client. If their procurement process is based on unfounded budgets, ignorance of risk and estimating disciplines, and ambiguity on quality, then they are flirting with disappointment, or worse.

If, as recommended, PMs gain commercial skills and experience, then the PM must be granted delegation commensurate with the value and criticality of her project. The use of an internal authority table, exemplified in Table 11.3, is a succinct way for all organizations to document delegations. These matters are, of course, confidential within the company and there is no proposal otherwise, though it might be advantageous for sponsoring managers to bring specific delegations more or less in line; for example, change request approvals.

Trust

A major challenge to the collaborative approach is abandoning the silo mentality and the reluctance to share information. Joint documents are not just prepared by one party and approved by the other, but worked out together in joint working sessions. In the process of working together, both parties must be comfortable sharing information. Simply put, people have to trust each other.

Trust, therefore, is a crucial ingredient for building commercial relationships. Commercial project failures can often arise from distrust and a lack of openness. So, trust and openness are important, although trust is always conditional and in some ways like the icing on the cake. It's difficult to establish and can easily dissolve, leading to a negative and non-productive project environment. Work still proceeds, but what is hard becomes harder.

There are some straightforward rules that contribute to trust building that can be lifted out of life and applied to projects. Understand the difference between making a commitment and a promise. Don't overpromise. If a promise is not going to be kept, advise ASAP and apologize; keep the next one. Never tell tales behind someone's back. Don't disparage the competition. Don't claim credit that isn't yours. Don't tell secrets; have confidential conversations, but keep them confidential. Tell the truth and differentiate truth from opinion. Build team confidence but don't blow smoke. If you ask a question, be sincere and don't brush off the answer. By all means, do deals and favors, but not to anyone's disadvantage. If you are asked explicitly for information, then provide it. If asked for confidential information that directly affects the requester ... well, now it's complicated, but I think they should be told. In summary, act with integrity.

If all this is akin to icing on the cake, then I will argue that the cake is the method and path being followed to achieve the result. In this context, it is the TCP: a methodology subscribed to by both buyer and seller to jointly guide stakeholders from solicitation through to completion. Progressively accepting commitments and responsibilities designated by the TCP and then delivering on them will therefore earn trust. It is demonstrated by actions, not demanded by words.

A third party role

The adoption of TCP by a client or a firm cannot be done unilaterally or even bilaterally. It must engage a sufficient mass of vendors and buyers to maintain a competitive environment and to ensure sufficient repeatability to make the investment worthwhile. Realistically, and in spite of the righteous words on trust, this can only be achieved by the sponsorship of a professional third party who, in return for a subscription, assumes ownership of the TCP and registers firms committed to the TCP methodology and adjudicates any disputes. The TCP owner also provides materials, updates, and training.

Future development

The reader may be familiar with the marriage analogy sometimes used in reference to a client and vendor contemplating a project contract. I ask your forbearance as I pursue this a little further to illustrate the argument for a third party role.

In today's world, it is commonplace to let the Internet do the hard work of locating and qualifying suitable partners. However, prudent interested parties don't just 'put it out there'. They will contract through a third party who will vet their profile and intent, pay attention to integrity, monitor the matches and follow-up, and maybe suggest some rules or guidance to determine if a marriage proposition would be workable. In some cultures, the Internet is redundant; one just engages a marriage broker.

The proposal for pursuit of a credible TCP program is similar. The third party is part consultant, part broker, and part trustee. It must be institutionalized, and so for the sake of a working name, it can be titled the TCP Institute, or TCPI. This is an outline of how this venture could proceed. There are several steps required:

Step 1 Feasibility. Based largely on the current definition, a group of vendor and client companies should be identified, canvassed on their best practices and their willingness to evaluate the proposal to develop a pilot version of the TCP. Presuming sufficiently positive evaluations, and an interest in continued participation, then a TCP development consortium can be formed. This should yield sponsorship, designation of a working group, and a development plan.

Step 2 Constitution of TCPI. An expected side result from Step 1 would be the preliminary formalization of the TCPI. Hopefully, there would be several existing and respected organizations that might have an interest in establishing a TCPI subsidiary. The consortium can decide how far to pursue the venture without a solid expression of interest from a would-be TCP owner, but it might be unwise to go further without a draft of a TCPI constitution.

Step 3 Pilot Development. This step will require sponsorship funding. The objective will be to assemble a minimum scope, minimum cost TCP version and a basic administration. This requires completion of a methodology design, draft documentation of practices and techniques, and assembly of templates and checklists using rudimentary technology.

Step 4 Pilot Evaluation. The pilot product will be subject to first-use by consortium members willing to test their next procurement and project delivery using the methods of the TCP, and testing the product along the way. This will require significant elapsed time, and the formal end of the pilot evaluation would be findings and recommendations from the consortium on next steps. This is a major program checkpoint.

Step 5 Version 1 Development. This step is dependent on the recommendations from the pilot, but on the positive assumption that required improvements are small scale and the pilot is workable, then most of the work is productization and specifications for implementation. A technology must be selected (web seems appropriate), a technical design drafted, and the methodology translated into software. Beta tests with the consortium would validate the product.

Step 6 Implementation and Launch. Implementation requires many activities. Formalization of the TCPI and details of the client/vendor subscription model must be completed. An alternative might be a TCP licensing model. A training program for subscribers must be developed and offered. Administrative matters must be resolved, including registration list access, advisement of engagements, pro forma contracts, and methods of subscriber support.

If these ideas foment a more collaborative method for vendors and buyers to improve project procurement efficiency, the credit will go to experience and perhaps an element of intuition and common sense. The expected benefits are not backed up by research findings or any relevant comparative data. However, pending some data being found on this topic, I conjecture there are measurable gains available beyond a handful of project stakeholders saving some time and money on their outsourced projects. Summed over a national scope, I imagine that the productivity gains from sourcing and delivering projects quicker, eliminating work on unfit opportunities, choosing the right vendor more often, estimating work more accurately, and the personal benefits of working as part of a genuine team, would create a positive uptick in national productivity.

Indisputably, there is a vacuum in the commercial project arena. Unless this initiative, or something similar, is taken into development, it is hard to see any reason why commercial projects should improve either in efficiency, in outcomes for stakeholders, or in the equanimity of the project principals. The opportunity is there.

My hope is that exposition of this vision for collaboration will inspire actions, and bring the dream to reality.

References

Listed in order of mention

Thorp, John. 1999. The Information Paradox: Realizing the Business Benefits of Information Technology, McGraw-Hill.
Unfortunately the paradox still remains, though thanks to John Thorp's groundbreaking analysis of business benefit methodology, there is much better awareness of what needs to be done.

PMI®. 2013. A Guide to the Project Management Body of Knowledge (PMBOK® Guide)—Fifth Edition, Project Management Institute, Inc.
The PMBOK® has become an industry standard in North America. It is based upon a detailed, theoretical analysis of the 47 or so processes and the many more techniques that are seen to comprise the work of the project manager.

OGC®. 2002. Managing Successful Projects with PRINCE2®, Office of Government Commerce (UK).
PRINCE2® offers an alternative view to the organization of project management and has become a well-known methodology in Europe, particularly in government institutions.

Kerzner, Harold. 2009. Project Management: A Systems Approach to Planning, Scheduling, and Controlling—Tenth Edition, John Wiley & Sons, Inc.
If I am checking my project management facts, Kerzner is my first port of call. It's all there.

Peters, Tom. 1994. The Pursuit of WOW! Pan Books.
Tom Peters is a respected though controversial business author whose barrage of action-oriented ideas in this title balances a focus on business process.

Fujitsu Consulting. 2003. Macroscope Productivity Centre—Delivering and maintaining information system solutions, Fujitsu Consulting Limited.
Fujitsu is the successor organization to DMR Group who were the original developers of the Macroscope methodology series.

Gawande, Atul. 2009. The Checklist Manifesto—How to Get Things Right, Picador.
A splendid argument on the power and value of the humble checklist, and I don't think project management is mentioned once. Dr. Gawande persuaded the World Health Organization to fund a trial around the world to introduce checklists into the operating theater leading to a remarkable drop in mortality rates.

Hornby, Robin. 2004. Ten Commandments of Project Management: A Brief Guide to the Art of Righteous Project Management, Tempest Management, Inc.
Perhaps more concerned with the art than the science of project management, this work explores critical behaviors of successful project managers, as well as presenting practical methods of planning, estimating, and risk analysis.

Merrill, David W. and Reid, Roger H. 1981. Personal Styles & Effective Performance, Chilton Book Company.
One of the earliest of the several analyses based on the Myers–Briggs type indicator, and perhaps the most useful for project work.

Taggart, Adrian. 2015. Project Management for Supplier Organizations, Gower Publishing Ltd.
One of the few titles to deal with the subject of commercial project management. Taggart provides an interesting analysis on the distinctions between buyer and supplier organizations and how that might account for some of the difficulties with contracted projects.

Boehm, Barry W. 2000. Software Cost Estimation with COCOMO II, Prentice Hall.
Those interested in exploring models and automated means of estimating software can start with an examination of COCOMO II.

Brooks Jr, Frederick P. 1974. The Mythical Man-Month, Addison-Wesley Publishing Company.
An essential read for estimators who would like to learn from IBMer Fred Brooks' visceral experiences with the connection between resource and schedule and how it could rapidly become non-linear.

Pirsig, Robert M. 1974. Zen and the Art of Motorcycle Maintenance: An Inquiry into Values, HarperCollins.
If, like me, you are intrigued by the philosophical overtones in quality, then Pirsig's classic might be of interest. It's not really about the 'bike'.

Crosby, Philip B. 1979. Quality Is Free: The Art of Making Quality Certain, McGraw-Hill.
This book launched a broad and generally successful appeal to US corporate executives to get on-board the quality movement.

Hackman, Richard J. and Oldham, Greg R. 1976. Motivation through the Design of Work: Test of a Theory, Academic Press, Inc.
This theory on motivation, leading to modeling based on Critical Psychological States, seems tailor-made for the work of the project manager and is worth study.

Verma, Vijay K. 1995. Human Resource Skills for the Project Manager, Project Management Institute, Inc.
A comprehensive account of the 'soft' skills that benefit the project manager.

O'Brien, Maureen. 1995. Who's Got the Ball? (And Other Nagging Questions about Team Life), Jossey-Bass, Inc.
The sports team analogy applied to project teams, but from the coaching perspective.

Maister, David H. 1982. Balancing the Professional Service Firm, Sloan Management Review MIT.
This early analysis of how to build a successful business model for services delivery has lost none of its relevance and utility.

Shapiro, Andrea. 2003. Creating Contagious Commitment: Applying the Tipping Point to Organizational Change, Strategy Perspective.

It has long perplexed me what 'change managers', who lurk in the folds of large, organizationally significant projects, actually do. Andrea Shapiro's work makes it very clear.

Barker, Joel. 2012. The Power of Vision DVD, Star Thrower Distribution, Inc.

This training video presents a profound view of what Vision really means and how it can impact the future of civilizations, children, adults enduring appalling stress, and, of course, the corporation. Watch it if you get the opportunity.

PMBOK®, PMI®, and PMP® are the registered trademarks of the Project Management Institute. PRINCE2® is the registered trademark of OGC.

Glossary

Specialized terminology, jargon, and abbreviations are used in this book. The glossary provides cross-references and definitions on how to interpret these terms within the context of commercial project management.

Term	Definition
Account team	A group of senior practitioners and vendor PMs, working on client (account) projects, led by the sales executive (aka account executive).
Activity	The lowest level of doing and estimating work; decomposition of a work packet.
ADR	Alternative dispute resolution.
AICPA	American Institute of Certified Public Accountants.
Application lifecycle	*See Project lifecycle.*
Authority table	A concept used by companies to manage financial or other authority delegations sometimes called a delegation matrix. The authority table is used to manage financial delegations, and to control use of templates and reviews based on financial or risk criteria.
Backlog	Value of sold work to be executed. Can also be expressed in terms of months.
Bid estimate	Formal project estimate summarized by phase and type of resource. Includes work hours, costs, list price, bid price, discount, and margin.
Bid review package	The core deliverables from the bid phase, including the proposal/SOW, the risk assessment, risk register, and bid estimate. These are input to the bid review to obtain final approvals. The term is not definitive, and other documents may be included.
Bleeding project	A project whose forecast costs exceed revenue; forecast margin is <0%. Similar to a black hole project that consumes endless resources.
Booking	An accounting record of the sold value; the booked planned revenue.
CAR	Corrective action report.
CBA	Cost/benefit analysis; a justification based on comparing costs with the monetary value of benefits.

(Continued)

Term	Definition
CCB	Change Control Board.
Contingency	An amount of effort, time, or money that is unallocated at the beginning of a project, but is available to the PM for allocation to new or underestimated activities; a response to risk.
Contract SOW	*See SOW.*
COQ	Cost of quality; the cost of conforming to quality plus the cost when non-conformance occurs.
COTS	Commercial off-the-shelf; usually a reference to packaged, pre-written software offered for sale.
CPE	Commercial project environment. A name coined for a standard description of the optimum contract environment.
CPFR	Collaborative planning forecasting and replenishment.
CPI	Consumer price index.
CPI	Cost performance index (BAC/EAC for completed deliverables, or use EV/AC if incomplete); an EV metric.
CR	Change request.
CSF	Critical success factor; a factor or condition seen as a prerequisite for meeting project objectives.
CSR	Customer status report.
Cure period	A period of time specified in contract within which the firm can rectify a situation non-compliant with the contract before a breach can be declared.
Defect	A failure, or deviation of the product from the technical specification, that requires rectification and rework.
Delegation matrix	*See Authority table.*
Deliverability	Capability of being delivered.
Deliverable	A result or product produced by project activities.
DM	Delivery manager.
DR	Discrepancy report.
EAC	Estimate at completion.
Earned value	A measure of work accomplishment based on the estimated $ value for the deliverable. For example, a deliverable estimated at $100 provides $100 of value to the project when complete, regardless of the actual cost to produce.
Earned value management	A formalized method of evaluating costs and schedule achievement against plans.
EMV	Expected monetary value; a metric used to evaluate alternatives by setting a value on an uncertain outcome. EMV = Probability % × $ Cost.
Error	A mistake, a correctable misunderstanding, a detectable deviation from requirements specifications, standards, procedures, that can be corrected before the product is built.
Escrow	An item of value held in trust by a third party, to be released to a second party (beneficiary) only if the first party (owner) fails to maintain certain agreed conditions.
ETC	Estimate to complete.
EV	*See Earned value.*
EVM	*See Earned value management.*
FAT	Factory acceptance test.
Firm	*See Professional services firm.*
FP	Fixed price contract.

Term	Definition
FTE	Full time equivalent (staff positions).
FUL	Fixed upper limit contract.
GAAP	Generally accepted accounting principles.
GIGO	Garbage in, garbage out.
IAS 18	IFRS IAS 18 (Revenue) outlines the accounting requirements for when to recognize revenue from the sale of goods, rendering of services, and for interest, royalties and dividends. Revenue is measured at the fair value of the consideration received or receivable and recognized when prescribed conditions are met, which depend on the nature of the revenue (Deloitte, www.iasplus.com/en/standards/standard16).
IFRS	International financial reporting standards.
IP	Intellectual property.
IPO	An input–process–output diagram.
Issue	An impediment to meeting a project objective.
IT	Information technology.
KPI	Key performance indicator.
Management reserve	A form of $ contingency retained by management.
MBTI	Myers–Briggs type indicator.
Methodology	A formal, repeatable method for performing work to build a product in a specific application area—construction, electronics, software, etc.
MSA	Master services agreement.
MTBF	Mean time between failures.
PARIS	Responsibility coding for a RAM; participate, accountable, review, input, sign-off.
Performance chain	An aspect of project performance that is moving the project work toward the project objectives. May default to four chains: delivery, finance, team, and client.
Phase	A grouping of similar activities to meet a definitive phase objective. A sequence of phases is a *lifecycle*.
PIP	Performance improvement program.
PMBOK®	*See Project management body of knowledge.*
PMI®	Project Management Institute.
PMO	Project Management Office.
PMP®	The Project Management Professional certification.
POC	Percent of completion.
POCL	Plan, organize, control, and lead.
PPT	People, process, technology—the quality triangle.
Practitioner	A generalized term for a professional resource who works for the services firm. The term suggests that they possess a body of practice knowledge whether it is technical, business, industrial, or management expertise.
PRINCE2®	PRojects IN Controlled Environments 2. A standard for project management published by Office of Government Commerce (UK) organized into eight processes: directing a project, planning, starting up a project, initiating a project, controlling a stage, managing project delivery, managing stage boundaries, closing a project.
Procedure	A precise instruction on how to achieve a repeated task; a step-by-step prescription. Usually, part of the decomposition of a process.

(Continued)

Term	Definition
Process	A general description of how inputs can be used to generate useful outputs, diagrammed in an IPO. In the methods context, suggests transformation of data into information, or a decision, or a new state; a process is usually decomposed into procedures.
Procurement SOW	*See SOW.*
Project accounting report	An essential report for the vendor PM that uses project accounting data to report status of project hours, costs, revenue, and margin against plan.
Professional services firm	A firm whose primary business is providing services to clients; staffing and delivering projects under contract to clients.
Project lifecycle	A sequence of phases that will accomplish the work of the project to build a product in an application area (aka application lifecycle, development lifecycle).
Project management	A structured approach to plan, organize, control, and lead the work of the project to meet project objectives.
Project management body of knowledge	A standard for project management, published by PMI, organized into 5 process groups (initiate, plan, execute, monitor and control, and close) and 10 knowledge areas (time, cost, scope, HR, communications, quality, risk, integration, procurement, stakeholders).
Proposal	A selling document presented to the client, usually in competition with other firms, providing information that can be assessed by the client. Will include pricing, the proposed solution documented as a SOW and/or technical specifications, the credentials of the firm, their experience in the proposed work, references, and any conditions of business.
PSM	Professional services manager.
PSR	Project status report.
QA	Quality assurance, or preventing defects.
QC	Quality control, or finding and fixing defects.
QFD	Quality function deployment.
QMC	Quality Management Council.
QMS	Quality Management System.
RAA	Responsibility, accountability, and authority.
RACI	Responsibility coding for a RAM; responsible, accountable, consulted, informed.
RAM	Responsibility assignment matrix.
RFI	Request for information.
RFP	Request for proposal.
Risk alert	A global risk metric that measures current performance of the project or a performance chain in terms of potential deviation from objectives. Usually represented as red, yellow, or green.
Risk facet	A generic aspect of the project or project family that generates risk. May default to six facets: team, contract, size, solution, technology, and customer.
Risk factor	A negative characteristic of a project risk facet that will have a detriment on project activities. Summed over time, this could cause a probable failure to meet one or more project objectives.

Term	Definition
Risk indicator	A risk metric that assesses the status, or health, of a link in the performance chain. There can be many risk indicators for each chain.
Risk rank	A global risk metric of the project that assesses the risk of a bid in terms of the project's deliverability. Usual range is 1 (very low) to 5 (very high).
ROT	Rule of thumb—an experience-based rule for top-down estimating.
RTM	Requirements traceability matrix, to prove the propagation of requirements into design and construction.
SAT	Site acceptance test.
Services firm	*See Professional services firm.*
Sigma	Greek letter, symbol for standard deviation.
SME	Subject matter expert.
SOP	Standard operating procedures.
SOP 97–2	Rules endorsed by AICPA governing revenue recognition for multi-element deliverables that may also be subject to VSOE fair value criteria.
SOR	Statement of role.
SOW	*See Statement of work.*
SOX	Sarbanes–Oxley Act.
Statement of work	A document intended to describe the scope of work to be assigned to the Services Firm, and how it is to be performed; usually authored by the firm in response to RFP, though sometimes originated by the client. Sometimes called a contract SOW or a procurement SOW.
SWOT	Strengths weaknesses opportunities threats.
T&C	Terms and conditions, usually in the contract.
T&M	Time and material contract.
Task	There is no formal definition for this term, though may be synonymous with activity, or may be taken as further decomposition of an activity, or may be an aggregation of activities.
TCP	Total collaborative procurement. A name coined for a proposed procurement methodology.
TOC	Table of contents.
TQM	Total quality management.
TR	Trouble report.
Triple constraint	The three continual preoccupations of the vendor PM—scope, cost, and schedule. Older texts sometimes refer to quality, not scope.
V&V	Verification and validation.
Validation	The assurance that a product, service, or system meets the needs of the customer and other identified stakeholders. It often involves acceptance and suitability assessment with external customers.
Vendor lifecycle	A sequence of phases that will manage the business priorities of a project as it moves from opportunity to bid, then through initiation, execution, and completion.
Vendor PM	Project manager of a commercial, for-profit project.

(Continued)

Term	Definition
Verification	The evaluation of whether or not a product, service, or system complies with a regulation, requirement, specification, or imposed condition. It is often an internal process.
VSOE	Vendor specific objective evidence.
WBS	Work breakdown structure, usually defines the scope baseline.
Work estimate	A structured account showing details of activity/work packet estimates (usually effort in hours) for the project; may be based on a standard template provided by the firm.
Work packet	A decomposition of a deliverable; the lowest level in a WBS (aka work package).

Index

For Product Safety Concerns and Information please contact our EU
representative GPSR@taylorandfrancis.com Taylor & Francis Verlag GmbH,
Kaufingerstraße 24, 80331 München, Germany

Printed and bound by CPI Group (UK) Ltd, Croydon, CR0 4YY
08/05/2025
01864398-0001